실전 문법
300제

저자 | (주)이앤미래(대표 이동기)

공무원 영어의 시작과 끝
이동기 영어

2026
이동기 영어
실전 문법 300제

# 이 책에 앞서 PREFACE

인사혁신처에서 발표한 출제 기조 전환에 따라 2025년 시험부터 공무원 영어 시험의 출제 유형이 달라졌습니다. 문법 문제의 경우 그동안 영작 문제, 단락 밑줄 문제, 영어 단문 문제의 세 가지 유형이 출제되었다면 2025년 시험부터 영작 문제, 영어 단문 문제가 출제되지 않고 빈칸 문제와 단락 밑줄 문제가 출제되고 있습니다. 인사혁신처는 이미 두 차례 예시 문제를 공개하여 출제 기조의 전환을 분명히 밝혔고, 2025년 국가직, 지방직 9급 시험은 그러한 출제 기조가 반영된 첫 시험이었습니다. 따라서 수험생들은 기존의 영작 문제나 영어 단문 문제에서 문법 포인트를 파악하는 방식과는 전혀 다른 빈칸 문제와 단락 밑줄 문제에서 문법 포인트를 빠르게 파악하는 방법을 배우고 연습하는 것이 필요합니다.

이동기 영어교육연구소는 인사혁신처의 출제 기조 전환에 대한 공지문과 두 차례 예시 문제, 2025년 기출문제의 분석뿐 아니라 이를 기반으로 유사성이 보이는 공무원 기출문제, 토익 문제, 수능 문제 등 다양한 시험들을 모두 분석하여 출제 가능한 유형들을 정리하여 공무원 영어 기본서인 [이동기 영어 신경향 ALL IN ONE]에 수록했습니다. 또한 이런 유형분석을 기반으로 인사혁신처에서 발표한 예시 문제와 가장 유사한 문제들, 그리고 출제 가능한 문제들을 직접 출제하고 여러 차례 감수를 거쳐 이번 [이동기 영어 실전 문법 300제]를 출간하게 되었습니다.

[이동기 영어 실전 문법 300제] 이 한 권으로 새롭게 바뀌는 시험에 완벽히 대비할 수 있다고 자신합니다.

2025년 8월 연구실에서

이동기 드림

# 교재 활용법 GUIDE

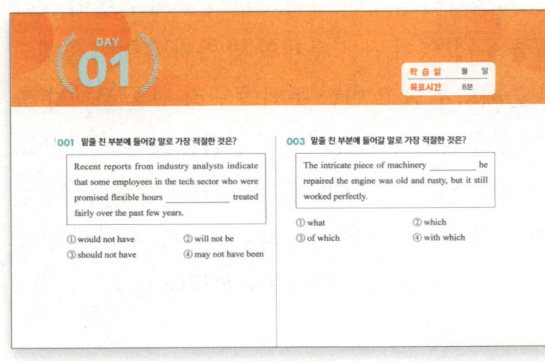

### STEP 1

하루 정해진 분량인 15개의 문제를 시간을 재며 먼저 풀어봅니다. 권장하는 문제 개수와 시간은 다음과 같습니다.

| 권장 문제 개수 | 15개/1일 |
| --- | --- |
| 권장 시간 | 8~10분 |

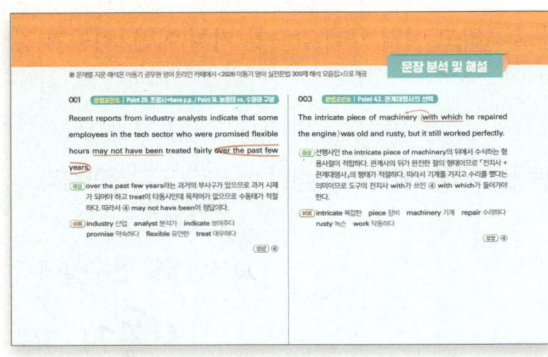

### STEP 2

필기노트를 보고 자신이 풀었던 방식과 맞는지 확인합니다. 이후 각 문제의 정답과 해설 부분을 읽어 꼼꼼히 학습합니다.

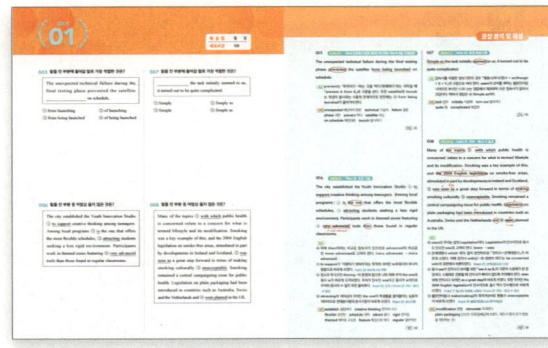

### STEP 3

300문제를 모두 푼 후 하루당 문제 개수를 늘려 복습합니다. 예를 들어 2~3일치를 하루에 풀며 복습합니다.

# 구성과 특징 STRUCTURE

### 1  엄선된 신경향 문법 300제
- 인사혁신처 신경향 출제 기조를 중심으로 선별된 신경향 문법 문제
- 난이도 중~상의 실전문제

### 2  자습에 최적화된 해설과 해석
- 강의의 핵심을 눈으로 확인할 수 있는 손글씨체 필기노트
- 전 문항 꼼꼼한 해설과 해석
- 정답 뿐 아니라 오답인 이유를 명쾌하게 설명
- 문제별 핵심 문법 포인트 수록

### 3  매일 학습을 고려한 문제 구성
- 문제구성에 있어 각기 다른 문법 포인트로 DAY별 문제를 구성
- 수준에 맞게 하루 15개, 또는 30개의 문제풀이 권장

### 4  온라인을 통한 학습 지원
- 동영상 강의(gong.conects.com)를 통해 시간은 적게 들고 문제풀이 방법은 정확히 학습하는 시간 효율적인 학습
- 카페(Naver '이동기 영어')를 통한 질문과 답변, 상담

# 차례 CONTENTS

| | | | |
|---|---|---|---|
| **DAY 01** | 010 | **DAY 11** | 090 |
| **DAY 02** | 018 | **DAY 12** | 098 |
| **DAY 03** | 026 | **DAY 13** | 106 |
| **DAY 04** | 034 | **DAY 14** | 114 |
| **DAY 05** | 042 | **DAY 15** | 122 |
| **DAY 06** | 050 | **DAY 16** | 130 |
| **DAY 07** | 058 | **DAY 17** | 138 |
| **DAY 08** | 066 | **DAY 18** | 146 |
| **DAY 09** | 074 | **DAY 19** | 154 |
| **DAY 10** | 082 | **DAY 20** | 162 |

※ 빠른 정답은 170p에 있습니다.

# 학습플랜 STUDY PLAN

## 20일 완성 학습 플랜
하루 15문제를 매일 풀어 20일을 완성합니다.

| 1일 완료 ☐ | 2일 완료 ☐ | 3일 완료 ☐ | 4일 완료 ☐ |
|---|---|---|---|
| DAY 01 | DAY 02 | DAY 03 | DAY 04 |

| 5일 완료 ☐ | 6일 완료 ☐ | 7일 완료 ☐ | 8일 완료 ☐ |
|---|---|---|---|
| DAY 05 | DAY 06 | DAY 07 | DAY 08 |

| 9일 완료 ☐ | 10일 완료 ☐ | 11일 완료 ☐ | 12일 완료 ☐ |
|---|---|---|---|
| DAY 09 | DAY 10 | DAY 11 | DAY 12 |

| 13일 완료 ☐ | 14일 완료 ☐ | 15일 완료 ☐ | 16일 완료 ☐ |
|---|---|---|---|
| DAY 13 | DAY 14 | DAY 15 | DAY 16 |

| 17일 완료 ☐ | 18일 완료 ☐ | 19일 완료 ☐ | 20일 완료 ☐ |
|---|---|---|---|
| DAY 17 | DAY 18 | DAY 19 | DAY 20 |

선별된
300문제로
깔끔하고
빈틈없이
정리하는 영문법

2026 이동기 영어

# 실전 문법

# 300제

# DAY 01

**001** 밑줄 친 부분에 들어갈 말로 가장 적절한 것은?

> Recent reports from industry analysts indicate that some employees in the tech sector who were promised flexible hours _____ treated fairly over the past few years.

① would not have  ② will not be
③ should not have  ④ may not have been

**002** 밑줄 친 부분 중 어법상 옳지 않은 것은?

> The school launched the Digital Learning Lab, an education center that ① <u>makes</u> it easier for students to focus. It provides personalized lessons ② <u>used</u> tablets, supports remote tutoring programs, and ③ <u>includes</u> interactive coding games. Teachers say it helps ④ <u>improve</u> student outcomes.

**003** 밑줄 친 부분에 들어갈 말로 가장 적절한 것은?

> The intricate piece of machinery _____ he repaired the engine was old and rusty, but it still worked perfectly.

① what  ② which
③ of which  ④ with which

**004** 밑줄 친 부분 중 어법상 옳지 않은 것은?

> The university opened the Center for Digital Innovation, ① <u>which supports</u> research in artificial intelligence and robotics. Many students visit ② <u>them</u> regularly ③ <u>to explore</u> new projects and collaborate with experts. They often share ideas through presentations ④ <u>featuring</u> cutting-edge solutions.

## 001 문법포인트 | Point 20. 조동사+have p.p. / Point 16. 능동태 vs. 수동태 구분

Recent reports from industry analysts indicate that some employees in the tech sector who were promised flexible hours may not have been treated fairly over the past few years.

**해설** over the past few years라는 과거의 부사구가 있으므로 과거 시제가 사용되어야 하고 treat이 타동사인데 목적어가 없는 것으로 볼 때 수동태가 적절하다. 따라서 ④ may not have been이 정답이다. 「조동사 + have p.p.」는 조동사를 사용한 과거 표현법이다.

**어휘** industry 산업   analyst 분석가   indicate 보여주다
promise 약속하다   flexible 유연한   treat 대우하다

정답 ④

## 002 문법포인트 | Point 32. 현재분사 vs. 과거분사

The school launched the Digital Learning Lab, an education center (that ① makes it easier for students to focus). It provides personalized lessons ② used tablets, supports remote tutoring programs, and ③ includes interactive coding games. Teachers say it helps ④ improve student outcomes.

**해설**
② lessons를 수식하는 분사가 필요한 자리. 의미상 lessons가 태블릿을 사용하는 능동의 의미이고 목적어인 tablets를 취하고 있으므로 현재분사 using으로 고쳐야 한다. (used → using)
① 관계대명사절의 동사는 선행사에 수 일치를 해야 한다. 선행사가 an education center로 단수이므로 단수 동사가 바르게 쓰였다. Point 27. 주어 - 동사 수 일치
③ provides, supports, includes가 등위접속사 and로 병렬로 바르게 연결되었다. Point 39. 등위접속사의 병렬 구조
④ help는 목적어로 to부정사와 동사원형(원형부정사) 둘 다 취할 수 있다. 원형부정사 improve가 목적어로 바르게 쓰였다. Point 06. 완전타동사와 동작의 목적어

**어휘** launch 시작하다   focus 집중하다   personalized 개인 맞춤형의
support 지원하다   remote 원격의   tutoring 교습
interactive 대화형의   improve 향상시키다   outcome 성과

정답 ②

## 003 문법포인트 | Point 43. 관계대명사의 선택

The intricate piece of machinery (with which he repaired the engine) was old and rusty, but it still worked perfectly.

**해설** 선행사인 the intricate piece of machinery의 뒤에서 수식하는 형용사절이 적합하다. 관계사의 뒤가 완전한 절의 형태이므로 「전치사 + 관계대명사」의 형태가 적절하다. 따라서 기계를 가지고 수리를 했다는 의미이므로 도구의 전치사 with가 쓰인 ④ with which가 들어가야 한다.

**어휘** intricate 복잡한   piece 장비   machinery 기계   repair 수리하다
rusty 녹슨   work 작동하다

정답 ④

## 004 문법포인트 | Point 24. 인칭대명사

The university opened the Center for Digital Innovation, ① (which supports research in artificial intelligence and robotics.) Many students visit ② them regularly ③ to explore new projects and collaborate with experts. They often share ideas through presentations ④ (featuring cutting-edge solutions).

**해설**
② them이 가리키는 것은 문맥상 the Center for Digital Innovation이므로 단수인 it으로 고쳐야 한다. (them → it)
① 선행사가 the Center for Digital Innovation이며, 동사 앞이므로 주격의 관계대명사 which가 바르게 쓰였다. 관계대명사절의 동사는 선행사에 맞추어 수 일치를 한다. 선행사가 단수이므로 단수인 supports가 바르게 쓰였다. Point 43. 관계대명사의 선택 / Point 27. 주어 - 동사 수 일치
③ to explore가 '탐구하기 위하여'라는 목적의 의미인 to부정사의 부사적 용법으로 바르게 쓰였다. Point 29. to부정사의 역할
④ featuring은 presentations를 수식하는 분사로 둘의 관계가 능동이고 뒤에 목적어가 있으므로 현재분사형으로 바르게 쓰였다. Point 32. 현재분사 vs. 과거분사

**어휘** innovation 혁신   research 연구   robotics 로봇 공학
explore 탐색하다   collaborate 협력하다   expert 전문가
presentation 발표   feature 특징으로 하다
cutting-edge 최첨단의   solution 해결책

정답 ②

## DAY 01

**005** 밑줄 친 부분에 들어갈 말로 가장 적절한 것은?

The unexpected technical failure during the final testing phase prevented the satellite _____ on schedule.

① from launching  ② of launching
③ from being launched  ④ of being launched

**006** 밑줄 친 부분 중 어법상 옳지 않은 것은?

The city established the Youth Innovation Studio ① to support creative thinking among teenagers. Among local programs ② is the one that offers the most flexible schedules, ③ attracting students seeking a less rigid environment. Participants work in themed zones featuring ④ very advanced tools than those found in regular classrooms.

**007** 밑줄 친 부분에 들어갈 말로 가장 적절한 것은?

_____ the task initially seemed to us, it turned out to be quite complicated.

① Simply  ② Simply as
③ Simple  ④ Simple as

**008** 밑줄 친 부분 중 어법상 옳지 않은 것은?

Many of the topics ① with which public health is concerned relate to a concern for what is termed lifestyle and its modification. Smoking was a key example of this, and the 2004 English legislation on smoke-free areas, stimulated in part by developments in Ireland and Scotland, ② was seen as a great step forward in terms of making smoking culturally ③ unacceptable. Smoking remained a central campaigning issue for public health. Legislation on plain packaging had been introduced in countries such as Australia, Swiss and the Netherlands and ④ were planned in the UK.

## 005 문법포인트 | Point 07. 완전자동사와 함께 사용되는 주요 전치사 / Point 30. 준동사의 형태 변화

The unexpected technical failure during the final testing phase prevented the satellite from being launched on schedule.

**해설** prevent는 '목적어가 ~하는 것을 막다/방해하다'라는 의미일 때 「prevent A from B」의 구문을 쓴다. 또한 satellite와 launch는 위성이 발사되는 수동의 관계이므로 빈칸에는 ③ from being launched가 들어가야 한다.

**어휘** unexpected 예상하지 못한  technical 기술적  failure 결함
phase 국면  prevent 막다  satellite 위성
on schedule 예정대로  launch 발사하다

정답 ③

## 006 문법포인트 | Point 36. 비교 구문

The city established the Youth Innovation Studio ① to support creative thinking among teenagers. (Among local programs) ② is the one that offers the most flexible schedules, ③ attracting students seeking a less rigid environment. Participants work in themed zones featuring ④ very advanced (→ more advanced) tools than those found in regular classrooms.

**해설**
④ 뒤에 than이라는 비교급 접속사가 있으므로 advanced의 비교급인 more advanced로 고쳐야 한다. (very advanced → more advanced)
① to support가 '지원하기 위하여'라는 목적의 의미인 to부정사의 부사적 용법으로 바르게 쓰였다. Point 29. to부정사의 역할
② 장소의 부사구인 Among ~이 문장의 앞으로 나와 뒤에 주어 the one과 동사 is가 바르게 도치되었다. 주어가 단수인 one이고 동사가 is이므로 주어와 동사의 수 일치 또한 올바르다. Point 50. 도치 / Point 27. 주어 - 동사 수 일치
③ attracting의 의미상의 주어인 the one이 학생들을 끌어들이는 능동의 의미이므로 현재분사형의 분사구문이 바르게 쓰였다. Point 33. 분사구문

**어휘** establish 설립하다  creative thinking 창의적 사고
flexible 유연한  schedule 계획  attract 끌다  rigid 경직된
themed 테마로 구성된  feature 특징으로 하다  regular 일반적인

정답 ④

## 007 문법포인트 | Point 42. 주요 양보구문

Simple as the task initially seemed to us, it turned out to be quite complicated.

**해설** 접속사를 이용한 양보구문의 경우 「형용사/부사/명사 + as/though + S + V」의 구문으로 써야 한다. seem이 보어를 취하는 불완전자동사이므로 부사인 ①과 ②는 정답에서 제외되며 ③은 접속사가 없어서 오답이다. 따라서 정답은 ④ Simple as이다.

**어휘** task 업무  initially 처음에  turn out 밝혀지다
quite 꽤  complicated 복잡한

정답 ④

## 008 문법포인트 | Point 27. 주어 - 동사 수 일치

Many of the topics ① (with which public health is concerned) relate to a concern for what is termed lifestyle and its modification. Smoking was a key example of this, and the 2004 English legislation on smoke-free areas, stimulated in part by developments in Ireland and Scotland, ② was seen as a great step forward in terms of making smoking culturally ③ unacceptable. Smoking remained a central campaigning issue for public health. Legislation on plain packaging had been introduced in countries such as Australia, Swiss and the Netherlands and ④ were (→ was) planned in the UK.

**해설**
④ were의 주어는 앞의 Legislation이다. Legislation이 단수이므로 동사도 단수인 was로 고쳐야 한다. (were → was)
① 관계대명사 which 뒤의 절이 완전하므로 「전치사+관계대명사」가 바르게 쓰였다. 이때 전치사 with는 '~와 관련이 되다'는 be concerned with의 표현에서 비롯되었다. Point 43. 관계대명사의 선택
② 동사 see가 전치사구 보어를 취한 「see A as B」의 구문이 수동태가 된 문장이다. 수동태로 전환될 때 전치사가 빠지지 않도록 주의해야 한다. seen 뒤에 전치사구 보어인 as a great step이 바르게 쓰였다. 또한 주어인 the 2004 English legislation이 단수이므로 동사 역시 단수형으로 바르게 쓰였다. Point 17. 동사의 유형별 수동태 / Point 27. 주어 - 동사 수 일치
③ 불완전자동사 make(making)의 목적격보어로 형용사 unacceptable이 바르게 쓰였다. Point 09. 불완전자동사의 목적격보어

**어휘** modification 변형  stimulate 자극하다
plain packaging 단순한 포장(담배갑에 브랜드, 제조사 명의 표기 방법을 제한하는 것)

정답 ④

## DAY 01

**009** 밑줄 친 부분에 들어갈 말로 가장 적절한 것은?

> Only after she left the company for good _____ how much she had contributed.

① realized her colleagues
② did realize her colleagues
③ did her colleagues realize
④ did her colleagues realized

**010** 밑줄 친 부분 중 어법상 옳지 않은 것은?

> Mozart began ① composing music at a very young age, astonishing audiences with his talent across Europe. He wrote operas, symphonies, and chamber works that remain widely ② performed today. His melodies were often more expressive than ③ that of his contemporaries with each piece ④ capturing deep emotion with elegance.

**011** 밑줄 친 부분에 들어갈 말로 가장 적절한 것은?

> _____ toward the evening, the rescue team refused to abandon the search.

① However the weather conditions became harshly
② However harsh the weather conditions became
③ However the weather conditions became harsh
④ However harshly the weather conditions became

**012** 밑줄 친 부분 중 어법상 옳은 것은?

> ① Despite she faced challenges shaped by societal prejudice, Marie Curie pursued science ② driven by a desire to benefit humanity. Had she been discouraged by early setbacks, she ③ might not achieve her groundbreaking discoveries. Her laboratory contained ④ equipments built by hand during years of limited funding.

## 009　문법포인트 | Point 50. 도치

(Only after she left the company for good) did her colleagues realize how much she had contributed.

**해설** 부정부사인 only가 붙은 부사절이 문장의 앞에 왔기 때문에 주절에 도치가 일어나야 하는데, 일반동사 realized가 주절의 동사로 사용되었기 때문에 「did + 주어 + 동사원형」의 형태가 되어야 한다. 따라서 빈칸에는 ③ did her colleagues realize가 와야 한다.

**어휘** for good 아주　contribute 기여하다　colleague 동료
realize 깨닫다

**정답** ③

## 011　문법포인트 | Point 42. 주요 양보구문

However harsh the weather conditions(S) became(V) toward the evening, the rescue team refused to abandon the search.

**해설** However가 이끄는 주요 양보구문이다. However가 수식하는 형용사나 부사는 반드시 붙여서 「However + 형용사/부사 + S + V」의 어순을 취해야 한다. 불완전자동사 became의 보어 자리에는 부사가 올 수 없으므로 however 뒤에 형용사를 사용하는 것이 올바르다. 따라서 정답은 ② However harsh the weather conditions became이다.

**어휘** harsh 혹독한　rescue 구조　refuse 거부하다
abandon 포기하다　search 수색

**정답** ②

## 010　문법포인트 | Point 38. 비교대상의 일치

Mozart began ① composing music at a very young age, astonishing audiences with his talent across Europe. He wrote operas, symphonies, and chamber works that remain widely ② performed today. His melodies were often more expressive than ③ that (→ those) of his contemporaries with each piece ④ capturing (능동) deep emotion with elegance.

**해설**
③ that은 문맥상 앞의 melodies와 비교되는 말이므로 복수인 those로 고쳐야 한다. (that → those)
① begin은 동명사와 to부정사를 모두 목적어로 취할 수 있다. 동명사 composing이 목적어로 바르게 쓰였다. Point 06. 완전타동사와 동작의 목적어
② remain의 보어로 과거분사 performed가 쓰였다. 선행사인 operas, symphonies, and chamber works가 연주된다는 수동의 의미이므로 과거분사가 바르게 쓰였다. Point 04. 불완전자동사의 보어
④ with 분사구문으로 목적어인 each piece가 깊은 감정을 사로잡는다는 능동의 의미이므로 현재분사가 바르게 쓰였다. Point 33. 분사구문

**어휘** compose 작곡하다　astonish 놀라게 하다　talent 재능
symphony 교향곡　chamber work 실내악 작품
perform 연주하다　expressive 표현력이 풍부한
contemporary 동시대인　capture 사로잡다　elegance 고귀함

**정답** ③

## 012　문법포인트 | Point 33. 분사구문

① Despite (→ Although) she faced(V) challenges shaped by societal prejudice, Marie Curie pursued science ② driven (수동) by a desire to benefit humanity. Had she been discouraged by early setbacks, she ③ might not achieve (→ might not have achieved) her groundbreaking discoveries. Her laboratory contained ④ equipments (→ equipment) built by hand during years of limited funding.

**해설**
② 주절의 주어인 Marie Curie가 이끌린다는 수동의 의미이므로 과거분사형인 driven이 바르게 쓰였다.
① despite는 전치사인데 뒤에 주어와 동사의 절이 왔으므로 같은 의미의 접속사 Although로 고쳐야 한다. (Despite → Although) Point 41. 부사절 접속사의 선택
③ 조건절의 동사가 가정법 과거완료이므로 주절도 가정법 과거완료 동사인 might not have achieved로 고쳐야 한다. (might not achieve → might not have achieved) Point 46. 기본 가정법
④ equipment는 절대 불가산명사이므로 복수형으로 쓸 수 없다. 단수로 고쳐야 한다. (equipments → equipment) Point 21. 명사의 이해

**어휘** challenge 어려움　shape 형성하다　societal 사회의
prejudice 편견　pursue 추구하다　desire 욕망
benefit 이롭게 하다　humanity 인류　discourage 막다
setback 차질　achieve 성취하다　groundbreaking 획기적인
laboratory 연구소　contain 포함하다　equipment 장비
limited 제한된　funding 재정 지원

**정답** ②

**013** 밑줄 친 부분에 들어갈 말로 가장 적절한 것은?

He forgot _____ the device before shipment, and the customer reported a malfunction on arrival.

① to test
② testing
③ to testing
④ test

**014** 밑줄 친 부분 중 어법상 옳지 않은 것은?

Historians still debate ① that the government should have done to prevent the tragedy that unfolded. Although some evidence ② was initially ignored, new documents have been analyzed hard, which made ③ it difficult to determine who was truly responsible. The mission seems ④ to have been planned without proper coordination among the teams involved.

**015** 밑줄 친 부분 중 어법상 옳은 것은?

The engineer ① works on renewable energy projects since 2010, gradually becoming used ② to manage complex systems. Last year, people accused her ③ of being manipulated by corporate interests, though the claims were never proven. Her team described her as ④ a such dedicated professional with a clear sense of purpose.

### 013  문법포인트 | Point 06. 완전타동사와 동작의 목적어

He forgot to test the device before shipment, and the customer reported a malfunction on arrival.

**해설** forget은 과거에 어떤 일을 한 것을 잊었다는 의미일 때는 목적어로 동명사를 쓰고, 앞으로 어떤 일을 할 것을 잊었다는 의미일 때는 목적어로 to부정사를 쓴다. 장치를 시험해야 할 것을 잊었다는 미래의 의미이므로 to부정사를 사용해야 한다. 따라서 정답은 ① to test이다.

**어휘** device 장치  shipment 배송  customer 고객
malfunction 오작동

**정답** ①

### 014  문법포인트 | Point 40. 명사절 접속사의 선택

Historians still debate ① that [→ what] the government should have done to prevent the tragedy that unfolded. Although some evidence ② was initially ignored, new documents have been analyzed hard, which made ③ it difficult to determine who was truly responsible. The mission seems ④ to have been planned without proper coordination among the teams involved.

**해설**
① 타동사 debate의 목적어로 명사절이 왔다. have done의 목적어가 없는 불완전한 절이므로 that은 what으로 고쳐야 한다. (that → what)
② 타동사 ignore의 목적어가 없으므로 수동태로 바르게 쓰였다. evidence는 불가산명사이므로 항상 단수 취급하므로 단수 동사 was가 쓰인 것도 바르다. Point 16. 능동태 vs. 수동태 구분 / Point 27. 주어 - 동사 수 일치
③ it은 가목적어이고 진목적어는 to determine ~이므로 가목적어, 진목적어 구문이 바르게 쓰였다. Point 24. 인칭대명사
④ seem은 보어로 to부정사를 취할 수 있다. 보이는 것보다 이전에 계획되었음을 표현하기 위해 완료 부정사가 쓰였고 The mission과 plan은 수동 관계이므로 수동형 완료부정사가 바르게 쓰였다. Point 04. 불완전자동사의 보어 / Point 30. 준동사의 형태 변화

**어휘** debate 논쟁하다  prevent 막다  unfold 밝혀지다
initially 처음에는  ignore 무시하다  analyze 분석하다
determine 결정하다  responsible 책임이 있는
coordination 조정

**정답** ①

### 015  문법포인트 | Point 07. 완전타동사와 함께 사용되는 주요 전치사 / Point 30. 준동사의 형태 변화

The engineer ① works [→ has worked] on renewable energy projects since 2010, gradually becoming used ② to manage [→ to managing] complex systems. Last year, people accused her ③ of being manipulated by corporate interests, though the claims were never proven. Her team described her as ④ a such dedicated professional [→ such a dedicated professional] with a clear sense of purpose.

**해설**
③ 'A를 B하다고 비난하다'라는 의미는 「accuse A of B」의 구문으로 표현하므로 「of + 동명사」가 바르게 쓰였다. 또한 그녀가 조정을 당했다는 수동의 관계이므로 수동형 동명사가 바르게 쓰였다.
① since 2010이라는 「since + 과거 시점」이 있으므로 현재 시제가 아닌 현재완료 시제로 써야 한다. (works → has worked) Point 12. 완료 시제
② '~에 익숙하다'는 「be used to -ing」를 써야 한다. 이때 be동사 대신 '되다'라는 의미를 나타내기 위해 become, get 등의 동사를 쓰기도 한다. 따라서 manage는 managing으로 고쳐야 한다. (to manage → to managing) Point 18. 조동사의 선택
④ 한정사 such 뒤에 관사 형용사 명사가 온다면 「such + 부정관사 + 형용사 + 명사」의 어순이 되어야 한다. (a such dedicated professional → such a dedicated a professional) Point 23. 관사의 위치

**어휘** renewable 재생 가능한  accuse 비난하다  manipulate 조종하다
prove 입증하다  dedicated 헌신적인  professional 전문가
clear 명확한  sense of purpose 목적의식

**정답** ③

### 016 밑줄 친 부분에 들어갈 말로 가장 적절한 것은?

The library, _____ I spent countless hours studying, has a vast collection of books.

① whose  ② that
③ which  ④ in which

### 017 밑줄 친 부분 중 어법상 옳지 않은 것은?

It was at the moment when she received the news ① that she appeared truly ② shocking, unable to say a word. ③ Had it not been for her mentor, she might not have overcome the pressure that came with such responsibility. The ceremony ended in the hall ④ where she had given her first presentation, a place she would never forget.

### 018 밑줄 친 부분에 들어갈 말로 가장 적절한 것은?

To improve productivity, the company encourages flexible work arrangements, such as starting earlier in the morning and _____ during quieter hours in the afternoon.

① finishes  ② finishing
③ to finish  ④ finished

### 019 밑줄 친 부분 중 어법상 옳지 않은 것은?

Some citizens continue to object ① to increasing surveillance in public spaces, arguing that it invades personal freedom. As concerns ② raise about data privacy, many demand that policies ③ be revised to better protect individual rights. In such situations, one cannot but ④ question the balance between security and liberty.

## 문장 분석 및 해설

### 016 문법포인트 | Point 43. 관계대명사의 선택

The library, (in which I spent countless hours studying), has a vast collection of books.

**해설** 문장 중간에 절이 삽입되었다. 문맥상 The library를 수식하는 관계대명사절로 만들어 주어야 한다. 빈칸 뒤에 절이 완전하므로 빈칸에는 ④ in which가 들어가야 한다. 장소의 관계부사인 where도 가능하다.

**어휘** countless 셀 수 없는  vas 방대한  collection 소장품

**정답** ④

### 017 문법포인트 | Point 32. 현재분사 vs. 과거분사

It was at the moment when she received the news ① that she appeared truly ② shocking, unable to say a word. ③ Had it not been for her mentor, she might not have overcome the pressure that came with such responsibility. The ceremony ended in the hall ④ (where she had given her first presentation), a place she would never forget.

**해설**
② 감정유발동사의 경우 주체가 감정을 일으키는 것이면 현재분사로, 감정을 느끼는 것이면 과거분사로 쓴다. 그녀가 충격을 받는, 즉 감정을 느끼는 상황이므로 과거분사로 써야 한다. (shocking → shocked)
① it ~ that 강조구문으로 전치사구인 at the moment ~가 바르게 강조되었다. Point 49. 강조
③ 「Had it not been for ~」는 '~이 없었다면'을 의미하는 가정법 과거완료의 표현으로 주절의 가정법 과거완료 동사와 호응하여 바르게 쓰였다. Point 47. 기타 가정법
④ 선행사가 장소인 hall이고 where 뒤가 완전한 절이므로 관계부사 where가 바르게 쓰였다. Point 44. 관계부사

**어휘** appear ~처럼 보이다  overcome 극복하다  pressure 압박감  responsibility 책임  ceremony 행사  presentation 발표

**정답** ②

### 018 문법포인트 | Point 39. 등위접속사의 병렬 구조

To improve productivity, the company encourages flexible work arrangements, such as starting earlier in the morning and finishing during quieter hours in the afternoon.

**해설** 등위접속사는 병렬 구조를 이루어야 한다. 등위접속사 and로 연결되므로 앞의 starting과 같은 동명사 ② finishing이 들어가야 한다.

**어휘** productivity 생산성  encourage 장려하다  flexible 유연한  work arrangement 근무 방식  such as ~ 같은

**정답** ②

### 019 문법포인트 | Point 11. 혼동하기 쉬운 동사의 불규칙 변화

Some citizens continue to object ① to increasing surveillance in public spaces, arguing that it invades personal freedom. As concerns ② raise about data privacy, many demand that policies ③ be revised to better protect individual rights. In such situations, one cannot but ④ question the balance between security and liberty.

**해설**
② raise는 타동사로 '~을 제기하다'를 의미한다. 목적어가 없으므로 수동태로 써야 한다. 또는 자동사 arise(생기다)나 rise(늘어나다)로 쓸 수 있다. (raise → are raised/arise/rise)
① object to의 to는 전치사이므로 목적어로 동명사 increasing이 바르게 쓰였다. Point 48. 전치사의 목적어
③ 명령, 주장, 요구, 제안 동사의 목적어로 that절이 오면 that절의 동사는 「(should) + 동사원형」으로 써야 한다. demand의 목적어인 that절에서 should가 생략된 be revised가 바르게 쓰였다. Point 19. 당위의 조동사 should
④ 「cannot but + 동사원형」은 '~하지 않을 수 없다'라는 뜻의 준동사 주요 표현이다. 동사원형 question이 와서 표현이 바르게 쓰였다. Point 31. 준동사 주요 표현

**어휘** object to ~에 반대하다  surveillance 감시  invade 침해하다  policy 정책  revise 개정하다  question 의문을 제기하다  security 안전  liberty 자유

**정답** ②

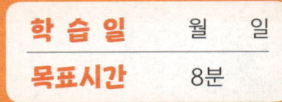

**020** 밑줄 친 부분에 들어갈 말로 가장 적절한 것은?

During the emergency meeting, several board members strongly opposed _____ the proposal without discussing the financial risks involved.

① approving
② being approved
③ to approving
④ to being approved

**021** 밑줄 친 부분 중 어법상 옳은 것은?

The old technician was used ① to working late into the night, but his new assistant clearly was not used to such a routine. The tools in the lab ② were belonged to a private collector and were only temporarily on loan. ③ Hardly the assistant had entered the workshop when he was told that a critical machine had failed. In a rush, the manager let the damaged device ④ examined by an outside expert.

**022** 밑줄 친 부분에 들어갈 말로 가장 적절한 것은?

The final exam featured _____ for the majority of students to complete within the allotted time.

① too a difficult question
② too difficult question
③ too difficult a question
④ a too difficult question

**023** 밑줄 친 부분 중 어법상 옳지 않은 것은?

One was a ① ten-year-old boy, and the other, with a serious look on his face, was two years older than him. They had arrived early, hoping to avoid attention after missing practice. Their coach had them ② punish for skipping it. Such ③ was the tension in the room that no one dared ④ to speak a word.

## 020  문법포인트 | Point 05. 완전타동사 / Point 06. 완전타동사와 동작의 목적어

During the emergency meeting, several board members strongly opposed approving the proposal without discussing the financial risks involved.

**해설** oppose는 완전타동사로 전치사 없이 목적어를 바로 취한다. 따라서 빈칸에는 동명사인 ① approving이 들어가야 한다. 제안을 승인한다는 능동의 의미이고 목적어인 the proposal을 통해 능동 관계를 확인할 수 있으므로 수동의 동명사 형태인 being approved는 적절하지 않다.

**어휘** board member 이사  strongly 강하게  oppose 반대하다
financial 재정적인  risk 위험  involved 관련된
approve 승인하다

**정답** ①

## 021  문법포인트 | Point 18. 조동사의 선택

The old technician was used ① to working late into the night, but his new assistant clearly was not used to such a routine. The tools in the lab ② were belonged to a private collector and were only temporarily on loan. ③ Hardly the assistant had entered the workshop when he was told that a critical machine had failed. In a rush, the manager let the damaged device ④ examined by an outside expert.

→ belonged to
→ Hardly had the assistant entered
→ be examined

**해설**
① 「be used to -ing」는 '~에 익숙하다'를 의미한다. 전치사 to 뒤에 동명사 working이 바르게 쓰였다.
② belong to는 자동사이므로 수동태로 쓸 수 없다. (were belonged to → belonged to) Point 17. 동사의 유형별 수동태
③ 「Hardly + had + S + p.p. when + S' + V'(과거 시제)」는 '~하자마자 …했다'를 의미하는 표현이다. Hardly가 부정부사이므로 문장의 앞으로 나오면 주어와 동사는 도치되어야 한다. (Hardly the assistant had entered → Hardly had the assistant entered) Point 15. 시제 관련 표현 / Point 50. 도치
④ let은 사역동사로 목적어와 목적격보어의 관계가 수동일 때 목적격보어는 「be + p.p.」로 써야 한다. 기계가 검사된다는 수동의 의미이므로 be examined로 고쳐야 한다. (examined → be examined) Point 10. 불완전타동사와 동작의 목적격보어

**어휘** technician 기술자  assistant 조수  routine 일상
collector 수집가  temporarily 임시로  on loan 빌린
workshop 작업장  critical 중요한  fail 고장 나다
in a rush 서둘러  damaged 손상된  device 기기
examine 검사하다  expert 전문가

**정답** ①

## 022  문법포인트 | Point 23. 관사의 위치

The final exam featured too difficult a question for the majority of students to complete within the allotted time.

**해설** too, so, how 등의 부사가 올 때 관사의 어순은 「too/so/how + 형용사 + a/an + 명사」와 같다. 따라서 정답은 ③ too difficult a question이다. 「too ~ to …」는 '너무 ~해서 …하지 못하다'는 의미의 to부정사 부사적 용법이다.

**어휘** feature 포함하다  majority 대다수  complete 완료하다
allotted 주어진

**정답** ③

## 023  문법포인트 | Point 10. 불완전타동사와 동작의 목적격보어

One was a ① ten-year-old boy, and the other, with a serious look on his face, was two years older than him. They had arrived early, hoping to avoid attention after missing practice. Their coach had them ② punish for skipping it. (Such) ③ was the tension in the room that no one dared ④ to speak a word.

→ punished

**해설**
② 사역동사의 목적어와 목적격보어 사이의 관계가 수동이면 목적격보어는 과거분사로 써야 한다. 두 아이가 벌을 받는 수동의 관계이므로 punish는 punished로 고쳐야 한다. (punish → punished)
① 측정단위명사(year)가 명사(boy)를 수식할 때 측정단위명사는 단수로 써야 한다. year가 단수로 바르게 쓰였다. Point 35. 주의할 형용사와 부사
③ 보어인 such가 문장의 앞으로 나왔으므로 주어와 동사는 도치되어야 한다. 주어 the tension과 동사 was의 도치가 바르게 쓰였다. 「Such + be동사 + 주어 + that + 결과절」은 '주어가 너무 ~해서 …하다'라는 뜻이다. Point 50. 도치
④ dare는 일반동사일 때 to부정사를 목적어로 취한다. to부정사가 목적어로 바르게 쓰였다. Point 06. 완전타동사와 동작의 목적어

**어휘** avoid 피하다  attention 관심  practice 연습  punish 벌을 주다
skip 거르다  tension 긴장감

**정답** ②

**024** 밑줄 친 부분에 들어갈 말로 가장 적절한 것은?

> With the final report _____ and the deadline approaching, the team resolved to extend their working hours through the weekend to meet expectations.

① complete
② completed
③ completing
④ completes

**025** 밑줄 친 부분 중 어법상 옳지 않은 것은?

> That she remained calm during the crisis ① surprising everyone. She spoke clearly and acted with confidence, ② impressing even the most skeptical members of the team. ③ Tired as she was, she continued working until the task was complete. I wish she ④ had taken a break earlier, but she refused to stop.

**026** 밑줄 친 부분에 들어갈 말로 가장 적절한 것은?

> The patient was taken to the emergency room who had already received proper first aid; someone with medical training _____ him earlier.

① should have treated
② shouldn't have treated
③ must have treated
④ couldn't have treated

**027** 밑줄 친 부분 중 어법상 옳은 것은?

> Scientists relied on data ① collected from remote sensors to understand climate patterns more accurately. The Earth ② revolved around the Sun, and this predictable movement ③ influencing seasonal changes across the globe. Reliable ④ informations played a key role in forming early climate models.

## 024 문법포인트 | Point 33. 분사구문

With the final report completed and the deadline approaching, the team resolved to extend their working hours through the weekend to meet expectations.

해설 「with + 목적어 + 목적격보어(분사/형용사)」는 '~가 ~하는 상황에서'라는 의미로 부대상황을 나타내는 분사구문이다. 빈칸에는 목적어 the final report에 대한 목적격보어가 들어가야 한다. 보고서가 완료된다는 수동의 관계이므로 빈칸에는 과거분사인 ② completed가 들어가야 한다.

어휘 deadline 마감일  approach 다가오다  resolve 결심하다
extend 연장하다  through (기간) 내내  expectation 기대
complete 완료하다

정답 ②

## 025 문법포인트 | Point 01. 문장의 구성

[That she remained calm during the crisis] ① surprising (→ surprised) everyone. She spoke clearly and acted with confidence, ② impressing even the most skeptical members of the team. ③ Tired as she was, she continued working until the task was complete. I wish she ④ had taken a break earlier, but she refused to stop.

해설
① that절이 주어로 나왔으며 문장에 동사가 없다. 따라서 surprising을 동사인 surprised로 고쳐 문장을 구성하는 것이 가장 적절하다. 글 전체가 과거에 관한 것이므로 과거 동사로 고쳐야 한다. (surprising → surprised) Point 01 문장의 구성
② 의미상의 주어인 she가 팀원들에게 깊은 인상을 주었다는 의미이므로 능동의 현재분사형 분사구문이 바르게 쓰였다. Point 33. 분사구문
③ 「형용사/부사/명사 + as/though + 주어 + 동사」의 접속사 양보구문이 바르게 쓰였다. Point 42. 주요 양보구문
④ I wish 뒤에는 가정법 동사가 온다. earlier로 과거의 일을 알 수 있으므로 과거에 대한 소망을 표현하는 가정법 과거완료인 had taken이 바르게 쓰였다. Point 47. 기타 가정법

어휘 calm 차분한  crisis 위기  surprise 놀라게 하다
confidence 자신감  impress 깊은 인상을 주다
skeptical 회의적인  complete 완료된

정답 ①

## 026 문법포인트 | Point 20. 조동사 + have p.p.

The patient was taken to the emergency room who had already received proper first aid; someone with medical training must have treated him earlier.

해설 지난 일에 대한 추측은 「must/may/would/cannot + have + p.p.」로 표현한다. 문맥상 의학 교육을 받은 사람이 그 환자를 치유했을 것이라는 추측을 나타내야 하므로 ③ must have treated가 적절하다. ④ couldn't have treated는 지난 일에 대한 부정적인 추측이므로 문맥상 어울리지 않는다.

어휘 proper 적절한  first aid 응급 처치  medical 의학적인
treat 치료하다

정답 ③

## 027 문법포인트 | Point 32. 현재분사 vs. 과거분사

Scientists relied on data ① collected from remote sensors to understand climate patterns more accurately. The Earth ② revolved (→ revolves) around the Sun, and this predictable movement ③ influencing (→ influences) seasonal changes across the globe. Reliable ④ informations (→ information) played a key role in forming early climate models.

해설
① collected는 data를 수식하는 과거분사로 data가 수집되는 수동의 의미이므로 과거분사가 바르게 쓰였다.
② 지구가 태양 주위를 도는 것은 과학적 사실이므로 현재 시제로 써야 한다. 따라서 revolved는 revolves로 고쳐야 한다 (revolved → revolves) Point 14. 시제일치와 예외
③ movement라는 주어만 있고 동사가 없는 문장이다. 따라서 influencing을 동사 influences로 고쳐야 한다. 역시 과학적 사실이므로 현재 시제로 고쳐야 한다. (influencing → influences) Point 01. 문장의 구성
④ information은 절대 불가산명사이므로 복수로 쓸 수 없다. 단수로 고쳐야 한다. (informations → information) Point 21. 명사의 이해

어휘 revolve 돌다  predictable 예측 가능한  influence 영향을 주다
seasonal 계절의  reliable 믿을 수 있는

정답 ①

**028** 밑줄 친 부분에 들어갈 말로 가장 적절한 것은?

Watching the sunset over the ocean, she _____ the peaceful moments spent by the shore during her childhood.

① reminded
② was reminded
③ reminded of
④ was reminded of

**029** 밑줄 친 부분 중 어법상 옳은 것은?

The team added new rules lest hackers ① should not bypass the firewall. They worked for hours, with their focus ② directed on every alert. Their leader ③ monitors the system for three years and once mentioned ④ all employees the need for stricter password policies.

**030** 밑줄 친 부분 중 어법상 옳은 것은?

She loves classical music, and ① so does her brother. At a ② recently rehearsal, she was heard ③ play a familiar melody, and it inspired everyone in the room. Her performance, ④ that required both precision and emotion, left a strong impression. The conductor's praise clearly reflected her growth as a musician.

## 028 문법포인트 | Point 17. 동사의 유형별 수동태

Watching the sunset over the ocean, she was reminded of the peaceful moments spent by the shore during her childhood.

**해설** 'A에게 B에 대해 떠오르게 하다'는 「remind A of B」로 수동태가 되면 「A be reminded of B」 형태가 된다. 이때 동사의 수동태형 뒤에 전치사 of를 누락시키지 않아야 한다. 따라서 정답은 ④ was reminded of이다.

**어휘** sunset 석양  ocean 바다  moment 순간  shore 해변  childhood 어린 시절

**정답** ④

## 029 문법포인트 | Point 33. 분사구문

The team added new rules lest hackers ① should not bypass the firewall. They worked for hours, with their focus ② directed on every alert. Their leader ③ monitors the system for three years and once mentioned ④ all employees the need for stricter password policies.

→ should bypass
→ has monitored
→ to all employees

**해설**
② with 분사구문으로 목적어인 focus를 겨냥되도록 한다는 수동의 관계이므로 과거분사인 directed가 바르게 쓰였다.
① lest는 부정의 의미를 포함한 접속사이므로 뒤에 다시 부정어를 쓸 수 없다. should not bypass를 should bypass로 고쳐야 한다. (should not bypass → should bypass) Point 41. 부사절 접속사의 선택
③ for three years로 보아 과거부터 현재까지 계속된 의미이므로 현재완료 시제로 고쳐야 한다. (monitors → has monitored) Point 12. 완료시제
④ mention은 4형식으로 쓸 수 없는 완전타동사이다. 따라서 간접목적어에 해당하는 all employees는 to all employees로 고쳐야 한다. (all employees → to all employees) Point 05. 완전타동사

**어휘** bypass 우회하다  firewall 방화벽  direct 겨냥하다  alert 경고  monitor 감시하다  mention 언급하다

**정답** ②

## 030 문법포인트 | Point 50. 도치

She loves classical music, and ① so does her brother. At a ② recently rehearsal, she was heard ③ play a familiar melody, and it inspired everyone in the room. Her performance, ④ that required both precision and emotion, left a strong impression. The conductor's praise clearly reflected her growth as a musician.

→ recent
→ to play
→ which

**해설**
① '~ 또한 그러하다'를 의미하는 so는 도치해야 한다. 이때 앞에 나온 동사가 일반동사이면 do를 대신 써야 한다. 앞에 love라는 일반동사가 있으므로 does가 바르게 쓰였다.
② recently가 명사 rehearsal을 수식하고 있다. 부사는 명사를 수식할 수 없으므로 형용사인 recent로 고쳐야 한다. (recently → recent) Point 34. 형용사 vs. 부사
③ 지각동사가 수동태로 전환될 때 원형부정사 목적격보어는 to부정사로 고쳐야 한다. 따라서 play는 to play로 고쳐야 한다. (play → to play) Point 17. 동사의 유형별 수동태
④ 관계대명사 that은 계속적 용법으로 쓸 수 없으므로 which로 고쳐야 한다. (that → which) Point 43. 관계대명사의 선택

**어휘** rehearsal 예행연습  familiar 익숙한  inspire 영감을 주다  performance 연주  precision 정확성  emotion 감정  impression 인상  conductor 지휘자  praise 칭찬  reflect 보여주다  musician 음악가

**정답** ①

**031** 밑줄 친 부분에 들어갈 말로 가장 적절한 것은?

Strict security measures kept unauthorized visitors _____ the laboratory.

① entering
② from entering
③ to enter
④ to enter into

**032** 밑줄 친 부분 중 어법상 옳지 않은 것은?

The contemporary art exhibition ① held to commemorate the gallery's 50th anniversary ② has raised global attention. Due to sponsorship changes, however, several installations ③ were deprived the necessary funding the night before the opening. Now, the gallery ④ in which the missing works were supposed to be displayed appears disjointed and incomplete, with the exhibition's overall coherence impaired.

**033** 밑줄 친 부분에 들어갈 말로 가장 적절한 것은?

Nobody who was there forgot _____ what had happened just moments before the explosion.

① witness
② witnessing
③ being witnessed
④ to witness

**034** 밑줄 친 부분 중 어법상 옳지 않은 것은?

The academic plan with multiple implementation phases at the universities ① is a critical framework that meets international standards, ② given broad recognition by leading scholars for its innovative curriculum. The new schedule is expected ③ to provide greater consistency for joint programs, making the academic year from these universities ④ widely recognizing across global networks.

## 문장 분석 및 해설

**031** 문법포인트 | Point 07. 완전타동사와 함께 사용되는 주요 전치사

Strict security measures kept unauthorized visitors from entering the laboratory.

[해설] keep, prevent, deter, stop, prohibit 등과 같이 금지를 의미하는 동사들은 뒤에 목적어가 나오고 그 목적어가 하지 못하게 하는 행위를 「from -ing」로 표현한다. 따라서 정답은 ②이다.

[어휘] strict 엄격한　security 보안　measure 조치
unauthorized 승인되지 않은　laboratory 실험실

[정답] ②

---

**032** 문법포인트 | Point 17. 동사의 유형별 수동태

The contemporary art exhibition ① (held to commemorate the gallery's 50th anniversary) ② has raised global attention. Due to sponsorship changes, however, several installations ③ were deprived the necessary funding the night before
→ were deprived of
the opening. Now, the gallery ④ (in which the missing works were supposed to be displayed) appears disjointed and incomplete, with the exhibition's overall coherence impaired.

[해설]
③ deprive는 목적어 뒤에 「of + 명사」의 형태로 빼앗긴 대상을 표현하는데, 수동태 전환 시에 전치사를 빠뜨리지 않도록 주의해야 한다. (were deprived → were deprived of)
① 수식받는 명사인 The contemporary art exhibition과 분사가 의미상 수동의 관계이므로 과거분사 held가 바르게 쓰였다. Point 32. 현재분사 vs. 과거분사
② raise는 '불러일으키다'라는 의미의 타동사이고 뒤에 목적어인 global attention이 있으므로 타동사 raise가 바르게 쓰였다. Point 11. 혼동하기 쉬운 동사의 불규칙 변화
④ 관계대명사 뒤에 완전한 절이 왔고 선행사가 장소를 의미하는 명사인 the gallery이므로 in which가 바르게 쓰였다. 참고로, in which 대신 관계부사인 where를 써도 된다. Point 43. 관계대명사의 선택

[어휘] contemporary 현대의　exhibition 전시회
commemorate 기념하다　raise (감정이나 반응) 불러일으키다
sponsorship 후원　installation 설치 작품
deprive A of B A에게 B를 빼앗다　funding 자금
disjointed 단절된　incomplete 미완성의　overall 전체적인
coherence 일관성　impair 손상하다

[정답] ③

---

**033** 문법포인트 | Point 06. 완전타동사와 동작의 목적어

Nobody (who was there) forgot witnessing what had happened just moments before the explosion.

[해설] forget은 한 일을 잊었다는 의미일 때는 동명사를, 해야 할 일을 잊었다는 의미일 때는 to부정사를 목적어로 취한다. 여기서는 목격했던 일을 잊지 못했다는 의미이므로 ② witnessing이 정답이다.

[어휘] explosion 폭발　witness 목격하다

[정답] ②

---

**034** 문법포인트 | Point 10. 불완전타동사와 동작의 목적격보어

The academic plan with multiple implementation phases at the universities ① is a critical framework that meets international standards, ② given broad recognition by leading scholars for its innovative curriculum. The new schedule is expected ③ to provide greater consistency for joint programs, making the academic year from these universities ④ widely recognizing across global networks.
→ widely recognized

[해설]
④ 사역동사의 목적격보어로 현재분사는 올 수 없다. 목적어인 the academic year와 목적격보어의 관계가 의미상 수동이므로 recognizing을 recognized로 고쳐야 한다. (widely recognizing → widely recognized)
① 문장의 주어는 단수 명사인 The academic plan이므로 be 동사의 단수형인 is가 바르게 쓰였다. Point 27. 주어 - 동사 수 일치
② 분사구문 given이 의미상 주어인 The academic plan과 문맥상 수동의 관계이므로 과거분사 given이 바르게 쓰였다. give는 수여동사로 쓰였으므로 과거분사 뒤에 여전히 직접목적어가 올 수 있다. Point 33. 분사구문
③ 불완전타동사 expect는 목적격보어로 to부정사를 취하며, 수동태로 전환 시에도 동사 뒤에 목적격보어인 to부정사가 그대로 온다. Point 17. 동사의 유형별 수동태

[어휘] academic 학사의　multiple 여러 개의　implementation 실행
phase 단계　critical 핵심적인　framework 틀
recognition 인정　innovative 혁신적인　consistency 일관성

[정답] ④

**035** 밑줄 친 부분에 들어갈 말로 가장 적절한 것은?

It took him months _____ enough courage to ask her out on a date.

① gather　　② gathering
③ to gather　④ to be gathered

**036** 밑줄 친 부분 중 어법상 옳지 않은 것은?

So urgent ① was the need for a revised climate model that several leading researchers recommended in 2010 the committee ② revise the methodology and ③ include new atmospheric variables in their projections, only to fail due to a lack of consensus. Had the committee accepted the proposal back then, more accurate forecasts ④ would have been generated now.

**037** 밑줄 친 부분에 들어갈 말로 가장 적절한 것은?

The CEO proposed that her company _____ a new marketing campaign to expand the customer base in emerging markets.

① launches　② launch
③ to launch　④ be launched

**038** 밑줄 친 부분 중 어법상 옳지 않은 것은?

One common risk of blood transfusions is an allergic reaction or fever ① caused by the immune system's response. There is also a chance of ② transmitting infections if the blood is not properly screened. Incompatible blood types can cause serious complications, such as hemolysis, ③ where red blood cells are destroyed. Additionally, repeated transfusions may lead to iron overload, ④ that can damage organs.

## 035 문법포인트 | Point 08. 수여동사

It took him months to gather enough courage to ask her out on a date.

**해설** '~가 ...하는 데 시간/돈이 걸리다/들다'는 「It + take/cost + 간접목적어(~) + 직접목적어(시간/돈) + to부정사」으로 나타낸다. 따라서 빈칸에는 to부정사가 들어가야 하므로 정답은 ③ to gather이다. 뒤에 목적어가 있으므로 ④ to be gathered는 들어갈 수 없다.

**어휘** ask ~ out on a date ~에게 데이트 신청을 하다

**정답** ③

## 036 문법포인트 | Point 46. 기본 가정법

(So urgent) ① was the need for a revised climate model that several leading researchers recommended in 2010 the committee ② revise the methodology and ③ include new atmospheric variables in their projections, only to fail due to a lack of consensus. Had the committee accepted the proposal back then, more accurate forecasts ④ would have been generated now.
→ would be generated

**해설**
④ 조건절에서는 과거 상황의 반대를 가정하고 (가정법 과거완료) 주절에서는 그로 인한 현재의 결과에 대한 아쉬움을 표현하는 (가정법 과거) 혼합가정법이다. 따라서 주절의 동사는 가정법 과거에 맞게 would be generated로 고쳐야 한다. (would have been generated → would be generated)
① 보어가 문장의 앞으로 나오면 주어와 동사를 도치시켜야 한다. 보어 urgent가 문두에 나와 동사 was와 주어인 the need가 바르게 도치되었다. Point 50. 도치
② 주장, 요구, 제안, 명령 동사의 목적어로 that절이 오면 that절의 동사는 「(should) + 동사원형」의 형태가 되어야 한다. 동사원형 revise가 바르게 쓰였다. Point 19. 당위의 조동사 should
③ the committee가 주어이고 두 개의 동사 revise와 include가 등위접속사 and를 통해 병렬로 바르게 연결되었다. Point 39. 등위접속사의 병렬구조

**어휘** urgent 긴급한  revise 개정하다  methodology 방법론  atmospheric 대기의  variable 변수  projection 예측  consensus 의견 합의  accept 받아들이다  proposal 제안  accurate 정확한  forecast 예측  generate 생성하다

**정답** ④

## 037 문법포인트 | Point 19. 당위의 조동사 should / Point 16. 능동태 vs. 수동태 구분

The CEO proposed that her company launch a new marketing campaign to expand the customer base in emerging markets.

**해설** 주장, 요구, 제안, 명령 동사가 that절을 목적어로 취할 경우, that절의 동사는 「(should) + 동사원형」의 형태가 되어야 한다. 또한 타동사 launch가 목적어와 함께 쓰였으므로 능동태가 되어야 한다. 따라서 이 두 가지를 만족하는 ② launch가 정답이다.

**어휘** propose 제안하다  campaign 광고  expand 확장하다  base 기반  emerging 신흥의  launch 시작하다

**정답** ②

## 038 문법포인트 | Point 43. 관계대명사의 선택

One common risk of blood transfusions is an allergic reaction or fever ① (caused by the immune system's response). There is also a chance of ② transmitting infections if the blood is not properly screened. Incompatible blood types can cause serious complications, such as hemolysis, ③ (where red blood cells are destroyed). Additionally, repeated transfusions may lead to iron overload, ④ that can damage organs.
→ which

**해설**
④ 관계대명사 that은 계속적 용법으로 쓸 수 없다. 선행사가 iron overload이므로 which로 고쳐야 한다. (that → which)
① 수식받는 명사인 reaction or fever와 cause는 유발된다는 의미로 수동 관계이다. 따라서 과거분사가 바르게 쓰였다. Point 32. 현재분사 vs. 과거분사
② 전치사 of의 목적어로 동명사가 바르게 쓰였다. Point 48. 전치사의 목적어
③ where 이후 절이 완전하므로 관계부사나 「전치사 + 관계대명사」만 가능하다. hemolysis가 장소는 아니지만 상황, 영역에 해당하는 단어가 선행사이면 where나 in which를 쓸 수 있다. Point 44. 관계부사

**어휘** blood transfusion 수혈  allergic 알레르기의  reaction 반응  fever 열  immune 면역의  transmit 전파하다  infection 감염  properly 제대로  screen 보호하다  incompatible 맞지 않는  blood type 혈액형  complications (pl.) 합병증  hemolysis 용혈  overload 과다  damage 손상시키다  organ 장기

**정답** ④

DAY 03  29

**039** 밑줄 친 부분에 들어갈 말로 가장 적절한 것은?

She tries to keep _____ her painting skills by attending workshops regularly.

① improve  ② improving
③ to improve  ④ for her to improve

**041** 밑줄 친 부분에 들어갈 말로 가장 적절한 것은?

Inflation has caused prices _____ steadily over the past years.

① rise  ② raise
③ to rise  ④ to raise

**040** 밑줄 친 부분 중 어법상 옳지 않은 것은?

Not until the final economic report revealed the impact of low literacy rates ① the government recognized the crisis and begin addressing the problem. Nevertheless, the lack of strategies among regions, which face different challenges, ② remains a major concern in national policy planning. Citizens argue that education is worth ③ funding and urge the government ④ to implement more effective measures.

**042** 밑줄 친 부분 중 어법상 옳은 것은?

Hospital administrators found ① it essential for nurses to attend regular training to ensure compliance with safety protocols. ② A great number of evidence supports the idea ③ what well-trained staff can reduce patient risk, but overworked nurses ④ don't rarely attend workshops offered by the hospital.

## 039  문법포인트 | Point 06. 완전타동사와 동작의 목적어

She tries to keep improving her painting skills by attending workshops regularly.

해설 동사 keep은 완전타동사로, 목적어로 동명사를 취한다. 따라서 정답은 ② improving이다.

어휘 attend 참석하다

정답 ②

## 040  문법포인트 | Point 15. 시제 관련 표현

(Not until the final economic report revealed the impact of low literacy rates) ① the government recognized the crisis
→ did the government recognize
and begin addressing the problem. Nevertheless, the lack of strategies among regions, which face different challenges, ② remains a major concern in national policy planning. Citizens argue that education is worth ③ funding and urge the government ④ to implement more effective measures.

해설
① 「Not until B A」 구문은 '~가 되어서야 (비로소) …하다'라는 뜻이며, 이때 주어와 동사는 도치된다. 일반동사의 과거형이 쓰였으므로 조동사 did를 주어 앞으로 보내고 주어 뒤에는 동사원형을 써야 한다. (the government recognized → did the government recognize)
② 동사 remains의 주어는 the lack이라는 단수 명사이므로 동사 역시 단수형인 remains가 바르게 쓰였다. Point 27. 주어 - 동사 수 일치
③ 「be + worth/worthy of + -ing」는 '~할 만한 가치가 있다'라는 뜻을 나타내는 표현이므로 worth 뒤에 funding이 바르게 쓰였다. Point 31. 준동사 주요 표현
④ 불완전타동사로 쓰인 urge는 목적어와 목적격보어가 의미상 능동의 관계일 때 to부정사를 목적격보어로 취한다. Point 10. 불완전타동사와 동작의 목적격보어

어휘 reveal 밝히다  impact 영향  literacy rate 식자율  crisis 위기
address 다루다  strategy 전략  urge 촉구하다
implement 시행하다  measures (pl.) 조치

정답 ①

## 041  문법포인트 | Point 10. 불완전타동사와 동작의 목적격보어

Inflation has caused prices to rise steadily over the past years.

해설 빈칸은 cause의 목적격보어인 to부정사가 되어야 하므로 「to + 동사원형」이 들어가야 한다. 또한 목적어가 없으므로 자동사인 rise가 들어가야 한다. 따라서 정답은 ③ to rise이다.

어휘 cause 일으키다

정답 ③

## 042  문법포인트 | Point 24. 인칭대명사

Hospital administrators found ① It essential for nurses
     가목
to attend regular training to ensure compliance with safety
진목
protocols. ② A great number of evidence supports the idea
                → A great deal of
③ [what well-trained staff can reduce patient risk], but
      → that
overworked nurses ④ don't rarely attend workshops
              → don't attend/rarely attend
offered by the hospital.

해설
① 목적어가 to부정사구나 명사절일 경우 목적어 자리에 가목적어 it을 쓰고 진목적어를 문장의 뒤로 보낸다. to attend ~가 진목적어이며 가목적어 it이 바르게 쓰였다.
② a great number of는 셀 수 있는 명사의 복수형을 수식하는 수 형용사인데 evidence는 셀 수 없는 명사이므로 양 형용사인 a great deal of로 고쳐야 한다. (A great number of → A great deal of) Point 21. 명사의 이해
③ 명사절 접속사 뒤에 완전한 절이 왔고 의미상 앞의 명사 the idea의 동격이므로 동격의 접속사 that으로 고쳐야 한다. (what → that) Point 40. 명사절 접속사의 선택
④ 부정부사는 자체적으로 부정의 의미를 가지고 있으므로 다른 부정부사와 함께 쓰이지 않는다. 따라서 don't 혹은 rarely를 삭제해야 한다. (don't rarely attend → don't attend/rarely attend) Point 35. 주의할 형용사와 부사

어휘 administrator 관리자  ensure 보장하다  compliance 준수
safety protocol 안전 수칙  evidence 증거  support 뒷받침하다
overworked 과로한

정답 ①

**043** 밑줄 친 부분에 들어갈 말로 가장 적절한 것은?

The museum _____ since renovations began.

① closes
② closed
③ is closed
④ has been closed

**044** 밑줄 친 부분 중 어법상 옳지 않은 것은?

A researcher published a report in 2018 ① showed that whales possess a communication system, ② only to discover that scientists still knew very little about it. It took years for her ③ to decode the signals, and the paper explained ④ how sound patterns vary depending on context.

**045** 밑줄 친 부분 중 어법상 옳지 않은 것은?

Vaccination programs contributed ① to preventing diseases, improving public trust, and reducing long-term medical costs. With them, health officials could keep ② reducing outbreaks at the early stages of spread, administering vaccines to vulnerable groups, and ③ monitoring regions to track the spread of new variants, which could be later contained in areas ④ designating to prevent further transmission.

## 043 문법포인트 | Point 12. 완료 시제

The museum has been closed since renovations began.

**해설** since 이하가 과거 시제이고 그 이후 계속되었다는 의미이므로, 현재완료 시제가 사용되어야 한다. close가 타동사인데 목적어가 없으므로 수동태가 들어야 하므로 ④ has been closed가 가장 적절하다.

**어휘** renovation 수리

정답 ④

## 044 문법포인트 | Point 01. 문장의 구성 / Point 32. 현재분사 vs. 과거분사

A researcher published a report in 2018 ① (showed) that whales possess a communication system, ② only to discover that scientists still knew very little about it. It took years for her ③ to decode the signals, and the paper explained ④ [how sound patterns vary depending on context].

**해설**
① 문장의 주어는 A researcher이고 동사는 published이다. 동사가 있으므로 showed는 동사가 아니라 a report를 후치 수식하는 분사여야 하는데, report가 보여주는 능동의 의미이고 뒤에 목적절이 이어지므로 과거분사를 현재분사로 고쳐야 한다. (showed → showing)
② to부정사의 부사적 용법의 하나로 「only to ~」는 '결국 ~하게 되다'라는 결과의 의미를 나타낸다. Point 29. to부정사의 역할
③ 「It + take/cost + 목적어(시간/노력/돈) + (for ~) + to...」는 '~가 ...하는 데 시간/돈이 걸리다/들다'라는 의미로 to부정사가 바르게 쓰였다. Point 08. 수여동사
④ 앞선 타동사 explained의 목적어로 접속사 how로 시작하는 명사절인 간접의문문이 올바른 어순으로 쓰였다. Point 02. 의문문의 어순

**어휘** whale 고래   possess 가지고 있다   decode 해독하다
signal 신호

정답 ①

## 045 문법포인트 | Point 32. 현재분사 vs. 과거분사

Vaccination programs contributed ① to preventing diseases, improving public trust, and reducing long-term medical costs. With them, health officials could keep ② reducing outbreaks at the early stages of spread, administering vaccines to vulnerable groups, and ③ monitoring regions to track the spread of new variants, which could be later contained in areas ④ designating to prevent further transmission.
(→ designated)

**해설**
④ 수식받는 명사인 areas와 분사의 관계가 의미상 수동이고, 타동사인 designate 뒤에 목적어가 없으므로 현재분사를 과거분사로 고쳐야 한다. (designating → designated)
① contribute to는 '~에 기여하다'라는 뜻이며, 여기서 to는 전치사이므로 동명사 목적어를 바르게 취하고 있다. Point 48. 전치사의 목적어
② keep은 동명사를 목적어로 취하는 완전타동사이므로 reducing이 목적어로 바르게 쓰였다. Point 06. 완전타동사와 동작의 목적어
③ keep의 목적어로 reducing, administering, monitoring이라는 세 개의 동명사가 and를 통해 병렬로 바르게 연결되었다. Point 39. 등위접속사의 병렬 구조

**어휘** vaccination 예방접종   contribute 기여하다   medical 의료의
health official 보건 당국   outbreak 발병
administer 접종시키다   vulnerable 취약한   track 추적하다
variant 변이   transmission 전파

정답 ④

## 046 밑줄 친 부분에 들어갈 말로 가장 적절한 것은?

The small business managed _____ the fierce competition by offering unique products and excellent customer service.

① to survive
② surviving
③ to survive to
④ surviving to

## 047 밑줄 친 부분 중 어법상 옳지 않은 것은?

The museum displayed restored paintings and sculptures ① discovered during the renovation. A curator remembered ② seeing similar artifacts in a private collection years ago, which caused the museum ③ to launch an investigation into it. During the inquiry, they came across documents that appeared to confirm the source of the artifacts and ④ suggesting a connection to the private collection.

## 048 밑줄 친 부분에 들어갈 말로 가장 적절한 것은?

Parental interference must have adversely affected their kids: too much parental involvement, especially in their early school years, appears to _____ their school performance as well as their relationship with friends over the past decade.

① hold back
② be held back
③ have held back
④ have been held back

## 049 밑줄 친 부분 중 어법상 옳지 않은 것은?

Plastic pollution has become a major issue, especially in oceans, ① where marine animals often mistake it for food. The durability of plastic means that it remains in ecosystems for decades, ② harming wildlife and disrupting food chains. Although scientists have sounded the alarm about the issue, there ③ has been few changes in global plastic consumption. Promoting recycling and ④ reducing single-use plastics are key steps toward sustainable change.

**046** 문법포인트 | Point 06. 완전타동사와 동작의 목적어

The small business managed to survive the fierce competition by offering unique products and excellent customer service.

해설) manage는 to부정사를 목적어로 취하므로 빈칸에는 ① to survive가 들어가야 한다. 위기나 안 좋은 상황을 견딘다는 뜻으로 뒤에 목적어 the fierce competition이 바르게 쓰였다.

어휘) manage 간신히 해내다  fierce 치열한  competition 경쟁
unique 독특한  product 제품  customer 고객
survive (위기 등을) 견뎌내다

정답 ①

**047** 문법포인트 | Point 39. 등위접속사의 병렬 구조

The museum displayed restored paintings and sculptures ① discovered during the renovation. A curator remembered ② seeing similar artifacts in a private collection years ago, which caused the museum ③ to launch an investigation into it. During the inquiry, they came across documents that appeared to confirm the source of the artifacts and ④ suggesting a connection to the private collection.
→ (to) suggest

해설)
④ 관계대명사절의 동사인 appeared의 목적어로 to confirm과 suggesting이 and를 통해 병렬 구조로 연결되어 있다. 따라서 suggesting은 to suggest로 고쳐야 한다. 두 개 이상의 to부정사가 등위접속사로 연결될 때 뒤의 to부정사는 to를 생략해서 쓸 수 있다. (suggesting → (to) suggest)
① 수식받는 명사 paintings and sculptures와 후치 수식하는 분사가 의미상 수동의 관계이므로 과거분사인 discovered가 바르게 쓰였다. Point 32. 현재분사 vs. 과거분사
② remember는 동명사를 목적어로 취할 때는 '과거에 실제로 한 일을 기억하다'는 의미가 되고, to부정사를 목적어로 취할 때는 '앞으로 할 일을 잊지 않고 기억하다'는 의미가 된다. 여기서는 years ago라는 과거 시점을 나타내는 부사구가 있으므로, 과거에 본 경험을 기억한다는 의미이므로 동명사 seeing이 바르게 쓰였다. Point 06. 완전타동사와 동작의 목적어
③ cause는 목적어와 목적격보어의 관계가 능동일 때 목적격보어로 to부정사를 쓴다. 박물관이 시작하도록 한 것이므로 to launch가 바르게 쓰였다. Point 10. 불완전타동사와 동작의 목적격보어

어휘) restore 복원하다  sculpture 조각상  renovation 보수 작업
artifact 유물  cause 하게 하다  launch 시작하다
investigation 조사  inquiry 조사
come across ~을 우연히 발견하다

정답 ④

**048** 문법포인트 | Point 30. 준동사의 형태 변화

Parental interference must have adversely affected their kids: too much parental involvement, especially in their early school years, appears to have held back their school performance as well as their relationship with friends over the past decade.

해설) 콜론 앞의 절에서 「must have p.p.」를 통해 부모의 간섭이 자녀에게 악영향을 미쳤다는 과거의 일을 추측했고, 같은 맥락의 내용이 콜론 이후에도 제시되었다. 부모의 개입이 appear보다 먼저 일어난 일이므로 완료 부정사인 ③ to have held back이 들어가야 한다.

어휘) parental 부모의  interference 간섭
adversely affect 악영향을 미치다  involvement 개입
performance 성적  hold back ~을 방해하다

정답 ③

**049** 문법포인트 | Point 27. 주어 - 동사 수 일치

Plastic pollution has become a major issue, especially in oceans, ① (where marine animals often mistake it for food). The durability of plastic means that it remains in ecosystems for decades, ② harming wildlife and disrupting food chains. Although scientists have sounded the alarm about the issue, (there) ③ has been few changes in global plastic consumption. Promoting recycling and ④ reducing single-use plastics are key steps toward sustainable change.
→ have been

해설)
③ There가 문두에 나온 도치 구문에서 동사는 뒤의 명사(주어)에 수 일치해야 하므로, 복수 명사인 few changes에 맞게 복수형 동사인 have been으로 고쳐야 한다. (has been → have been)
① 선행사가 장소 명사인 oceans이고, where 뒤에 완전한 절이 이어졌으므로 장소의 관계부사 where가 바르게 쓰였다. Point 44. 관계부사
② harm의 의미상 주어는 주절의 주어인 it이고 주절 동사에 대한 부대 상황을 설명하는 분사구문이다. 의미상 주어와 분사가 능동의 관계이고 분사 뒤에 목적어가 있으므로 현재분사가 바르게 쓰였다. Point 33. 분사구문
④ 등위접속사 and를 통해 동명사 Promoting과 병렬 구조로 연결되어 주어 역할을 하고 있다. Point 39. 등위접속사의 병렬 구조

어휘) pollution 오염  especially 특히  marine 해양의
mistake A for B A를 B로 오인하다  durability 내구성
ecosystem 생태계  harm 해를 입히다  wildlife 야생동물
disrupt 와해시키다  sound 울리다  alarm 경종
consumption 소비  promote 촉진하다  single-use 일회용의
sustainable 지속 가능한

정답 ③

**050** 밑줄 친 부분에 들어갈 말로 가장 적절한 것은?

> More significant than the awards themselves ____ the recognition that the team has received from the international community.

① is ② are
③ have ④ has

**051** 밑줄 친 부분 중 어법상 옳지 않은 것은?

> The foundation selected ten entrepreneurs, ① all of whom had launched startups ② designing to address environmental issues. It was ③ so remarkable an initiative, not merely to fund their projects ④ but also to provide mentorship and global exposure, that it attracted attention from leading organizations worldwide.

**052** 밑줄 친 부분에 들어갈 말로 가장 적절한 것은?

> They imagined themselves ____ around the world.

① travel ② traveling
③ to travel ④ traveled

**053** 밑줄 친 부분 중 어법상 옳지 않은 것은?

> During the internal audit, the manager pointed out ① that the employees had failed to include. The omitted files turned out ② to be documents that were scheduled ③ to be submitted two weeks earlier. To resolve the issue quickly, the manager had the revised documents ④ reviewed by an external consultant before sending them again.

## 050 문법포인트 | Point 27. 주어-동사 수 일치 / Point 50. 도치

(More significant than the awards themselves) is the recognition that the team has received from the international community.

**해설** 보어인 형용사 significant가 도치되어 문장 앞으로 나왔고, 주어는 the recognition이다. 따라서 빈칸에는 be동사의 단수형이 와야 하므로 정답은 ① is이다. have는 보어를 가질 수 없어 ④는 들어갈 수 없다.

**어휘** significant 중요한   recognition 인정
international community 국제사회

**정답** ①

## 051 문법포인트 | Point 32. 현재분사 vs. 과거분사

The foundation selected ten entrepreneurs, ① all of whom had launched startups ② designing to address environmental issues. It was ③ so remarkable an initiative, not merely to fund their projects ④ but also to provide mentorship and global exposure, that it attracted attention from leading organizations worldwide.

**해설**
② 수식받는 명사인 startups와 후치 수식하는 분사가 고안된 스타트업이라는 수동의 의미이므로 현재분사가 아닌 과거분사로 수식해야 한다. (designing → designed)
① all of 뒤에 선행사 ten entrepreneurs를 수식하는 관계대명사 whom이 바르게 쓰였다. 전치사 of의 목적어 역할을 해야 하므로 목적격 관계대명사 whom이 옳다. Point 43. 관계대명사의 선택
③ so, as, too, how는 뒤에 「형용사 + a/an + 명사」의 어순이 되어야 한다. 어순이 바르게 쓰였다. Point 23. 관사의 위치
④ 등위상관접속사로 연결된 요소는 문법상 같은 형태이어야 하므로, 「not only[merely] A but also B」에서 A와 B 자리에 모두 to부정사가 바르게 쓰였다. Point 39. 등위접속사의 병렬 구조

**어휘** foundation 재단   entrepreneur 기업가   launch 시작하다
remarkable 놀라운   initiative 계획   fund 자금을 지원하다
exposure 홍보

**정답** ②

## 052 문법포인트 | Point 10. 불완전타동사와 동작의 목적격보어

They imagined themselves traveling around the world.

**해설** imagine은 목적어와 목적격보어가 능동의 관계일 경우 현재분사를, 수동의 관계일 경우 과거분사를 목적격보어로 취한다. 빈칸은 목적격보어 자리이고 그들이 세계 일주를 하는 능동의 관계이므로 빈칸에는 ② traveling이 들어가야 한다.

**어휘** imagine 상상하다   travel around the world 세계 여행을 하다

**정답** ②

## 053 문법포인트 | Point 40. 명사절 접속사의 선택

During the internal audit, the manager pointed out ① that the employees had failed to include. The omitted files turned out ② to be documents that were scheduled ③ to be submitted two weeks earlier. To resolve the issue quickly, the manager had the revised documents ④ reviewed by an external consultant before sending them again.

**해설**
① 접속사 that 뒤에 include의 목적어가 없는 불완전한 절이 왔으므로, that을 what으로 바꾸어야 한다. (that → what)
② turn out은 to부정사를 보어로 취할 수 있는 불완전자동사이다. Point 04. 불완전자동사의 보어
③ to부정사를 목적격보어로 취하는 schedule이 수동태가 되어 to부정사 목적격보어가 수동태 뒤에 바르게 쓰였다. 원래 목적어인 documents와 submit은 의미상 수동의 관계이므로, '문서들이 제출되도록 예정되었다'는 의미를 나타내기 위해 to be submitted처럼 수동형 부정사가 사용된 것도 바르다. Point 17. 동사의 유형별 수동태 / Point 30. 준동사의 형태 변화
④ 사역동사 have는 목적어와 목적격보어의 관계가 수동일 때 목적격보어로 과거분사를 취하므로 reviewed가 바르게 쓰였다. Point 10. 불완전타동사와 동작의 목적격보어

**어휘** internal 내부의   audit 감사   point out 지적하다
include 포함하다   omit 빠뜨리다   submit 제출하다
resolve 해결하다   revised 개정된   review 검토하다
external 외부의

**정답** ①

**054** 밑줄 친 부분에 들어갈 말로 가장 적절한 것은?

Medals _____ the team in recognition of their outstanding performance.

① gave to
② gave
③ were given
④ were given to

**055** 밑줄 친 부분 중 어법상 옳지 않은 것은?

By the time the session began, the participants ① had overlooked a key instruction, which later caused serious confusion. A safety document, a set of standard lab rules, ② was provided to everyone beforehand. During the task, they had no choice but ③ relying on the written rules and ④ attend to their assigned roles carefully.

**056** 밑줄 친 부분에 들어갈 말로 가장 적절한 것은?

He gave us _____ that we had no reason to doubt his expertise.

① so convinced an explanation
② such convinced an explanation
③ so a convincing explanation
④ such a convincing explanation

**057** 밑줄 친 부분 중 어법상 옳지 않은 것은?

If it ① had not been for the technician's quick response, the entire data center would have collapsed. According to the report, critical failures were found in the cooling unit, ② which sensors had malfunctioned. The damage cost from this incident was far higher than ③ that of last winter, as the incident affected ④ hundreds of stored devices.

## 문장 분석 및 해설

### 054 | 문법포인트 | Point 17. 동사의 유형별 수동태

Medals were given to the team in recognition of their outstanding performance.

**[해설]** 수여동사의 경우 두 개의 목적어가 있으므로 각각을 주어로 하는 수동태 문장이 가능하다. 다만 직접목적어를 주어로 하는 수동태로 변환되는 경우 간접목적어 앞에 전치사를 써 주어야 한다. 따라서 정답은 ④ were given to이다.

**[어휘]** in recognition of ~을 인정하는   outstanding 뛰어난   performance 성과

**[정답]** ④

---

### 055 | 문법포인트 | Point 31. 준동사 주요 표현

By the time the session began, the participants ① had overlooked a key instruction, which later caused serious confusion. A safety document, a set of standard lab rules, ② was provided to everyone beforehand. During the task, they had no choice but ③ relying on the written rules and ④ attend to their assigned roles carefully.
(→ to rely)

**[해설]**
③ 「have no choice but to do」는 '~할 수밖에 없다'라는 의미를 나타낸다. but 뒤에는 to부정사가 와야 하므로 relying을 to rely로 고쳐야 한다. (relying → to rely)
① 세션이 시작되는 시점보다 참가자들이 지시 사항을 간과한 시점이 더 이전이라는 의미로 과거완료가 바르게 쓰였다. Point 12. 완료 시제
② provide는 타동사인데 뒤에 목적어가 없이 전치사구가 왔고, 주어와 의미상 수동의 관계이므로 수동태가 바르게 쓰였다. 또한 주어가 단수 명사이므로 동사 역시 단수형이 쓰였다. Point 16. 능동태 vs. 수동태 구분 / Point 27. 주어 - 동사 수 일치
④ 문맥상 to rely와 등위접속사 and로 병렬 연결되므로 (to) attend가 바르게 쓰였다. to부정사가 병렬로 연결되는 경우 뒤의 to는 생략할 수 있다. 또한 완전자동사 attend는 전치사 to와 함께 쓰여 '~에 주의를 기울이다'라는 의미를 나타낸다. Point 39. 등위접속사의 병렬 구조 / Point 03. 완전자동사

**[어휘]** overlook 간과하다   instruction 지시 사항   confusion 혼란   safety 안전   beforehand 사전에   rely on ~에 의존하다   attend to ~에 주의를 기울이다   assign 할당하다

**[정답]** ③

---

### 056 | 문법포인트 | Point 23. 관사의 위치 / Point 32. 현재분사 vs 과거분사

He gave us such a convincing explanation that we had no reason to doubt his expertise.

**[해설]** such와 명사가 함께 쓰일 때는 「such + a/an + 형용사 + 명사」의 형태가 되어야 한다. 명사 explanation 앞에서 분사가 수식하고 있는데 문맥상 '설득력을 가지고 있는' 능동의 관계이므로 현재분사 convincing을 써야 한다. 따라서 정답은 ④ such a convincing explanation이다.

**[어휘]** convince 설득하다   explanation 설명   expertise 전문 지식

**[정답]** ④

---

### 057 | 문법포인트 | Point 43. 관계대명사의 선택

If it ① had not been for the technician's quick response, the entire data center would have collapsed. According to the report, critical failures were found in the cooling unit, ② which sensors had malfunctioned. The damage cost (→ whose) from this incident was far higher than ③ that of last winter, as the incident affected ④ hundreds of stored devices.

**[해설]**
② which 뒤에 완전한 절이 왔고 문맥상 which sensors가 cooling unit의 소유격에 해당하므로 which는 소유격인 whose로 고쳐야 한다. (which → whose)
① '~이 없었다면'이라는 의미를 지닌 가정법 과거완료는 「If it had not been for ~, 주어 + 조동사 (과거형) + have p.p.」로 표현하므로 조건절의 동사가 바르게 쓰였다. Point 46. 기타 가정법
③ 이번 사고의 손해 비용과 지난 겨울의 손해 비용을 비교하고 있으므로 단수 명사인 The damage cost를 지칭하는 단수 대명사 that이 바르게 쓰였다. Point 38. 비교대상의 일치
④ hundred 같은 수 단위명사는 특정 숫자와 함께 쓰일 때 단수로, 막연하게 큰 수를 의미할 때는 복수로 쓰이므로, 막연히 큰 수를 의미하는 hundreds of가 바르게 쓰였다. Point 35. 주의할 형용사와 부사

**[어휘]** response 대응   entire 전체의   collapse 붕괴되다   failure 고장   malfunction 오작동하다   damage 손해   incident 사고   store 저장하다

**[정답]** ②

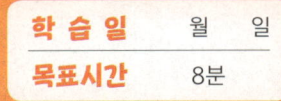

**058** 밑줄 친 부분에 들어갈 말로 가장 적절한 것은?

The car owner had the broken window _____.

① fix
② fixing
③ being fixed
④ fixed

**060** 밑줄 친 부분 중 어법상 옳지 않은 것은?

The internship program offers students valuable experience in the field and connects them with professionals ① who can guide their career paths. Participants ② are given responsibilities appropriate to their skills, and they are allowed ③ to continue the internship as long as they ④ will meet the required performance standards. The program also provides weekly feedback and networking opportunities with alumni.

**059** 밑줄 친 부분 중 어법상 옳지 않은 것은?

Much more significant than the drop in exports ① was the decline in consumer spending, which affected the overall economy ② considerable. This trend has been analyzed in a recent report. The report outlines ③ what economists expected to happen, with the market ④ stabilized after the initial shock.

## 058 문법포인트 | Point 10. 불완전타동사와 동작의 목적격보어

The car owner had the broken window fixed.

**해설** 사역동사 have는 목적어와 목적격보어를 가지며 목적어와 목적격보어의 관계가 능동이면 원형부정사(동사원형)를, 수동이면 과거분사를 목적격보어로 취한다. 깨진 창문이 수리되는 수동의 의미이므로 목적격보어인 빈칸에는 ④ fixed가 들어가야 한다.

**어휘** owner 소유자  broken 깨진  fix 수리하다

정답 ④

## 059 문법포인트 | Point 34. 형용사 vs. 부사

(Much more significant than the drop in exports) ① was the decline in consumer spending, which affected the overall economy ② considerable. (→ considerably) This trend has been analyzed in a recent report. The report outlines ③ [what economists expected to happen], with the market ④ stabilized after the initial shock.

**해설**
② affect는 완전타동사로 이 문장에서 목적어는 the overall economy이다. 이때 considerable은 영향을 얼마나 크게 미쳤는지를 나타내기 위해 affected를 수식한다. 동사는 부사로 수식하므로 considerable은 부사인 considerably로 고쳐야 한다. (considerable → considerably)
① 주격 보어인 Much more significant가 강조되면서 문두로 나간 형태로 주어는 단수 명사인 the decline이다. 따라서 단수 동사가 바르게 쓰였다. Point 50. 도치 / Point 27. 주어 - 동사 수 일치
③ 접속사 뒤에 타동사 expected의 목적어가 없는 불완전한 절이 왔다. outlines의 목적어인 명사절을 이끄는 동시에 expected의 목적어 역할을 할 수 있는 what이 바르게 쓰였다. Point 40. 명사절 접속사의 선택
④ with 분사구문에서 목적어인 the market과 목적격보어인 분사의 관계가 의미상 수동이므로 과거분사 stabilized가 바르게 쓰였다. Point 33. 분사구문

**어휘** significant 중요한  drop 감소  export 수출  decline 감소
affect 영향을 주다  overall 전체의  considerable 상당한
trend 추세  analyze 분석하다  outline 요약하다
stabilize 안정화시키다  initial 초기의

정답 ②

## 060 문법포인트 | Point 14. 시제일치와 예외

The internship program offers students valuable experience in the field and connects them with professionals ① (who can guide their career paths). Participants ② are given responsibilities appropriate to their skills, and they are allowed ③ to continue the internship as long as they ④ will meet (→ meet) the required performance standards. The program also provides weekly feedback and networking opportunities with alumni.

**해설**
④ as long as, when, if 등의 시간과 조건의 부사절에서 미래 시제는 현재 시제로 표현해야 한다. 따라서 will meet은 meet으로 고쳐야 한다. (will meet → meet)
① 선행사가 사람인 professionals이므로 주격 관계대명사로 who가 바르게 쓰였다. Point 43. 관계대명사의 선택
② 수여동사인 give는 수동태 전환 시 간접목적어가 주어가 되고, 직접목적어는 수동태 동사 뒤에 그대로 써 준다. 따라서 목적어가 수동태 동사 뒤에 왔지만 are given이 바르게 쓰였다. Point 17. 동사의 유형별 수동태
③ allow는 5형식 능동태 문형에서 목적격보어로 to부정사를 취한다. 이때 allow가 수동태가 되면 목적격보어인 to부정사는 수동태 동사 뒤에 그대로 써주어야 한다. 수동태 동사 뒤에 to부정사가 바르게 쓰였다. Point 17. 동사의 유형별 수동태

**어휘** field 현장  connect 연결하다  responsibility 책임
appropriate 적합한  skill 능력
performance standard 성과 기준
alumnus 졸업생 (pl. alumni)

정답 ④

**061** 밑줄 친 부분에 들어갈 말로 가장 적절한 것은?

_____, I will support him.

① Whoever may be he
② Whoever he may be
③ Whomever he may be
④ Whomever may be he

**062** 밑줄 친 부분 중 어법상 옳지 않은 것은?

The IT department recently introduced a new system for data security. ① Having designed to protect sensitive information, the system automatically detects suspicious activity and ② sends alerts. Employees are expected to follow the updated protocol carefully, ③ knowing that a single mistake could lead to serious consequences. The department also offered workshops to help staff ④ understand the new procedures more clearly.

**063** 밑줄 친 부분에 들어갈 말로 가장 적절한 것은?

She discovered from the documentary that the Great Depression _____ in 1929.

① breaks out
② broke out
③ were broken out
④ had broken out

**064** 밑줄 친 부분 중 어법상 옳은 것은?

The forgetting curve is a concept ① proposed by a German psychologist. It illustrates how ② does memory fade over time. Through his experiments, he discovered that without repetition, information is quickly forgotten after it is learned. A notable feature of this curve is the sharp decline in memory that ③ is occurred within just a few hours after learning. However, by reviewing the material at the right intervals, the rate of forgetting can be slowed. This curve ④ widely uses in developing effective review and study strategies.

## 061 　문법포인트 | Point 42. 주요 양보구문

Whoever he may be, I will support him.

[해설] 복합관계사절은 문장에서 명사절이나 부사절이 될 수 있다. 주절이 완전한 절이므로 빈칸이 있는 절은 부사절이 되어야 한다. be의 보어가 되면서 부사절을 이끌 수 있는 것은 whoever이므로 정답은 ② Whoever he may be이다. whomever는 목적격이므로 보어 역할로 사용할 수 없다.

[정답] ②

## 062 　문법포인트 | Point 33. 분사구문

The IT department recently introduced a new system for data security. ① Having designed to protect sensitive information, the system automatically detects suspicious activity and ② sends alerts. Employees are expected to follow the updated protocol carefully, ③ knowing that a single mistake could lead to serious consequences. The department also offered workshops to help staff ④ understand the new procedures more clearly.

[해설]
① 주절의 주어 the system과 동사 design은 설계되다라는 수동의 관계이다. 또한 이미 설계된 것은 과거이므로 완료분사구문의 수동형이 필요하다. 따라서 Having been designed로 고쳐야 하고 Having been은 생략 가능하므로 Designed로 쓸 수 있다. (Having designed → Having been designed/Designed)
② sends의 주어는 the system으로 detects와 함께 and에 의해 바르게 병렬로 연결되었다. Point 39. 등위접속사의 병렬 구조
③ 의미상의 주어인 주절의 주어 Employees와 능동의 관계이고 목적어가 있으므로 능동의 knowing이 바르게 쓰였다. Point 33. 분사구문
④ help 동사는 목적격보어에 to부정사 또는 원형부정사(동사원형)를 취할 수 있다. 동사원형인 understand가 help의 목적격보어로 바르게 쓰였다. Point 10. 불완전타동사와 동작의 목적격보어

[어휘] recently 최근에　security 보안　sensitive 민감한
automatically 자동으로　detect 감지하다
suspicious 의심스러운　alert 경고　protocol 지침
lead to ~을 초래하다　serious 심각한　consequence 결과
procedure 절차

[정답] ①

## 063 　문법포인트 | Point 14. 시제일치와 예외 / Point 03. 완전자동사

She discovered from the documentary that the Great Depression broke out in 1929.

[해설] 역사적 사실은 항상 과거 시제로 써야 한다. 대공황이 발생한 것은 역사적 사실이므로 빈칸에는 과거 시제인 ② broke out이 들어가야 한다. 또한, break out은 완전자동사이므로 수동태로 쓸 수 없어 ③은 답이 될 수 없다.

[어휘] Great Depression 대공황　break out 발생하다

[정답] ②

## 064 　문법포인트 | Point 32. 현재분사 vs. 과거분사

The forgetting curve is a concept ① (proposed by a German psychologist). It illustrates [how ② does memory fade over time]. Through his experiments, he discovered that without repetition, information is quickly forgotten after it is learned. A notable feature of this curve is the sharp decline in memory (that ③ is occurred within just a few hours after learning). However, by reviewing the material at the right intervals, the rate of forgetting can be slowed. This curve ④ widely uses in developing effective review and study strategies.

[해설]
① 수식받는 명사 concept와 propose는 개념이 제안되는 수동의 관계이므로 과거분사인 proposed가 바르게 쓰였다.
② 타동사 illustrates의 목적어로 간접의문문이 쓰인 구조다. 간접의문문은 「의문사 + 주어 + 동사」의 어순이 되어야 하므로 does memory fade는 memory fades로 고쳐야 한다. (does memory fade → memory fades) Point 02. 의문문의 어순
③ 자동사인 occur는 수동태가 불가하다. 따라서 현재 시제의 단수형인 occurs로 고쳐야 한다. (is occurred → occurs) Point 17. 동사의 유형별 수동태
④ use는 타동사인데 목적어가 없으므로 be동사를 넣어 수동태 동사로 고쳐야 한다. (widely uses → is widely used) Point 16. 능동태 vs. 수동태 구분

[어휘] forgetting 망각　curve 곡선　concept 개념　propose 제안하다
psychologist 심리학자　illustrate 보여주다　memory 기억(력)
fade 사라지다　over time 시간이 지남에 따라　experiment 실험
repetition 반복　notable 뚜렷한　feature 특징　sharp 급격한
decline 감소　review 복습하다; 복습　interval 간격
effective 효과적인

[정답] ①

**065** 밑줄 친 부분에 들어갈 말로 가장 적절한 것은?

> I made it a rule _____ for each day's to-do list in the morning.

① plan　　② to plan
③ planed　④ planning

**066** 밑줄 친 부분 중 어법상 옳지 않은 것은?

> The team launched a new customer service platform last month. In order ① to reduce wait times and improve user satisfaction, the platform uses AI that responds to basic questions automatically. Customers ② interacting with the system for the first time ③ is guided through each step, which makes ④ it easier for them to complete simple tasks without speaking to an agent.

**067** 밑줄 친 부분에 들어갈 말로 가장 적절한 것은?

> The manuscript was nearly destroyed when it _____ by a lawnmower in the backyard.

① ran over　　② was run
③ was run over　④ was running over

**068** 밑줄 친 부분 중 어법상 옳지 않은 것은?

> Environmental regulations are reviewed ① every two year to address industries that contributed to air pollution. Analysts recommend that the updated guidelines ② be explained to company representatives. However, some companies insist on strictly ③ cutting costs instead of adopting the stricter measures ④ proposed during economic downturns.

## 065 문법포인트 | Point 31. 준동사 주요 표현

I made it a rule to plan for each day's to-do list in the morning.
(it = 가O, to plan = 진O)

해설 '~하는 것을 규칙으로 삼다'는 「make it a rule to부정사」로 나타내므로 답은 ② to plan이다.

정답 ②

## 066 문법포인트 | Point 27. 주어 – 동사 수 일치

The team launched a new customer service platform last month. In order ① to reduce wait times and improve user satisfaction, the platform uses AI that responds to basic questions automatically. Customers ② (interacting with the system for the first time) ③ is guided through each step, which makes ④ it easier for them to complete simple tasks without speaking to an agent.
(interacting = 능동, is → are, it = 가O, to complete = 진O)

해설
③ is의 주어는 복수 명사인 Customers이므로 복수 동사인 are로 고쳐야 한다. (is → are)
① 「in order to + 동사원형」은 '~하기 위하여'라는 목적을 표현하는 to부정사의 부사적 용법이다. 문맥에 맞게 to부정사가 바르게 쓰였다. Point 29. to부정사의 역할
② 수식받는 Customers와 interact는 능동의 관계이므로 현재분사가 바르게 수식하고 있다. Point 32. 현재분사 vs. 과거분사
④ 5형식의 불완전타동사의 목적어로 to부정사 또는 명사절이 올 경우 대신 가목적어로 it을 써 주고 진목적어는 목적격보어 뒤에 써주어야 한다. 가목적어 it과 진목적어 to complete가 바르게 쓰였다. Point 24. 인칭대명사

어휘 launch 출시하다  reduce 줄이다  satisfaction 만족도
respond 응답하다  interact 상호작용하다  complete 완료하다
agent 직원

정답 ③

## 067 문법포인트 | Point 17. 동사의 유형별 수동태

The manuscript was nearly destroyed when it was run over by a lawnmower in the backyard.
(over = 목(X))

해설 run over가 하나의 타동사처럼 목적어를 취한다. 수동태가 될 경우에도 over가 누락되지 않아야 한다. 따라서 ③ was run over가 정답이다.

어휘 manuscript 원고  nearly 거의  destroy 훼손하다
lawnmower 잔디 깎는 기계  backyard 뒤뜰
run ~ over ~을 (차 등으로) 치다

정답 ③

## 068 문법포인트 | Point 25. 부정대명사

Environmental regulations are reviewed ① every two year to address industries that contributed to air pollution. Analysts recommend that the updated guidelines ② be explained to company representatives. However, some companies insist on strictly ③ cutting costs instead of adopting the stricter measures ④ (proposed during economic downturns).
(every two → every two years/every second year, (should) + R, proposed = 수동)

해설
① '~마다'는 「every + 기수 + 복수 (기간) 명사」 또는 「every + 서수 + 단수 (기간) 명사로, 나타내므로, 기수인 two 뒤에는 복수 명사 years를 써야 한다. 또는 서수를 써서 every second year로 고쳐도 된다. (every two year → every two years/every second year)
② 주장, 요구, 제안, 명령 동사의 목적어로 that절이 오면 that절의 동사는 「(should) + 동사원형」의 형태가 되어야 한다. be explained가 바르게 쓰였다. Point 19. 당위의 조동사 should
③ insist on은 '~을 주장하다'라는 의미이다. 전치사 on 뒤에 동명사 cutting이 바르게 쓰였다. Point 28. 동명사의 역할 / Point 48. 전치사의 목적어
④ 수식받는 명사인 the stricter measures와 분사가 의미상 수동의 관계이므로 과거분사인 proposed가 바르게 쓰였다. Point 32. 현재분사 vs. 과거분사

어휘 environmental 환경의  regulation 규제  address 다루다
contribute to ~에 일조하다  pollution 오염  analyst 분석가
representative 대표자  insist 고집하다  strictly 엄격하게
adopt 채택하다  propose 제안하다  downturn 경제 불황

정답 ①

**069** 밑줄 친 부분에 들어갈 말로 가장 적절한 것은?

> I suggested _____ a new approach for solving the problem which had been annoying us.

① them
② them for
③ to them
④ them that

**070** 밑줄 친 부분 중 어법상 옳지 않은 것은?

> The upgraded processor in the new model is ① as twice fast as the one ② used in the previous version. According to internal tests, the device also consumes 30% less energy while ③ maintaining the same level of performance. The software offers a new interface ④ in which settings are easier to access and customize.

**071** 밑줄 친 부분에 들어갈 말로 가장 적절한 것은?

> Under no circumstances _____ a personal preference on others.

① you should not impose
② you should impose
③ should you not impose
④ should you impose

**072** 밑줄 친 부분 중 어법상 옳지 않은 것은?

> Deep research refers to a thorough and systematic investigation of a specific topic ① that goes beyond simple information retrieval. It involves comparing, analyzing, and ② identifying information from various sources, taking into account the credibility and context of the data. Its goal is ③ to uncover hidden meanings or patterns beyond surface-level facts. ④ Although the significant time and effort required, deep research leads to more accurate and in-depth conclusions.

## 069 문법포인트 | Point 05. 완전타동사

I suggested to them a new approach for solving the problem which had been annoying us.

**해설** 동사 suggest는 4형식으로 쓸 수 없으므로 간접목적어가 올 경우 전치사와 함께 「to + 사람」의 형태로 와야 한다. 따라서 정답은 ③ to them이다.

**어휘** suggest 제안하다   approach 접근법   solve 해결하다
annoying 짜증나게 하는

정답 ③

## 070 문법포인트 | Point 37. 비교 사용 표현

The upgraded processor in the new model is ① as twice fast as the one ② used in the previous version. According to internal tests, the device also consumes 30% less energy while ③ maintaining the same level of performance. The software offers a new interface ④ in which settings are easier to access and customize.

**해설**
① 배수사는 비교급 앞에 위치해야 한다. 즉 「배수사 + as 형/부 as」의 어순이 되어야 한다. (as twice fast as → twice as fast as)
② the one을 분사가 수식하는 구조이다. the one과 use는 사용되는 이란 수동 관계이므로 과거분사 used가 바르게 사용되었다. Point 32. 현재분사 vs. 과거분사
③ 접속사가 생략되지 않은 분사구문이다. maintaining의 의미상 주어는 주절의 주어인 the device로 장치가 유지한다는 능동의 의미이고 뒤에 목적어가 있으므로 능동의 현재분사가 바르게 사용되었다. 분사구문 앞에 의미를 명확히 하기 위해 접속사를 삭제하지 않고 그대로 둘 수 있다. Point 33. 분사구문
④ in which 뒤에 절이 완전하고 선행사인 interface가 상황, 영역에 해당하므로 in which가 바르게 쓰였다. 관계부사 where도 가능하다. Point 43. 관계대명사의 선택

**어휘** previous 이전의   internal 내부의   device 장치
consume 소비하다   maintain 유지하다   performance 성능
access 접근하다   customize 맞춤화하다

정답 ①

## 071 문법포인트 | Point 35. 주의할 형용사와 부사 / Point 50. 도치

Under no circumstances should you impose a personal preference on others.

**해설** under no circumstances는 '어떤 일이 있더라도 ~해서는 안 된다'를 의미하는 부정부사구이다. 부정부사는 다른 부정부사와 함께 쓸 수 없고, 문두에 오면 뒤 절의 형태는 도치되어 「조동사 + 주어 + 동사원형」이 되어야 한다. 따라서 정답은 ④이다.

**어휘** circumstance 상황   preference 선호   impose 강요하다

정답 ④

## 072 문법포인트 | Point 41. 부사절 접속사의 선택

Deep research refers to a thorough and systematic investigation of a specific topic ① that goes beyond simple information retrieval. It involves comparing, analyzing, and ② identifying information from various sources, taking into account the credibility and context of the data. Its goal is ③ to uncover hidden meanings or patterns beyond surface-level facts. ④ Although the significant time and effort required, deep research leads to more accurate and in-depth conclusions.

**해설**
④ 절이 아니라 명사구가 이어지므로 접속사 Although와 의미가 같은 전치사 Despite나 In spite of로 고쳐야 한다. (Although → Despite/In spite of)
① that 뒤에 주어 없이 동사가 바로 나오므로 선행사 topic을 수식하는 관계대명사 that이 바르게 쓰였다. Point 43. 관계대명사의 선택
② involve는 목적어로 동명사를 취하는 동사이다. 목적어인 동명사 comparing, analyzing, identifying 세 개가 and에 의해 병렬로 바르게 연결되었다. Point 39. 등위접속사의 병렬 구조
③ 명사의 역할을 하는 to부정사가 be동사 is의 보어로 바르게 사용되었다. Point 29. to부정사의 역할

**어휘** refer to ~을 의미하다   thorough 철저한   systematic 체계적인
investigation 조사   retrieval 검색   analyze 분석하다
identify 식별하다   various 다양한   source 출처
take ~ into account ~을 고려하다   credibility 신뢰성
context 맥락   uncover 밝혀내다   surface 표면
significant 상당한   accurate 정확한   in-depth 심층적인
conclusion 결론

정답 ④

**073** 밑줄 친 부분에 들어갈 말로 가장 적절한 것은?

> The police _____ the series of burglaries that occurred in the neighborhood.

① is investigating   ② are investigating
③ is investigated    ④ are investigated

**075** 밑줄 친 부분 중 어법상 옳지 않은 것은?

> Sleep plays a critical role in overall health. Studies show that people ① deprived of sleep are more likely to experience stress and memory issues. The body's immune system is also affected, making ② that harder to fight infections. ③ Although the benefits of sleep are well known, many people still fail ④ to get enough rest.

**074** 밑줄 친 부분 중 어법상 옳지 않은 것은?

> Marie Curie was not merely a brilliant scientist ① nor a determined pioneer. She conducted groundbreaking research ② that changed the way people understood radioactivity. Her discoveries were important, but her dedication ③ to advancing science stood out just as much. ④ Despite the barriers she faced as a woman in science, she remained focused and refused to give up.

## 073  문법포인트 | Point 21. 명사의 이해 / Point 16. 능동태 vs. 수동태 구분

The police are investigating the series of burglaries that occurred in the neighborhood.

**해설** investigate 뒤에 목적어가 있으므로 능동태가 되어야 한다. 주어 The police는 항상 복수 취급하는 집합명사이므로 복수 동사를 써야 한다. 따라서 정답은 ② are investigating이다.

**어휘** a series of 일련의   burglary 절도 사건   neighborhood 인근   investigate 조사하다

정답 ②

## 074  문법포인트 | Point 39. 등위접속사의 병렬 구조

Marie Curie was not merely a brilliant scientist ① nor (→ but also) a determined pioneer. She conducted groundbreaking research ② that changed the way people understood radioactivity. Her discoveries were important, but her dedication ③ to advancing science stood out just as much. ④ Despite the barriers (she faced as a woman in science), she remained focused and refused to give up.

**해설**
① 'A뿐만 아니라 B도'라는 뜻의 등위상관접속사는 「not merely[only] A but also B」이다. 따라서 nor를 but also로 고쳐야 한다. (nor → but also)
② that 뒤에 주어가 없는 불완전한 절이므로 관계대명사 that이 바르게 쓰였다. Point 43. 관계대명사의 선택
③ to는 전치사이므로 명사 또는 동명사가 목적으로 올 수 있다. 목적어로 동명사 advancing이 바르게 쓰였다. Point 48. 전치사의 목적어
④ the barriers라는 명사구가 목적어로 왔으므로 전치사인 Despite가 바르게 쓰였다. Point 41. 부사절 접속사의 선택

**어휘** brilliant 뛰어난   determined 결단력 있는   pioneer 선구자   conduct 수행하다   groundbreaking 혁신적인   radioactivity 방사능   dedication 헌신   advance 발전시키다   stand out 두드러지다   barrier 장벽   focused 집중된

정답 ①

## 075  문법포인트 | Point 24. 인칭대명사

Sleep plays a critical role in overall health. Studies show that people ① (deprived of sleep) [수동, 목(X)] are more likely to experience stress and memory issues. The body's immune system is also affected, making ② that [가O→it, 진O] harder to fight infections. ③ Although the benefits of sleep are well known, many people still fail ④ to get enough rest.

**해설**
② 5형식 문형에서 to부정사가 목적어로 올 때는 대신 가목적어 it를 쓰고 진목적어는 목적격보어 뒤에 두어야 한다. 따라서 가목적어 it을 써야 하므로 that을 it으로 고쳐야 한다. (that → it)
① deprived of sleep이 명사 people을 수식하는 구조다. '박탈당하다'라는 수동의 의미이므로 과거분사가 바르다. Point 32. 현재분사 vs. 과거분사
③ 뒤에 완전한 절이 나왔으므로 양보의 부사절 접속사 Although가 바르게 쓰였다. Point 41. 부사절 접속사의 선택
④ fail은 to부정사를 목적어로 취하므로 목적어 to get이 바르게 쓰였다. Point 06. 완전타동사와 동작의 목적어

**어휘** critical 중요한   overall 전반적인   deprive 박탈하다   immune system 면역 체계   infection 감염   benefit 이점   rest 휴식

정답 ②

**076** 밑줄 친 부분에 들어갈 말로 가장 적절한 것은?

> The company didn't give any explanation for the accident, _____ an apology.

① still less  ② much more
③ still more  ④ much least

**077** 밑줄 친 부분 중 어법상 옳지 않은 것은?

> So far, technological progress in transportation ① has changed the way people travel in their daily lives, including the shortening of long-distance trips by high-speed trains and commercial flights. Ride-sharing apps have changed ② how do people get around within cities. These changes have occurred mostly in the last few decades, and ③ they will likely affect the decisions ④ that people make about where to live and work.

**078** 밑줄 친 부분에 들어갈 말로 가장 적절한 것은?

> The investors, impressed by her presentation, decided _____ the project.

① fund  ② to fund
③ funding  ④ to be funded

**079** 밑줄 친 부분 중 어법상 옳지 않은 것은?

> The logistics network has recently experienced several unexpected issues. There ① are still a great number of unused supplies stored in remote facilities, but they ② may have been overlooked, with information about them ③ excluding from recent logistics reports. It turns out that it was the outdated reporting system ④ that caused the oversight.

## 076  문법포인트 | Point 37. 비교 사용 표현

The company didn't give any explanation for the accident, still less an apology.

**[해설]** 부정의 의미를 강화하는 뜻의 '~은 말할 것도 없이'는 still less, much less로 나타낸다. 긍정의 의미를 강화할 때는 still more, much more를 쓴다.

**[어휘]** explanation 설명   accident 사고   apology 사과

정답 ①

## 077  문법포인트 | Point 02. 의문문의 어순

So far, technological progress in transportation ① has changed the way people travel in their daily lives, including the shortening of long-distance trips by high-speed trains and commercial flights. Ride-sharing apps have changed ② how do people get around within cities. (→ how people get) These changes have occurred mostly in the last few decades, and ③ they will likely affect the decisions ④ that people make about where to live and work.

**[해설]**
② have changed의 목적어 자리에 간접의문문이 사용되었다. 간접의문문은 「의문사 + 주어 + 동사」의 어순이 되어야 하므로 how people get으로 고쳐야 한다. (how do people get → how people get)
① '지금까지'를 의미하는 부사 so far는 완료 시제와 주로 사용된다. 지금까지 계속해서 변화했다는 의미이므로 현재완료 시제가 사용되었고, 주어가 progress이므로 단수형 동사인 has changed가 바르게 쓰였다. Point 12. 완료 시제 / Point 27. 주어 - 동사 수 일치
③ 앞선 명사인 these changes를 가리키는 대명사인 they가 복수 형태로 바르게 쓰였다. Point 24. 인칭대명사
④ that 이후에 목적어가 없는 불완전한 절이 왔으므로 선행사 decisions를 수식하는 관계대명사 that이 바르게 쓰였다. Point 43. 관계대명사의 선택

**[어휘]** progress 발달   transportation 교통수단
shorten 단축하다   long-distance 장거리의
commercial 상업의   ride-sharing 승차 공유
get around 이동하다   mostly 대부분   decade 십 년
affect 영향을 미치다

정답 ②

## 078  문법포인트 | Point 06. 완전타동사와 동작의 목적어

The investors, (impressed by her presentation), decided to fund the project.

**[해설]** decide는 to부정사를 목적어로 취하는 동사이므로 ② to fund가 정답이다. fund 뒤에 the project라는 목적어가 있으므로 ④는 정답이 될 수 없다.

**[어휘]** investor 투자자   impress 감명을 주다   fund 자금을 대다

정답 ②

## 079  문법포인트 | Point 33. 분사구문

The logistics network has recently experienced several unexpected issues. (There) ① are still a great number of unused supplies stored in remote facilities, but they ② may have been overlooked, with information about them ③ excluding (→ excluded) from recent logistics reports. It turns out that it was the outdated reporting system ④ that caused the oversight.

**[해설]**
③ with 분사구문으로 목적어인 information about them과 목적격보어인 분사가 의미상 수동의 관계이므로 현재분사를 과거분사로 고쳐야 한다. (excluding → excluded)
① There be 구문에서 be동사는 뒤에 나오는 명사에 일치시켜야 하는데, 명사가 a great number of unused supplies라는 복수이므로 be동사 역시 복수형 are가 바르게 쓰였다. Point 27. 주어 - 동사 수 일치
② 과거에 일어났을 수도 있는 일에 대해 추측하거나 가능성을 말하는 「may have p.p.」가 바르게 쓰였다. Point 20. 조동사 + have p.p.
④ 「it ~ that」 강조구문으로 it과 that 사이에 강조 대상인 주어가 오고, that 이하에는 원래 문장의 나머지 부분인 동사와 목적어가 와서 바르게 쓰였다. Point 49. 강조

**[어휘]** logistics 물류   unexpected 예기치 못한   supply 물자
remote 외딴   facility 시설   overlook 간과하다   outdated 낡은
oversight 간과

정답 ③

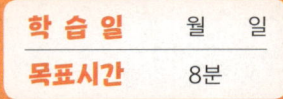

**080** 밑줄 친 부분에 들어갈 말로 가장 적절한 것은?

> Children should be exposed to _____ different languages from an early age to enhance their cognitive development.

① learn     ② learning
③ learned   ④ have learned

**082** 밑줄 친 부분에 들어갈 말로 가장 적절한 것은?

> He prefers to work from home rather than _____ to the office.

① commuting   ② to commuting
③ to commute  ④ commutes

**081** 밑줄 친 부분 중 어법상 옳지 않은 것은?

> Many inventions have changed daily life, but it is electricity ① <u>what</u> has made the biggest difference. Before the widespread use of electric power, people had difficulty ② <u>performing</u> daily tasks after sunset due to limited availability of reliable light source. Since electricity was introduced, people ③ <u>have had</u> many of their daily activities ④ <u>done</u> efficiently and conveniently. From cooking to communication, this invisible force powers modern life.

**083** 밑줄 친 부분 중 어법상 옳은 것은?

> Artificial intelligence is transforming industries at an unprecedented pace. One of its main applications ① <u>include</u> customer service automation, ② <u>which</u> chatbots can handle common queries. Experts warn ③ <u>what</u> while AI increases efficiency, it also raises ethical concerns that need ④ <u>to be addressed</u> carefully.

## 080 문법포인트 | Point 48. 전치사의 목적어

Children should be exposed to learning different languages from an early age to enhance their cognitive development.

**해설** '~하는 것에 노출되다'라는 말은 「be exposed to -ing」로 나타낸다. to는 전치사이므로 반드시 동명사가 와야 한다. 따라서 정답은 ② learning이다.

**어휘** enhance 향상시키다   cognitive 인지의

정답 ②

## 082 문법포인트 | Point 37. 비교 사용 표현 / Point 38. 비교대상의 일치

He prefers to work from home rather than to commute to the office.

**해설** 동사 prefer는 「prefer -ing to -ing」 또는 「prefer to + 동사원형 rather than (to) + 동사원형」의 형태로 쓴다. 빈칸의 비교대상이 to work로 to부정사의 형태이므로 빈칸도 to부정사 형태로 써야 한다. 따라서 정답은 ③ to commute이다. 이때 to는 생략 가능하다.

**어휘** prefer 선호하다   commute 통근하다

정답 ③

## 081 문법포인트 | Point 49. 강조

Many inventions have changed daily life, but it is electricity ① what (→ that) has made the biggest difference. Before the widespread use of electric power, people had difficulty ② performing daily tasks after sunset due to limited availability of reliable light source. Since electricity was introduced, people ③ have had many of their daily activities ④ done efficiently and conveniently. From cooking to communication, this invisible force powers modern life.

**해설**
① what 앞에 완전한 절이 있으므로 그 뒤에 what이 이끄는 명사절이 올 수 없다. 또한 what 뒤에는 주어가 없는 불완전한 절이 이어지는데 맥락상 주어는 앞의 electricity이고 it은 특별한 의미를 지니고 있지 않다. 따라서 it-that 강조 구문이므로 what을 that으로 고쳐야 한다. (what → that)
② 「have difficulty (in)-ing」는 '~을 하는 데 어려움을 겪다'라는 뜻으로 performing이 바르게 쓰였다. Point 31. 준동사 주요 표현
③ 「since + 과거 시점」이 주어졌고, 그 이후부터 현재까지 이어져 온 활동을 설명하고 있으므로 현재완료 시제인 have had가 바르게 쓰였다. Point 12. 완료 시제
④ 사역동사 have는 목적어와 목적격보어가 수동 관계일 때 목적격보어에 과거분사를 써야 한다. 일상 활동이 수행되는 수동의 의미이므로 과거분사 done이 바르게 쓰였다. Point 10. 불완전타동사와 동작의 목적격보어

**어휘** invention 발명품   electricity 전기   widespread 널리 퍼진   electric 전기의   power 동력; 동력을 제공하다   perform 수행하다   sunset 일몰   limited 제한적인   availability 이용 가능성   reliable 신뢰할 수 있는   efficiently 효율적으로   invisible 보이지 않는   force 힘

정답 ①

## 083 문법포인트 | Point 30. 준동사의 형태 변화

Artificial intelligence is transforming industries at an unprecedented pace. One of its main applications ① include (→ includes) customer service automation, ② which (→ where) chatbots can handle common queries. Experts warn ③ what (→ that) while AI increases efficiency, it also raises ethical concerns that need ④ to be addressed carefully.

**해설**
④ need의 목적어로 to부정사가 바르게 쓰였다. address의 의미상의 주어는 관계대명사 that의 선행사인 ethical concerns이다. 윤리적 문제들이 해결되어야 한다는 수동의 의미이므로 수동형 부정사가 필요하다. 따라서 to be addressed는 바르게 쓰였다.
① include의 주어는 One이다. 단수 주어이므로 단수 동사형인 includes로 고쳐야 한다. (include → includes) Point 27. 주어 - 동사 수 일치
② which 이하가 완전한 절이므로 관계대명사인 which는 올 수 없고, 선행사 customer service automation이 맥락상 '상황'을 제시하는 역할을 하므로 관계부사 where로 고쳐야 한다. (which → where) Point 44. 관계부사
③ warn의 뒤에 목적어 역할을 하는 절이 이어지는데, 이 목적절은 while이 이끄는 종속절과 주절로 구성된 복문이다. 복문 전체를 이끌 수 있는 접속사는 that뿐이므로 what을 that으로 고쳐야 한다. (what → that) Point 40. 명사절 접속사의 선택

**어휘** artificial 인공의   intelligence 지능   transform 변화시키다   unprecedented 전례 없는   pace 속도   main 주요한   application 활용   automation 자동화   handle 처리하다   query 문의   expert 전문가   efficiency 효율성   raise 제기하다   ethical 윤리적인   concern 문제   address 해결하다

정답 ④

**084** 밑줄 친 부분에 들어갈 말로 가장 적절한 것은?

> He's always early for meetings, so he _____ value punctuality highly.

① must  ② cannot
③ should  ④ ought to

**085** 밑줄 친 부분 중 어법상 옳지 않은 것은?

> The Great Wall of China, ① whose purpose was to protect the country from invasions, ② was built over many centuries. Stretching more than 13,000 miles, it passes through mountains, deserts, and plains. ③ Although parts of it have been damaged by time, much of the wall still remains today. For historians and travelers alike, visiting the wall is worth ④ experienced, as it tells a story of strength, unity, and human effort.

**086** 밑줄 친 부분에 들어갈 말로 가장 적절한 것은?

> Residents were made _____ the area due to the approaching hurricane.

① evacuate  ② to evacuate
③ evacuating  ④ to be evacuated

**087** 밑줄 친 부분 중 어법상 옳지 않은 것은?

> ① Commonly though artificial sweeteners have become recently, their long-term effects remain a subject of debate. Some believe they are superior ② to sugar, but many nutritionists warn ③ that they can be harmful, as certain compounds are ④ intense enough to disrupt metabolic responses in the body.

## 084 문법포인트 | Point 18. 조동사의 선택

He's always early for meetings, so he must value punctuality highly.

**해설** '~임이 틀림없다[분명하다]'라는 강한 긍정의 추측은 조동사 must로 나타낸다. 회의에 항상 일찍 오는 것을 근거로 그가 시간 엄수를 중시한다고 추측하고 있다. 따라서 정답은 ① must이다.

**어휘** value 중시하다  punctuality 시간 엄수  highly 매우

정답 ①

## 085 문법포인트 | Point 31. 준동사의 주요 표현

The Great Wall of China, ① (whose purpose was to protect the country from invasions), ② was built over many centuries. Stretching more than 13,000 miles, it passes through mountains, deserts, and plains. ③ Although parts of it have been damaged by time, much of the wall still remains today. For historians and travelers alike, visiting the wall is worth ④ experienced, as it tells a story of strength, unity, and human effort.
→ experiencing

**해설**
④ 「be worth -ing」는 '~할 만한 가치가 있다'를 의미하고, -ing는 능동의 형태이지만 수동의 의미를 가진다. 따라서 experiencing으로 고쳐야 한다. (experienced → experiencing)
① whose 이하의 절이 완전하지만 주어인 purpose에 관사나 소유격이 없는 상태다. 문맥상 The Great Wall of China와 purpose는 소유의 관계가 성립되어 '만리장성의 목적'이라는 의미를 나타내므로 소유격 관계대명사인 whose가 바르게 쓰였다. Point 43. 관계대명사의 선택
② 주어는 The Great Wall of China이므로 단수이고 건설된다는 수동의 의미이므로 수동태가 바르게 쓰였다. Point 27. 주어 - 동사 수 일치 / Point 16. 능동태 vs. 수동태 구분
③ 뒤에 주어와 동사가 있는 올바른 부사절의 형태이므로 접속사 Although가 바르게 쓰였다. Point 41. 부사절 접속사의 선택

**어휘** purpose 목적  invasion 침입  century 세기  stretch 뻗어 있다  desert 사막  plain 평원  damage 훼손하다  historian 역사가  alike 둘 다  strength 힘  unity 단결

정답 ④

## 086 문법포인트 | Point 17. 동사의 유형별 수동태

Residents were made to evacuate the area due to the approaching hurricane.

**해설** 사역동사인 make는 능동태일 경우 목적격보어에 동사원형을 쓰지만 수동태가 되면 동사원형인 목적격보어를 반드시 to부정사 형태로 고쳐야 한다. 따라서 수동태 동사인 were made 뒤에는 ② to evacuate가 들어가야 한다.

**어휘** resident 주민  approaching 다가오는  evacuate 대피시키다

정답 ②

## 087 문법포인트 | Point 42. 주요 양보구문 / Point 34. 형용사 vs. 부사

① Commonly though artificial sweeteners have become recently, their long-term effects remain a subject of debate. Some believe they are superior ② to sugar, but many nutritionists warn ③ [that they can be harmful, as certain compounds are ④ intense enough to disrupt metabolic responses in the body].
→ Common

**해설**
① 「형용사/부사/분사/명사 + as/though + S + V」의 접속사 양보구문이다. 동사인 have become은 보어를 취하는 불완전자동사이고, 부사인 commonly는 보어가 될 수 없으므로 형용사인 common으로 고쳐야 한다. (Commonly → Common)
② superior는 라틴 비교 표현으로 비교 대상 앞에 than이 아니라 to를 사용해야 하므로 to가 바르게 쓰였다. Point 37. 비교 사용 표현
③ warn의 목적어 자리에 명사절이 사용되었고, 접속사 뒤의 절이 완전하므로 접속사 that이 바르게 쓰였다. Point 40. 명사절 접속사의 선택
④ 「형용사/부사 + enough to부정사」의 구문은 '~할 만큼 충분히 (형용사/부사)하다'의 의미이다. enough가 형용사를 뒤에서 바르게 수식하고 있다. Point 34. 형용사 vs. 부사

**어휘** artificial 인공의  sweetener 감미료  recently 최근에  long-term 장기적인  effect 효과  subject 주제  superior 우수한  nutritionist 영양학자  compound 화합물  intense 강력한  disrupt 방해하다  metabolic 신진대사의  response 반응

정답 ①

**088** 밑줄 친 부분에 들어갈 말로 가장 적절한 것은?

> It's not just about winning the game _____ about playing with integrity and sportsmanship.

① and     ② but
③ or      ④ nor

**089** 밑줄 친 부분 중 어법상 옳지 않은 것은?

> Many students who study overseas have difficulty ① adjusted to a new environment at first. However, neither a foreign environment nor language barriers ② prevent them from building close friendships with their fellow students. ③ Having been exposed to diverse perspectives, these students often return home with a deeper understanding of the world. Ultimately, these programs help students better ④ adapt to the world and understand it more deeply.

**090** 밑줄 친 부분 중 어법상 옳지 않은 것은?

> The city planned ① to expand public green spaces as part of its long-term development plan. In densely populated neighborhoods ② which residents lack access to natural shade, summer temperatures often reach dangerous levels. A recent report confirmed ③ that when additional trees were planted along major streets, the local temperature dropped by several degrees. If this measure had not been introduced, the city ④ would have continued to experience extreme heat during the summer.

## 088  문법포인트 | Point 39. 등위접속사의 병렬 구조

It's not just about winning the game but about playing with integrity and sportsmanship.

**해설** 앞의 not just로 보아 「not only ~ but (also)」의 등위상관접속사임을 알 수 있다. 이 상관접속사로 두 개의 전치사구인 about winning the game과 about playing with integrity and sportsmanship이 병렬로 연결되는 것을 알 수 있다. 따라서 정답은 ② but이다.

**어휘** integrity 성실함   sportsmanship 스포츠맨 정신

**정답** ②

## 089  문법포인트 | Point 31. 준동사 주요 표현

Many students (who study overseas) have difficulty ① adjusted to a new environment at first. However, neither a foreign environment nor language barriers ② prevent them from building close friendships with their fellow students. ③ Having been exposed to diverse perspectives, these students often return home with a deeper understanding of the world. Ultimately, these programs help students better ④ adapt to the world and understand it more deeply.

**해설**
① '~하는 데 어려움을 겪다'라는 의미는 「have difficulty (in) + -ing」로 표현해야 하므로 동명사 adjusting으로 고쳐야 한다. (adjusted → adjusting)
② 「neither A nor B」가 주어일 때 동사는 B와 수 일치를 해야 한다. language barriers가 복수이므로 복수형 동사인 prevent가 바르게 쓰였다. Point 27. 주어 - 동사 수 일치
③ 분사와 분사구문의 의미상 주어인 these students가 수동의 관계로 '노출된다'를 의미하며, 분사구문의 시제는 주절의 동사인 return보다 이전 시점이므로 완료 수동형 분사구문인 Having been exposed가 바르게 쓰였다. Point 33. 분사구문
④ 준사역동사 help의 목적격보어로 동사원형인 adapt가 바르게 쓰였다. Point 10. 불완전타동사와 동작의 목적격보어

**어휘** overseas 해외에서   adjust 적응하다   barrier 장벽   fellow 동료   expose 노출하다   diverse 다양한   perspective 관점   ultimately 궁극적으로

**정답** ①

## 090  문법포인트 | Point 44. 관계부사

The city planned ① to expand public green spaces as part of its long-term development plan. In densely populated neighborhoods ② which residents lack access to natural shade, summer temperatures often reach dangerous levels. A recent report confirmed ③ that when additional trees were planted along major streets, the local temperature dropped by several degrees. If this measure had not been introduced, the city ④ would have continued to experience extreme heat during the summer.

**해설**
② 선행사가 장소를 나타내는 neighborhoods이고 관계사절이 완전하므로 관계대명사 which가 아닌 관계부사 where 또는 in which로 써야 한다. (which → where/in which)
① plan은 목적어로 to부정사를 취하는 동사이므로 to expand가 바르게 쓰였다. Point 06. 완전타동사와 동작의 목적어
③ confirm의 목적어로 명사절이 사용되었다. 접속사 뒤의 절이 완전하므로 명사절 접속사 that은 바르게 쓰였다. Point 40. 명사절 접속사의 선택
④ If절의 동사가 had p.p.의 형태이므로 가정법 과거완료가 사용된 것을 알 수 있다. 가정법 과거완료의 주절은 「주어 + 조동사 (과거형) + have p.p.」의 형태로 사용되어야 하므로 would have continued가 옳게 쓰였다. Point 46. 기본가정법

**어휘** expand 확장하다   long-term 장기의   densely 밀집하게   resident 주민   access 접근 기회   confirm 확인하다   degree 도   measure 조치

**정답** ②

## DAY 07

**091** 밑줄 친 부분에 들어갈 말로 가장 적절한 것은?

> The rainy weather was not _____ to force the games to cease.

① badly enough  ② enough badly
③ bad enough  ④ enough bad

**092** 밑줄 친 부분 중 어법상 옳지 않은 것은?

> The faculty ① discussed revising the curriculum, emphasizing the need for flexibility ② so that students can manage diverse academic paths. They suggested that the department ③ assigns faculty advisors more systematically. In response, the coordinator appears ④ confident that these changes will better support individual learning goals.

**093** 밑줄 친 부분에 들어갈 말로 가장 적절한 것은?

> Her diligent practice reminds me ____ achieving excellence through dedication and perseverance.

① of  ② with
③ from  ④ for

**094** 밑줄 친 부분 중 어법상 옳은 것은?

> After the opening of the new interactive science center, there was debate among educators about ① if it prioritized entertainment over instruction. The exhibition aimed to encourage both exploring scientific concepts and ② to apply them to real-world situations. Organizers supported the belief ③ what students learn best when they are engaged in the process. However, some educators claimed that the exhibits were too superficial ④ to offer students any meaningful insight.

## 091 문법포인트 | Point 34. 형용사 vs. 부사

The rainy weather was not bad enough to force the games to cease.

**해설** was의 보어가 되어야 하므로 형용사 bad가 적절하고 부사 badly는 올 수 없다. enough가 부사로서 형용사나 다른 부사를 수식할 때 수식받는 단어의 뒤에서 수식하므로 enough는 bad의 뒤에 와야 한다. 따라서 정답은 ③ bad enough이다.

**어휘** force (억지로) ~시키다   cease 중단되다

정답 ③

## 092 문법포인트 | PPoint 19. 당위의 조동사 should

The faculty ① discussed revising the curriculum, emphasizing the need for flexibility ② so that students can manage diverse academic paths. They suggested that the department ③ assigns (→ assign) faculty advisors more systematically. In response, the coordinator appears ④ confident that these changes will better support individual learning goals.

**해설**
③ 제안 동사 suggest의 목적어 자리에 온 that절의 동사는 「(should) + 동사원형」의 형태가 되어야 하므로 동사의 단수형인 assigns를 동사원형인 assign으로 고쳐야 한다. (assigns → assign)
① 완전타동사 discuss는 전치사 없이 목적어를 바로 취할 수 있으므로 동명사구가 목적어로 바르게 쓰였다. Point 05. 완전타동사
② 주절 뒤에 목적을 나타내는 부사절 접속사 so that이 '~하기 위해서, ~할 수 있도록'이라는 의미로 바르게 쓰였다. Point 41. 부사절 접속사의 선택
④ 불완전자동사 appear의 보어로 형용사 confident가 바르게 쓰였다. Point 04. 불완전자동사의 보어

**어휘** faculty 교수진   discuss 논의하다   revise 개정하다
curriculum 교육과정   emphasize 강조하다   flexibility 유연성
diverse 다양한   assign 배정하다   in response 이에 대응하여
confident 자신감이 있는

정답 ③

## 093 문법포인트 | Point 07. 완전타동사와 함께 사용되는 주요 전치사

Her diligent practice reminds me of achieving excellence through dedication and perseverance.

**해설** 'A에게 B를 상기시키다'는 「remind A of B」로 나타내므로 정답은 ① of이다.

**어휘** diligent 근면한   practice 연습   remind 상기시키다
achieve 달성하다   excellence 탁월함   dedication 헌신
perseverance 인내

정답 ①

## 094 문법포인트 | Point 29. to부정사의 역할

After the opening of the new interactive science center, there was debate among educators about ① [if (→ whether) it prioritized entertainment over instruction]. The exhibition aimed to encourage both exploring scientific concepts and ② to apply (→ applying) them to real-world situations. Organizers supported the belief ③ [what (→ that) students learn best when they are engaged in the process]. However, some educators claimed that the exhibits were too superficial ④ to offer students any meaningful insight.

**해설**
④ 「too + 형용사/부사 + to부정사」 구문은 '너무 ~해서 …할 수 없다'라는 의미이므로 to offer가 바르게 쓰였다.
① 접속사 if가 이끄는 명사절은 전치사의 목적어와 주어로 쓰일 수 없고 타동사의 목적어로만 쓰이므로 if를 whether로 고쳐야 한다. (if → whether) Point 40. 명사절 접속사의 선택
② 「both A and B」의 구조로 exploring과 병렬 구조를 이루어야 하므로 to apply를 applying으로 고쳐야 한다. (to apply → applying) Point 39. 등위접속사의 병렬 구조
③ 접속사 뒤에 완전한 절이 이어졌고, 그 절이 의미상 the belief를 부연하고 있으므로 what을 동격의 접속사 that으로 고쳐야 한다. (what → that) Point 40. 명사절 접속사의 선택

**어휘** interactive 체험형의   debate 논쟁   prioritize 우선시하다
instruction 교육   exhibition 전시   encourage 장려하다
explore 탐구하다   apply 적용하다   organizer 주최자
engage 몰두시키다   process 과정   superficial 피상적인
offer 제공하다   insight 통찰

정답 ④

**095** 밑줄 친 부분에 들어갈 말로 가장 적절한 것은?

> She inherited _____ from her grandmother, each piece holding sentimental value and cherished memories.

① a number of jewelry
② quite a few jewelries
③ a variety of jewelries
④ a good deal of jewelry

**096** 밑줄 친 부분 중 어법상 옳은 것은?

> The more people learn about climate change, ① the greater their sense of urgency becomes. As awareness grows, many communities cannot help ② to adopt stricter environmental practices. The government, ③ which policies were introduced last year, continue to monitor industrial carbon emissions closely. In recent years, the number of cities participating in green initiatives ④ have increased significantly.

**097** 밑줄 친 부분에 들어갈 말로 가장 적절한 것은?

> _____ we achieve in life often reflects our passion and commitment to our pursuits.

① That          ② What
③ Which         ④ Where

**098** 밑줄 친 부분 중 어법상 옳은 것은?

> The school recently renovated its library, making it ① far more modern than before. The entrance area, ② which wheelchair access was once limited, was widened and fitted with automatic doors. The school also had the lighting system ③ upgrade to reduce energy consumption. A new self-checkout machine was installed, ④ allowed students to borrow materials without waiting in line at the service desk.

## 095 문법포인트 | Point 21. 명사의 이해

She inherited a good deal of jewelry from her grandmother, each piece holding sentimental value and cherished memories.

**해설** jewelry는 불가산명사로 복수 명사를 수식하는 a number of(많은)나 quite a few(꽤 많은), a variety of(여러 가지의)로 수식할 수 없다. 양 형용사의 수식을 받아야 하므로 ④ a good deal of jewelry가 정답이다.

**어휘** inherit 물려받다  hold 지니다  sentimental 감상적인  value 가치  cherished 소중한  memory 추억

**정답** ④

## 096 문법포인트 | Point 37. 비교 사용 표현

The more people learn about climate change, ① the greater their sense of urgency becomes. As awareness grows, many communities cannot help ② to adopt stricter environmental practices. The government, ③ which policies were introduced last year, continue to monitor industrial carbon emissions closely. In recent years, the number of cities participating in green initiatives ④ have increased significantly.

**해설**
① 「The 비교급 S' + V', the 비교급 S + V」 구문은 '~할수록 …하다'라는 의미이다. 불완전자동사 become의 보어인 형용사가 the greater로 바르게 표현되었다.
② 「cannot help -ing」의 구문은 '~하지 않을 수 없다'라는 의미이므로 to adopt를 adopting으로 고쳐야 한다. (to adopt → adopting) Point 31. 준동사 주요 표현
③ 선행사인 The government와 관계사절의 주어인 policies가 문맥상 소유의 관계이므로 which를 소유격 관계대명사 whose로 고쳐야 한다. (which → whose) Point 43. 관계대명사의 선택
④ 「the number of + 복수 명사」는 '~의 수'라는 의미로 단수 취급한다. 문장의 주어가 단수이므로 동사 또한 단수형인 has increased로 고쳐야 한다. (have increased → has increased) Point 27. 주어 - 동사 수 일치

**어휘** urgency 위기  awareness 인식  adopt 채택하다  strict 엄격한  policy 정책  carbon emission 탄소 배출  participate 참여하다  initiative 정책  significantly 상당히

**정답** ①

## 097 문법포인트 | Point 40. 명사절 접속사의 선택

What we achieve in life often reflects our passion and commitment to our pursuits.

**해설** 주절의 동사는 reflects이고 주어 자리에 we achieve in life라는 불완전한 절이 나왔다. 따라서 불완전한 절을 이끌어 명사절로 만들 수 있는 ② What이 들어가야 한다.

**어휘** achieve 성취하다  reflect 반영하다  passion 열정  commitment 헌신  pursuit 추구

**정답** ②

## 098 문법포인트 | Point 36. 비교 구문

The school recently renovated its library, making it ① far more modern than before. The entrance area, ② which wheelchair access was once limited, was widened and fitted with automatic doors. The school also had the lighting system ③ upgrade to reduce energy consumption. A new self-checkout machine was installed, ④ allowed students to borrow materials without waiting in line at the service desk.

**해설**
① 형용사의 비교급은 far, much, still 등이 수식할 수 있으므로 more modern을 부사 far가 바르게 수식하고 있다.
② 선행사가 장소를 나타내는 The entrance area이고, 관계절이 완전하므로 관계대명사 which를 in which나 관계부사 where로 고쳐야 한다. (which → in which/where) Point 44. 관계부사
③ 사역동사 have는 목적어와 목적격보어의 관계가 능동이면 목적격보어에 동사원형을, 수동이면 과거분사를 써야 한다. the lighting system이 업그레이드된다는 수동의 의미이므로 과거분사 upgraded로 고쳐야 한다. (upgrade → upgraded) Point 10. 불완전타동사와 동작의 목적격보어
④ 의미상 주어인 A self-checkout machine와 분사가 의미상 능동의 관계이고 분사 뒤에 목적어가 있으므로 과거분사를 현재분사인 allowing으로 고쳐야 한다. (allowed → allowing) Point 33. 분사구문

**어휘** recently 최근에  renovate 개조하다  access 접근  fit 설치하다  consumption 소비  install 설치하다  material 자료

**정답** ①

**099** 밑줄 친 부분에 들어갈 말로 가장 적절한 것은?

> It will not be long before the technology _____ enough to make space tourism accessible to everyone.

① advances
② will advance
③ advanced
④ has advanced

**101** 밑줄 친 부분에 들어갈 말로 가장 적절한 것은?

> The environmental group _____ the construction of the new factory near the river.

① opposes to
② opposes
③ was opposed
④ oppose with

**100** 밑줄 친 부분 중 어법상 옳은 것은?

> ① Whoever wishes to participate in the Gyeongbokgung Music Festival is welcome to join the organizing committee. The organizers are making detailed plans lest any important aspect ② should not be overlooked. The fusion of traditional and modern music will sound ③ beautifully to the audience, and everyone will be ④ satisfying with the stunning performances and the palace's night scenery.

**102** 밑줄 친 부분 중 어법상 옳지 않은 것은?

> A famous author once ① mentioned a quiet coastal village in her novel, and since then, it has become a must-visit place for fans of the novel. Tourists often stop ② to take photos at various spots, trying to capture the mood of the story in every frame. Local officials found ③ it amazing that a single story could change the future of a town. They even restored the old lighthouse, ④ which unique structure now attracts the most tourists in the village.

## 099 문법포인트 | Point 15. 시제 관련 표현 / Point 14. 시제일치와 예외

It will not be long before the technology advances enough to make space tourism accessible to everyone.

**해설** 「It will not be long before S + V」라는 표현은 '머지않아 ~할 것이다'라는 의미이다. 이때 before절 동사의 시제는 미래 시제 대신 현재 시제를 써야 한다. 따라서 정답은 ① advances이다.

**어휘** technology 기술  space 우주  tourism 관광
accessible 이용 가능한  advance 발전하다

**정답** ①

## 100 문법포인트 | Point 45. 복합관계사

① [Whoever wishes to participate in the Gyeongbokgung Music Festival] is welcome to join the organizing committee. The organizers are making detailed plans lest any important aspect ② should not be overlooked. The fusion of traditional and modern music will sound ③ beautifully to the audience, and everyone will be ④ satisfying with the stunning performances and the palace's night scenery.

**해설**
① 복합관계사가 이끄는 명사절의 주어가 없으므로 주격인 Whoever가 바르게 쓰였다.
② lest는 부정의 의미를 포함하고 있는 접속사이므로 해당 절 내에서 부정어구를 다시 사용하지 않아야 한다. 따라서 should not be를 should be로 고쳐야 한다. (should not be → should be) Point 41. 부사절 접속사의 선택
③ 불완전자동사 sound는 부사가 아니라 형용사를 보어로 취하므로 beautifully를 beautiful로 고쳐야 한다. (beautifully → beautiful) Point 04. 불완전자동사의 보어
④ 감정유발동사 satisfy는 '만족시키다'라는 뜻이다. 주어인 everyone이 감정의 대상으로서 만족감을 느낀다는 수동의 의미를 나타내므로 과거분사 satisfied로 고쳐야 한다. (satisfying → satisfied) Point 32. 현재분사 vs. 과거분사

**어휘** participate 참가하다  organize 조직하다  committee 위원회
organizer 주최자  detailed 상세한  aspect 측면
overlook 간과하다  stunning 멋진  scenery 풍경

**정답** ①

## 101 문법포인트 | Point 05. 완전타동사

The environmental group opposes the construction of the new factory near the river.

**해설** oppose는 타동사이므로 전치사 없이 바로 뒤에 목적어를 취한다. 뒤에 목적어가 있으므로 능동태인 ② opposes가 정답이다.

**어휘** environmental 환경의  oppose 반대하다  construction 건설

**정답** ②

## 102 문법포인트 | Point 43. 관계대명사의 선택

A famous author once ① mentioned a quiet coastal village in her novel, and since then, it has become a must-visit place for fans of the novel. Tourists often stop ② to take photos at various spots, trying to capture the mood of the story in every frame. Local officials found ③ it amazing that a single story could change the future of a town. They even restored the old lighthouse, ④ which unique structure now attracts the most tourists in the village.

**해설**
④ 관계사절이 완전하고, 선행사인 the old lighthouse와 관계사절의 주어가 문맥상 소유의 관계이므로 관계대명사 which를 소유격 관계대명사인 whose로 고쳐야 한다. (which → whose)
① mention은 완전타동사라서 전치사 없이 목적어를 취한다. Point 05. 완전타동사
② stop 뒤에 동명사가 오면 '~하기를 그만두다'의 의미가 되고, to부정사가 오면 '~하기 위해 멈추다'의 의미가 된다. 사진을 찍기 위해 멈췄다는 의미로 to부정사가 바르게 쓰였다. Point 06. 완전타동사와 동작의 목적어
③ 동사 find의 진목적어인 that절이 목적격보어의 뒤로 이동하고 목적어 자리에는 가목적어 it이 바르게 쓰였다. Point 12. 인칭대명사

**어휘** mention 언급하다  coastal 해안의  spot 장소
capture 담아내다  mood 분위기  official 공무원
restore 복원하다  lighthouse 등대

**정답** ④

**103** 밑줄 친 부분에 들어갈 말로 가장 적절한 것은?

> They spent the evening listening to the waves _____ against the shore.

① crashed  ② crashing
③ to crash  ④ to be crashed

**104** 밑줄 친 부분 중 어법상 옳지 않은 것은?

> The training session began with an overview of the roles and responsibilities for each position. The supervisor warned the new employees ① of common mistakes during their first project. By the time the training ended, everyone ② had acquired the ability ③ to handle their tasks confidently. Even if unexpected events ④ are happened to them in the future, they will overcome the challenges by helping one another.

**105** 밑줄 친 부분 중 어법상 옳지 않은 것은?

> The charity campaign received ① far more support than expected, drawing attention from both local and international media. Volunteers were sent to areas ② where clean water and medical supplies were desperately needed by residents. One report captured a touching scene of volunteers ③ delivering aid to isolated communities. Many of the volunteers were devoted ④ to help disaster victims recover their livelihoods.

### 103 [문법포인트 | Point 10. 불완전타동사와 동작의 목적격보어]

They spent the evening listening to the waves crashing against the shore.

**[해설]** 지각동사는 목적어와 목적격보어를 가지며 목적어와 목적격보어의 관계가 능동이면 원형부정사(동사원형) 또는 현재분사를, 수동의 관계이면 과거분사를 목적격보어로 취한다. listen to가 지각동사로 목적어인 the waves가 해변에 부딪치는 능동의 의미이므로 목적격보어 자리인 빈칸에는 ② crashing이 들어가야 한다.

**[어휘]** wave 파도  shore 해안  crash 부딪치다

[정답] ②

### 104 [문법포인트 | Point 17. 동사의 유형별 수동태]

The training session began with an overview of the roles and responsibilities for each position. The supervisor warned the new employees ① of common mistakes during their first project. By the time the training ended, everyone ② had acquired the ability ③ to handle their tasks confidently. Even if unexpected events ④ are happened (→ happen) to them in the future, they will overcome the challenges by helping one another.

**[해설]**
④ 자동사 happen은 목적어를 취하지 않으므로 목적어가 주어로 전환되는 수동태로 쓸 수 없다. 따라서 능동태인 happen으로 고쳐야 한다. (are happened → happen)
① warn은 「warn A of B」의 형태로 'A에게 B를 경고하다'라는 뜻을 가진다. Point 07. 완전타동사와 함께 사용되는 주요 전치사
② 기준 시점인 부사절의 시제가 과거이고, 주절은 그보다 이전에 시작되어 완료된 일을 나타내므로 과거완료 had acquired가 바르게 쓰였다. Point 12. 완료 시제
③ to handle이 명사 the ability를 후치 수식하는 to부정사의 형용사적 용법으로 바르게 쓰였다. Point 29. to부정사의 역할

**[어휘]** session 기간  overview 개요  responsibility 책임  supervisor 감독자  confidently 자신 있게  unexpected 예상치 못한  overcome 극복하다

[정답] ④

### 105 [문법포인트 | Point 48. 전치사의 목적어]

The charity campaign received ① far more support than expected, drawing attention from both local and international media. Volunteers were sent to areas ② where clean water and medical supplies were desperately needed by residents. One report captured a touching scene of volunteers ③ delivering aid to isolated communities. Many of the volunteers were devoted ④ to help (→ to helping) disaster victims recover their livelihoods.

**[해설]**
④ be devoted to는 '~에 헌신하다'라는 뜻이며, 이때 to는 전치사로 동명사를 목적어로 취한다. 따라서 to help를 helping으로 고쳐야 한다. (to help → to helping)
① 형용사의 비교급은 far, much, still 등의 수식을 받으므로 부사 far가 more를 강조하여 바르게 쓰였다. Point 36. 비교 구문
② 선행사가 장소를 나타내는 areas이고, 관계사 뒤에 완전한 절이 왔으므로 관계부사 where가 바르게 쓰였다. Point 44. 관계부사
③ 전치사 of의 목적어로 동명사인 delivering이 옳게 쓰였다. 동명사 앞의 volunteers는 동명사의 의미상의 주어이다. Point 48. 전치사의 목적어

**[어휘]** charity 자선  volunteer 자원봉사자  medical supplies 의약품  desperately 절실하게  resident 주민  touching 감동적인  isolate 고립시키다  devote 헌신시키다  disaster 재해  victim 피해자  livelihood 생계

[정답] ④

**106** 밑줄 친 부분에 들어갈 말로 가장 적절한 것은?

The park, _____ families often gather for picnics, is located near the river.

① which   ② what
③ where   ④ whose

**108** 밑줄 친 부분에 들어갈 말로 가장 적절한 것은?

The report highlights _____ the company achieved last year.

① who    ② how
③ what   ④ that

**107** 밑줄 친 부분 중 어법상 옳은 것은?

Many ancient farming techniques ① using by early civilizations were designed to improve crop yields and soil quality. These methods often included irrigation systems ② to distribute water efficiently across the fields. In some regions, it was believed ③ what rotating crops would prevent soil exhaustion and maintain fertility. Farmers also built terraces, ④ which helps reduce soil erosion on steep slopes.

**109** 밑줄 친 부분 중 어법상 옳지 않은 것은?

Since Aphra Behn was known as the first female English writer in the early 17th century, some of the most influential English women ① have been writers, poets, and essayists. Their literary contributions have not only enriched cultural landscapes but also ② sparked important conversations about gender, identity, and societal norms. In response to this rich literary legacy, institutions like Lifelong Education Center ③ offering writing courses, ④ led by expert tutors, where you could delve into these pioneering female authors.

## 106 문법포인트 | Point 44. 관계부사

The park, (where families often gather for picnics), is located near the river.

**[해설]** 빈칸 뒤에 완전한 절이 왔고 장소를 의미하는 The park가 선행사이므로 빈칸에는 장소의 관계부사 ③ where가 들어가는 것이 적절하다.

**[정답]** ③

## 108 문법포인트 | Point 40. 명사절 접속사의 선택

The report highlights [what the company achieved last year].

**[해설]** highlight가 타동사로서 명사절을 목적어로 취하고 있는데, 이 명사절은 동사 achieve의 목적어가 없어 불완전하므로 빈칸에는 명사절 접속사와 주어 역할을 동시에 하는 what이 들어가야 한다.

**[정답]** ③

## 107 문법포인트 | Point 29. to부정사의 역할

Many ancient farming techniques ① (using by early civilizations) were designed to improve crop yields and soil quality. These methods often included irrigation systems ② (to distribute water efficiently across the fields). In some regions, it was believed ③ [what rotating crops would prevent soil exhaustion and maintain fertility]. Farmers also built terraces, ④ (which helps reduce soil erosion on steep slopes).

**[해설]**
② to distribute는 앞의 irrigation systems를 수식하는 형용사적 용법으로 바르게 쓰였다.
① 타동사 use의 목적어가 없으며 using이 수식하는 기술과의 관계가 수동이므로 using은 used로 고쳐야 한다. (using → used) Point 32. 현재분사 vs. 과거분사
③ what은 believe의 목적어가 되는 명사절을 이끄는 접속사인데 뒤의 절이 완전하므로 that으로 고쳐야 한다. (what → that) Point 40. 명사절 접속사의 선택
④ 관계대명사 절의 동사는 선행사에 수 일치를 해야 한다. which의 선행사가 terraces로 복수이므로 동사도 복수인 help가 되어야 한다. (which helps → which help) Point 27. 주어 - 동사 수 일치

**[어휘]** ancient 고대의   farming 농업   civilization 문명   design 고안하다   crop 작물   yield 생산   irrigation 관개   distribute 분배하다   rotating crop 윤작   exhaustion 피폐   fertility 생산력   terrace 계단식 밭   erosion 침식   steep 가파른   slope 경사지

**[정답]** ②

## 109 문법포인트 | Point 01. 문장의 구성 / Point 16. 능동태 vs. 수동태 구분

Since Aphra Behn was known as the first female English writer in the early 17th century, some of the most influential English women ① have been writers, poets, and essayists. Their literary contributions have not only enriched cultural landscapes but also ② sparked important conversations about gender, identity, and societal norms. In response to this rich literary legacy, institutions like Lifelong Education Center ③ offering writing courses, ④ (led by expert tutors), where you could delve into these pioneering female authors.

**[해설]**
③ 문장의 동사가 없으므로 분사가 아닌 동사가 와야 한다. 주어 institutions와 offer의 관계가 능동이고, 뒤에 writing courses라는 목적어가 있으므로 능동태로 써야 한다. (offering → offer)
① 「since + 과거(시점)」는 완료 시제와 자주 사용되는 부사구이다. Behn이 최초의 여성 작가로 알려진 시점 이후부터 지금까지의 상황을 이야기하고 있으므로 현재완료 시제인 have been이 바르게 쓰였다. Point 12. 완료 시제
② sparked가 enriched와 등위상관접속사 「not only A but also B(A뿐만 아니라 B도)」를 통해 병렬 구조로 바르게 연결되었다. Point 39. 등위접속사의 병렬 구조
④ 수식을 받는 명사구 writing courses와 lead의 관계가 수동이고, 분사 뒤에 목적어가 없으므로 과거분사 led가 바르게 사용되었다. Point 32. 현재분사 vs. 과거분사

**[어휘]** essayist 수필가   enrich 풍부하게 하다   spark 유발하다   delve into ~을 탐구하다   pioneering 선구적인   legacy 유산

**[정답]** ③

**110** 밑줄 친 부분에 들어갈 말로 가장 적절한 것은?

> The volunteers, along with their coordinator, _____ to various countries for charity work.

① have traveled　　② has traveled
③ have been traveled　　④ has been traveled

**112** 밑줄 친 부분에 들어갈 말로 가장 적절한 것은?

> Among the known forms of matter _____ in this lecture are the proton, neutron, electron and Z-particle.

① discuss　　② discussing
③ discussed　　④ to discuss about

**111** 밑줄 친 부분 중 어법상 옳지 않은 것은?

> All strokes should be treated as a medical emergency and taken ① as seriously as a heart attack, because ② hundreds of stroke patients die needlessly every year. Many doctors have stressed how important it is that stroke ③ be treated in the same way as heart disease and cancer for lives to be saved and the risk of disability reduced. They said among three causes of death in England ④ strokes were on top.

**113** 밑줄 친 부분 중 어법상 옳지 않은 것은?

> The key to a comfortable workspace ① lies not in luxurious furniture but in user-friendly design ② that supports health and productivity. Chairs and desks should be adjustable to accommodate different body types and preferences. Attention should be given to ③ whomever uses the workspace to ensure they can work efficiently and without discomfort. Investing in user-friendly solutions can reduce strain and contribute to a ④ much more beneficial environment for sustained focus and well-being.

## 110 문법포인트 | Point 27. 주어-동사 수 일치 / Point 16. 능동태 vs. 수동태 구분

The volunteers, along with their coordinator, have traveled to various countries for charity work.

**해설** along with their coordinator는 수식어이고, 주어는 The volunteers로 복수이므로 동사도 복수이어야 하고 travel은 자동사이므로 수동태로 쓸 수 없다. 따라서 정답은 ① have traveled이다.

**어휘** coordinator 실무책임자　charity work 자선 활동

**정답** ①

## 111 문법포인트 | Point 50. 도치

All strokes should be treated as a medical emergency and taken ① as seriously as a heart attack, because ② hundreds of stroke patients die needlessly every year. Many doctors have stressed [how important it is that stroke ③ be treated in the same way as heart disease and cancer for lives to be saved and the risk of disability reduced]. They said (among three causes of death in England) ④ strokes were on top.
→ were strokes

**해설**
④ among은 장소의 부사구로 among이 문두로 가면 주어와 동사는 도치되어야 한다. 따라서 strokes와 were는 도치되어야 한다. (strokes were → were strokes)
① 「as ~ as」는 원급비교로 이 사이에는 형용사 또는 부사의 원급이 들어가야 하므로 seriously가 바르게 쓰였다. Point 36. 비교 구문
② 수단위명사가 막연히 큰 수를 의미할 때는 수형용사 없이 복수형으로 쓴다. 수백 명을 의미하는 hundreds가 바르게 쓰였다. Point 35. 주의할 형용사와 부사
③ important와 같은 판단의 형용사가 쓰인 문장에서 진주어 that절의 동사는 「(should) + 동사원형」으로 써야 한다. should가 생략된 be treated가 바르게 쓰였다. Point 19. 당위의 조동사 should

**어휘** stroke 뇌졸중　disability 장애　on top 가장 높은

**정답** ④

## 112 문법포인트 | Point 32. 현재분사 vs. 과거분사

(Among the known forms of matter (discussed in this lecture)) are the proton, neutron, electron and Z-particle.

**해설** Among 전치사구가 강조되어 문두로 나가고 주어와 동사가 도치되었다. 문장의 주동사는 are이므로 빈칸에는 앞선 명사를 수식하는 분사가 와야 한다. 수식을 받는 명사구 forms of matter와 discuss의 관계가 수동이고, discuss가 취하는 목적어가 없으므로 과거분사 형태로 와야 한다. 따라서 정답은 ③ discussed이다.

**어휘** matter 물질　lecture 강의　proton 양성자　neutron 중성자　electron 전자　particle 입자　discuss 논의하다

**정답** ③

## 113 문법포인트 | Point 45. 복합관계사

The key to a comfortable workspace ① lies not in luxurious furniture but in user-friendly design ② (that supports health and productivity). Chairs and desks should be adjustable to accommodate different body types and preferences. Attention should be given to ③ [whomever uses the workspace to ensure they can work efficiently and without discomfort]. Investing in user-friendly solutions can reduce strain and contribute to a ④ much more beneficial environment for sustained focus and well-being.
→ whoever

**해설**
③ whomever 이하의 절에 주어가 없으므로 목적격인 whomever를 주격인 whoever로 고쳐야 한다. (whomever → whoever)
① 맥락상 '있다, 위치해 있다'의 의미가 되어야 하므로 자동사 lie가 바르게 쓰였다. lay는 타동사로 '눕히다, 놓다'라는 뜻으로 목적어와 함께 써야 한다. Point 11. 혼동하기 쉬운 동사의 불규칙 변화
② user-friendly design이라는 선행사가 있고, that 이하에 주어가 없으므로 주격 관계대명사 that이 바르게 쓰였다. which로 쓸 수도 있다. Point 43. 관계대명사의 선택
④ 비교급 more beneficial을 much가 바르게 수식하고 있다. much 외에도 far, by far, still, even, a lot, rather, a little이 비교급을 수식할 수 있다. Point 36. 비교 구문

**어휘** comfortable 편안한　adjustable 조정 가능한　accommodate 수용하다　preference 선호도　efficiently 효율적으로　strain 중압감　contribute to ~에 기여하다　beneficial 유익한

**정답** ③

**114** 밑줄 친 부분에 들어갈 말로 가장 적절한 것은?

However _____, she managed to complete it on time.

① the task seemed difficultly
② the task seemed difficult
③ difficultly the task seemed
④ difficult the task seemed

**116** 밑줄 친 부분에 들어갈 말로 가장 적절한 것은?

_____ building in the world was built by a Korean company in 2010.

① The most tall    ② The tallest
③ The most tallest ④ The more tall

**115** 밑줄 친 부분 중 어법상 옳지 않은 것은?

Economic instability can cause unemployment rates to soar, leaving many people without steady income. The rising inflation is an unpleasant consequence that ① affects daily life, which makes essentials more expensive and hard ② to afford. Government policies must address these issues effectively, lest you ③ should not see further social unrest and widespread dissatisfaction. Immediate and decisive action is crucial to stabilize the situation, restore public confidence, and ④ ensure economic recovery.

**117** 밑줄 친 부분 중 어법상 옳지 않은 것은?

Whether students discover their academic interests by chance or through careful planning, they will find themselves ① drawn to various academic disciplines. Courses need ② to be chosen based on personal interests and career goals. Consider three students: one pursues engineering, and ③ the other opts for literature, while the third selects economics. Each discipline offers unique insights and challenges, yet all ④ contribute to the diverse fabric of knowledge and learning on campus.

## 114  문법포인트 | Point 42. 주요 양보구문

However difficult the task seemed, she managed to complete it on time.

**해설** 뒤에 주절이 있고 However로 시작하는 것으로 보아 However 양보절이 되어야 함을 알 수 있다. However는 '얼마나', '아무리'를 의미하여 다른 형용사나 부사를 수식하는데 이때 수식받는 형용사나 부사는 반드시 붙여 써야 한다. 불완전자동사 seem의 보어가 와야 하므로 형용사가 먼저 오고 뒤에 주어와 동사가 사용되어서 ④ difficult the task seemed가 정답이다.

**어휘** manage (어떻게든) 해내다   on time 시간을 어기지 않고

**정답** ④

## 115  문법포인트 | Point 41. 부사절 접속사의 선택

Economic instability can cause unemployment rates to soar, leaving many people without steady income. The rising inflation is an unpleasant consequence (that ① affects daily life,) (which makes essentials more expensive and hard ② to afford.) Government policies must address these issues effectively, lest you ③ should not see further social unrest and widespread dissatisfaction. Immediate and decisive action is crucial to stabilize the situation, restore public confidence, and ④ ensure economic recovery.
→ should see

**해설**
③ lest는 부정의 의미를 내포한 접속사이므로 다시 부정어구를 사용하지 않아야 한다. 따라서 should not을 should로 고쳐야 한다. (should not → should)
① 주격 관계대명사 절의 동사는 선행사에 수를 일치시킨다. 선행사가 an unpleasant consequence로 단수이므로 affects가 바르게 쓰였다. Point 27. 주어 - 동사 수 일치
② to부정사가 앞에 있는 형용사 hard를 수식하는 부사적 용법으로 바르게 쓰였다. Point 29. to부정사의 역할
④ ensure가 등위접속사 and를 통해 stabilize, restore와 병렬 구조로 바르게 연결되었다. Point 39. 등위접속사의 병렬 구조

**어휘** instability 불안정   unemployment rate 실업률   soar 급증하다   consequence 결과   essential 필수품   address 해결하다   unrest (사회·정치적인) 불안   dissatisfaction 불만   immediate 즉각적인   decisive 결정적인   action 조치   crucial 결정적인   stabilize 안정화하다   confidence 신뢰   ensure 보장하다

**정답** ③

## 116  문법포인트 | Point 36. 비교 구문

The tallest building in the world was built by a Korean company in 2010.

**해설** 최상급은 「the + 형용사·부사의 최상급」으로 나타내며, '가장 ~한'이라는 의미이다. 따라서 정답은 ② The tallest이다.

**정답** ②

## 117  문법포인트 | Point 25. 부정대명사

Whether students discover their academic interests by chance or through careful planning, they will find themselves ① drawn to various academic disciplines. Courses need ② to be chosen based on personal interests and career goals. Consider three students: one pursues engineering, and ③ the other opts for literature, while the third selects economics. Each discipline offers unique insights and challenges, yet all ④ contribute to the diverse fabric of knowledge and learning on campus.
→ another

**해설**
③ 세 명 또는 세 물건을 지칭할 때는 one, another, the other(the third)로 차례로 지칭한다. (the other → another)
① find는 목적어와 목적격보어의 관계가 수동이면 목적격보어로 과거분사를 취한다. 자신들이 끌리는 수동의 의미이므로 drawn이 바르게 쓰였다. Point 10. 불완전타동사와 동작의 목적격보어
② to부정사의 의미상의 주어는 주어인 Courses이고 이 주어가 선택되는 수동의 의미이므로 수동형 to부정사가 바르게 쓰였다. need의 목적어로 to부정사가 바르게 쓰였다. Point 31. 준동사 주요 표현 / Point 06. 완전타동사와 동작의 목적어
④ 자동사 contribute와 전치사 to가 함께 쓰여 '~의 원인이다, ~을 초래하다'를 의미한다. 주어가 all이므로 동사도 복수형으로 잘 쓰였다. Point 03. 완전자동사

**어휘** by chance 우연히   draw 끌다   discipline 지식   career 직업   pursue 추구하다   opt for ~을 선택하다   contribute 기여하다

**정답** ③

DAY 08

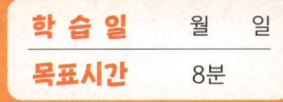

**118** 밑줄 친 부분에 들어갈 말로 가장 적절한 것은?

> It might cost you a lot of money _____ the old car engine to make it run again.

① repair
② repairing
③ to repair
④ to be repaired

**119** 밑줄 친 부분 중 어법상 옳지 않은 것은?

> There was ① a great deal of excitement in town the other day. A horse got out of a farm and came into town. It walked across the school grounds and through several busy streets, and then it ② lay down in the middle of the main street. All traffic stopped, and quite a few people ③ tried to lead it away, but no one could move it. However, when a farmer ④ was appeared, it got up and followed him.

**120** 밑줄 친 부분 중 어법상 옳지 않은 것은?

> It was thought ① that remote work would reduce productivity due to concerns about supervision and collaboration. However, people ② whom a flexible schedule is essential, have shown increased efficiency when ③ given the autonomy to manage their own time. Consequently, many companies are now reconsidering ④ their office space needs and embracing hybrid work models.

## 118 문법포인트 | Point 08. 수여동사

It might cost you a lot of money to repair the old car engine to make it run again.

**해설** '~가 …하는 데 시간/돈이 걸리다/들다'는 「It + take/cost + 간접목적어(~) + 직접목적어(시간/돈) + to …」로 나타낸다. 따라서 빈칸에는 to부정사가 들어가야 하므로 정답은 ③ to repair이다.

**어휘** run 작동하다  repair 수리하다

**정답** ③

## 119 문법포인트 | Point 17. 동사의 유형별 수동태

There was ① a great deal of excitement in town the other day. A horse got out of a farm and ② came into town. It walked across the school grounds and through several busy streets, and then it ② lay down in the middle of the main street. All traffic stopped, and quite a few people ③ tried to lead it away, but no one could move it. However, when a farmer ④ was appeared, it got up and followed him.

**해설**
④ appear는 자동사라서 목적어를 취하지 않으므로 목적어가 주어로 전환되어야 하는 수동태로 쓰일 수 없다. 그러므로 be동사 없이 appeared로 써야 한다. (was appeared → appeared)
① a great deal of는 '대량의, 아주 많은'의 의미로 셀 수 없는 명사 앞에 쓰인다. Point 21. 명사의 이해
② 뒤에 목적어가 없고 주어가 it인데 lays가 아니므로 lay는 lie의 과거형이다. 문맥상 '말이 길 한가운데 누웠다'는 뜻이므로, 자동사 lie의 과거형인 lay가 옳다. Point 11. 혼동하기 쉬운 동사의 불규칙 변화
③ try가 to부정사를 목적어로 취하면 '~하려 노력하다'의 의미가 된다. 말을 끌어내려 노력했다는 의미로 바르게 쓰였다. Point 06. 완전타동사와 동작의 목적어

**어휘** excitement 소동  lie down 눕다  main street 대로
quite a few 꽤 많은

**정답** ④

## 120 문법포인트 | Point 43. 관계대명사의 선택

It was thought ① that remote work would reduce productivity due to concerns about supervision and collaboration. However, people ② whom a flexible schedule is essential, have shown increased efficiency when ③ given the autonomy to manage their own time. Consequently, many companies are now reconsidering ④ their office space needs and embracing hybrid work models.

**해설**
② 선행사는 people이고 관계사 뒤에 완전한 절이 왔다. 문맥상 'essential for people'이 되어야 자연스러우므로 전치사 for를 넣어 for whom으로 고쳐야 한다. (whom → for whom)
① that 이하에 완전한 절이 왔고, It이 가주어이므로 that절이 진주어 역할을 하고 있다. Point 40. 명사절 접속사의 선택
③ 주절의 주어 people과 give의 관계가 수동이므로 과거분사 given이 바르게 왔다. give는 목적어를 두 개 취하는 동사이므로 뒤에 목적어 the autonomy가 남을 수 있다. Point 33. 분사구문
④ many companies를 받는 소유격 their가 바르게 쓰였다. Point 24. 인칭대명사

**어휘** remote work 원격 근무  supervision 감독
collaboration 협업  flexible 유연한  efficiency 효율성
autonomy 자율성  reconsider 재고하다  embrace 수용하다
hybrid work model 하이브리드 근무제: 사내 출근과 원격 근무를 결합한 근무 형태

**정답** ②

**121** 밑줄 친 부분에 들어갈 말로 가장 적절한 것은?

_____ effective habits with letting go of useless habits is essential when learning a new thing.

① Develop
② Developed
③ Developing
④ To be developed

**122** 밑줄 친 부분 중 어법상 옳지 않은 것은?

Preserving biodiversity is crucial in a forest ① which diverse species thrive, as each plant and animal plays a vital role in the ecosystem, ② contributing to its overall health and balance. Similarly, maintaining a streamlined and organized environment can enhance productivity and ③ efficiency in both personal and professional settings. By minimizing distractions and optimizing resources, individuals can focus more ④ effectively on their tasks and goals.

**123** 밑줄 친 부분에 들어갈 말로 가장 적절한 것은?

The sooner we start the project, _____ to meet the deadline.

① the more easy it will be
② the easier it will be
③ the more it will be easy
④ the more it will be easier

**124** 밑줄 친 부분 중 어법상 옳은 것은?

The ancient pyramids of Egypt continue to captivate historians and archaeologists alike. The Pyramid of Giza is a ① 481-foot-tall monument showcasing the architectural skill of ② their builders. These structures, ③ building thousands of years ago, have withstood the test of time and still hold many secrets. Scholars are aware that much remains ④ to discover about the techniques and labor used in their construction.

## 121 문법포인트 | Point 01. 문장의 구성

Developing effective habits with letting go of useless habits is essential when learning a new thing.

**해설** 주절의 동사가 be동사 단수형인 is이므로 복수형 명사인 habits는 주어가 될 수 없다. 따라서 빈칸에는 effective habits를 목적어로 취하는 동명사나 to부정사의 능동형이 들어가야 한다.

**어휘** effective 효과적인  let go of ~을 버리다  essential 꼭 필요한

정답 ③

## 122 문법포인트 | Point 44. 관계부사

Preserving biodiversity is crucial in a forest ① which (→ where) diverse species thrive, as each plant and animal plays a vital role in the ecosystem, ② contributing to its overall health and balance. Similarly, maintaining a streamlined and organized environment can enhance productivity and ③ efficiency in both personal and professional settings. By minimizing distractions and optimizing resources, individuals can focus more ④ effectively on their tasks and goals.

**해설**
① which 이하에 완전한 절이 왔고, a forest라는 장소를 수식하고 있으므로 which를 관계부사 where로 고쳐야 한다. (which → where)
② 분사구문의 분사 contributing의 의미상 주어는 each plant and animal이고, 분사와의 관계가 능동이므로 현재분사 contributing이 바르게 쓰였다. Point 33. 분사구문
③ 명사 efficiency가 명사 productivity와 and로 바르게 병렬되었다. Point 39. 등위접속사의 병렬 구조
④ 동사 focus를 수식하므로 부사 effectively가 바르게 쓰였다. more는 effectively를 수식하여 부사의 비교급 형태로 쓰였다. Point 34. 형용사 vs. 부사

**어휘** preserve 보존하다  biodiversity 생물 다양성  diverse 다양한  streamlined 능률적인  distraction 방해  optimize 최적화하다

정답 ①

## 123 문법포인트 | Point 37. 비교 사용 표현

The sooner we start the project, the easier it will be to meet the deadline.

**해설** '~할수록 …하다'는 「The 비교급 S' + V', the 비교급 S + V」로 나타낸다. 따라서 정답은 ② the easier it will be이다.

**어휘** meet (기한 등을) 지키다  deadline 마감일

정답 ②

## 124 문법포인트 | Point 35. 주의할 형용사와 부사

The ancient pyramids of Egypt continue to captivate historians and archaeologists alike. The Pyramid of Giza is a ① 481-foot-tall monument showcasing the architectural skill of ② their (→ its) builders. These structures, ③ building (→ built) thousands of years ago, have withstood the test of time and still hold many secrets. Scholars are aware that much remains ④ to discover (→ to be discovered) about the techniques and labor used in their construction.

**해설**
① 수단위명사는 수사와 함께 써서 다른 명사를 수식할 경우 단수로 써야 하므로 foot이 단수로 바르게 쓰였다.
② their가 지칭하는 것은 The Pyramid of Giza로 단수이므로 단수인 its로 고쳐야 한다. (their → its) Point 24. 인칭대명사
③ 분사구문인 building의 의미상의 주어는 주절의 주어인 These structures이고 이들이 세워진다는 수동의 의미이므로 과거분사형으로 써야 한다. (building → built) Point 33. 분사구문
④ 주어인 much가 발견된다는 수동의 의미이므로 수동형 to부정사로 고쳐야 한다. (to discover → to be discovered) Point 30. 준동사의 형태 변화

**어휘** captivate 마음을 사로잡다  archaeologist 고고학자  monument 기념물  showcase 보여주다  architectural 건축학의  builder 건설자  withstand 견디다

정답 ①

**125** 밑줄 친 부분에 들어갈 말로 가장 적절한 것은?

> _____ depends on the availability of the venue.

① When will the concert take place
② When take place the concert
③ When the concert will take place
④ When dose the concert take place

**126** 밑줄 친 부분 중 어법상 옳지 않은 것은?

> The attractions highlighted by the travel agency ① is now experiencing even greater popularity. They attempt ② to create appealing packages that showcase the best experiences available. These efforts allow travelers ③ to discover new destinations while ④ ensuring a memorable and enriching vacation.

**127** 밑줄 친 부분 중 어법상 옳지 않은 것은?

> In spite of the heavy rain, the community fair continued as planned. The fair featured several booths and activities, each aimed ① to support local poor families. Organizers found ② impossible for everyone to attend all the sessions due to the limited space. However, the enthusiasm of the attendees made the event a great success. The atmosphere was ③ lively, as if the rain ④ had never been a concern.

**128** 밑줄 부분 중 어법상 옳지 않은 것은?

> A team of Carilion's neurosurgeons and residents traveled to the other side of the world to provide Nepal's largest hospital ① with resources. This partnership means ② thousands of Nepalese citizens can get advanced treatments they otherwise would never have been able to. Since Dr. Srijan Adhikari, a neurosurgeon resident at Carilion Clinic, ③ started his residency five years ago, his goal ④ was to help the Nepalese community by sharing medical knowledge.

## 125 문법포인트 | Point 02. 의문문의 어순

[When the concert will take place] depends on the availability of the venue.

**해설** 빈칸은 동사 앞에 있으므로 주어 역할을 하는 절이 와야 한다. 문장에서 명사처럼 주어, 목적어, 보어 역할을 할 수 있는 의문사절을 간접의문이라고 한다. 간접의문의 어순은 「의문사 + 주어 + 동사」이므로 ③ When the concert will take place이 정답이다.

**어휘** depend on ~에 달려 있다  availability 이용 가능성  venue 장소  take place 열리다

**정답** ③

## 126 문법포인트 | Point 27. 주어-동사 수 일치

The attractions (highlighted by the travel agency) ① is (→ are) now experiencing even greater popularity. They attempt ② to create appealing packages that showcase the best experiences available. These efforts allow travelers ③ to discover new destinations while ④ ensuring a memorable and enriching vacation.

**해설**
① is의 주어는 The attractions로 복수이므로 동사도 복수인 are가 되어야 한다. (is → are)
② attempt는 to부정사를 목적어로 취하는 타동사이다. to create가 목적어로 바르게 쓰였다. Point 06. 완전타동사와 동작의 목적어
③ allow는 to부정사를 목적격보어로 취한다. to discover가 목적격보어로 바르게 쓰였다. Point 10. 불완전타동사와 동작의 목적격보어
④ 의미를 강조하기 위해 접속사를 그대로 둔 채 만든 분사구문이다. 주절의 주어가 확신한다는 능동의 의미이고 분사 뒤에 목적어가 있으므로 현재분사형이 바르게 쓰였다. Point 33. 분사구문

**어휘** attraction 명소  highlight 강조하다  popularity 인기  appealing 매력적인  package 관광상품  showcase 보여주다

**정답** ①

## 127 문법포인트 | Point 06. 완전타동사와 동작의 목적어 / Point 24. 인칭대명사

In spite of the heavy rain, the community fair continued as planned. The fair featured several booths and activities, each aimed ① to support local poor families. Organizers found ② impossible (→ it impossible) for everyone to attend all the sessions due to the limited space. However, the enthusiasm of the attendees made the event a great success. The atmosphere was ③ lively, as if the rain ④ had never been a concern.

**해설**
② find는 목적어가 to부정사일 때 가목적어 it을 쓰고 진목적어는 목적격보어 뒤로 보낸다. impossible이라는 목적격보어가 있고 진목적어인 to attend가 뒤에 있으므로 가목적어 it을 목적격보어 앞에 넣어주어야 한다. (impossible → it impossible)
① 앞에 위치한 each aimed는 의미상의 주어인 each를 갖는 분사구문으로 '각각은 목표가 설정되었다'는 의미이다. 그 뒤에 '~하도록'을 의미하는 to부정사의 부사적 용법으로 to support가 올바르게 쓰였다. Point 29. to부정사의 역할
③ lively는 부사가 아닌 형용사이므로 was의 보어로 형용사인 lively가 바르게 쓰였다. Point 04. 불완전자동사의 보어
④ as if 가정법의 시제를 선택할 때, 주절의 시간과 동일한 시간을 의미할 때는 가정법 과거를, 주절의 시간보다 앞선 시간을 의미할 때는 가정법 과거완료를 사용한다. as if 뒤에 가정법 과거완료가 와서 주절의 시제보다 앞에 있었던, 즉 비가 내렸던 상태를 바르게 나타내었다. Point 47. 기타 가정법

**어휘** fair 바자회  feature 특징을 이루다  organizer 주최자  attend 참석하다  enthusiasm 열정  lively 활기찬  concern 문제

**정답** ②

## 128 문법포인트 | Point 12. 완료 시제

A team of Carilion's neurosurgeons and residents traveled to the other side of the world to provide Nepal's largest hospital ① with resources. This partnership means ② thousands of Nepalese citizens can get advanced treatments they otherwise would never have been able to. Since Dr. Srijan Adhikari, a neurosurgeon resident at Carilion Clinic, ③ started his residency five years ago, his goal ④ was (→ has been) to help the Nepalese community by sharing medical knowledge.

**해설**
④ 앞에 「since + 과거시점」이 있으므로 시제는 현재완료로 써야 한다. 따라서 was를 has been으로 고쳐야 한다. (was → has been)
① provide는 「provide A with B」의 구문으로 'A에게 B를 제공하다'를 의미한다. 전치사 with가 바르게 쓰였다. Point 07. 완전타동사와 함께 사용되는 주요 전치사
② 수단위 명사는 특정한 수와 함께 쓰이면 단수로 쓰고, 막연히 많은 수를 의미할 경우 복수로 써야 한다. '수천'을 의미하는 thousands의 복수형이 바르게 쓰였다. Point 35. 주의할 형용사와 부사
③ 과거를 의미하는 five years ago가 있으므로 과거 시제가 바르게 쓰였다. Point 14. 시제일치와 예외

**어휘** neurosurgeon 신경외과 의사  resident 수련의  provide 제공하다  partnership 협력  residency 레지던트 근무  share 공유하다

**정답** ④

**129** 밑줄 친 부분에 들어갈 말로 가장 적절한 것은?

> It's not nice to _____ someone who is trying their best.

① laugh  ② laugh for
③ laugh to  ④ laugh at

**130** 밑줄 친 부분 중 어법상 옳지 않은 것은?

> Malaria kills young children every minute, most of ① them are Africans. Since the research into the disease first began, trials have revealed a vaccine ② produced by the research institute has the potential to be the most effective weapon ever developed against it. The breakthrough is an ③ even bigger achievement than the Covid-19 vaccine. When the pandemic struck in 2020, the team's focus switched from the malaria vaccine to ④ developing a Covid-19 vaccine.

**131** 밑줄 친 부분 중 어법상 옳은 것은?

> The zoos have restricted visitor access to certain animals to prevent them from ① exposing to foot-and-mouth disease (FMD). Indonesia is currently battling an outbreak of the ② high contagious disease. The zoos' chief executive said paid encounters with giraffes, kangaroos and elephants ③ were cancelled, following briefings about the risk ④ what the foot-and-mouth disease poses to the animals' health.

**132** 밑줄 친 부분 중 어법상 옳지 않은 것은?

> The Administrator decided ① to mail 31,342 copies of the settlement notice to potential settlement members of the class action. No settlement members ② have opposed to any aspect of the settlement. Never ③ have any requests been made to be excluded from the settlement. The Administrator suggests that the proposed settlement ④ be fair and reasonable.

## 129 문법포인트 | Point 03. 완전자동사

It's not nice to laugh at someone who is trying their best.

**해설** laugh는 완전자동사라서 목적어를 취하려면 전치사와 함께 써야 한다. 맥락상 「laugh at + 명사」의 형태로 '~을 비웃다'의 뜻을 전달해야 하므로 정답은 ④ laugh at이다.

**어휘** try one's best 최선을 다하다   laugh at ~을 비웃다

정답 ④

## 130 문법포인트 | Point 43. 관계대명사의 선택

Malaria kills young children every minute, (most of ① them are Africans). Since the research into the disease first began, trials have revealed a vaccine (② produced by the research institute) has the potential to be the most effective weapon ever developed against it. The breakthrough is an ③ even bigger achievement than the Covid-19 vaccine. When the pandemic struck in 2020, the team's focus switched from the malaria vaccine to ④ developing a Covid-19 vaccine.

**해설**
① 두 개의 절이 접속사 없이 연결되어 있으므로 대명사 역할과 접속사 역할을 동시에 할 수 있는 목적격 관계대명사가 와야 한다. 선행사가 사람이므로 whom으로 고쳐야 한다. (them → whom)
② vaccine과 produce는 의미상 수동의 관계이므로 과거분사 produced가 바르게 쓰였다. Point 32. 현재분사 vs. 과거분사
③ 비교급을 수식하여 강조하는 부사에는 much, far, by far, still, even, a lot 등이 있다. even이 비교급인 bigger를 강조하여 바르게 쓰였다. Point 36. 비교 구문
④ 「from A to B」는 'A부터 B까지'라는 의미이다. from과 to는 전치사이므로 뒤에는 (동)명사 형태가 나와야 한다. 따라서 동명사인 developing이 바르게 쓰였다. Point 48. 전치사의 목적어

**어휘** reveal 밝히다   breakthrough 획기적인 발명   achievement 성취

정답 ①

## 131 문법포인트 | Point 16. 능동태 vs. 수동태 구분

The zoos have restricted visitor access to certain animals to prevent them from ① exposing to foot-and-mouth disease (FMD). Indonesia is currently battling an outbreak of the ② high contagious disease. The zoos' chief executive said paid encounters (with giraffes, kangaroos and elephants) ③ were cancelled, following briefings about the risk ④ (what the foot-and-mouth disease poses to the animals' health).

**해설**
③ were cancelled의 주어는 paid encounters이며 「with ~ elephants」는 주어를 후치 수식하고 있는 전치사구이다. 주어가 복수이므로 복수 동사 were가 바르게 쓰였다. 또한 유료 만남이 '취소한' 것이 아니라, '취소된' 것이므로 수동태가 바르게 쓰였다.
① exposing의 의미상의 주어인 them이 구제역에 '노출되는 것'을 막는 것이므로 수동형이 되어야 한다. 따라서 being exposed로 고쳐야 한다. (exposing → being exposed) Point 30. 준동사의 형태 변화
② high는 높이를 나타내는 부사이고 highly는 정도를 나타내는 부사이다. contagious는 '전염성이 있는'이라는 뜻으로 성질이나 상태를 표현하므로 정도를 나타내는 부사 highly의 수식을 받아야 한다. (high → highly) Point 35. 주의할 형용사와 부사
④ what이 이끄는 절이 문맥상 risk를 수식하는데, what은 선행사가 있으면 쓸 수 없으므로 관계대명사 which 또는 that으로 고쳐야 한다. (what → which/that) Point 43. 관계대명사의 선택

**어휘** restrict 제한하다   access 접근   expose 노출시키다
foot-and-mouth disease 구제역: 가축의 입이나 발굽에 생기는 전염병
outbreak 발생   contagious 전염성이 있는
chief executive 최고경영자   paid 유료의   encounter 만남
following ~후에   pose 제기하다

정답 ③

## 132 문법포인트 | Point 05. 완전타동사

The Administrator decided ① to mail 31,342 copies of the settlement notice to potential settlement members of the class action. No settlement members ② have opposed to any aspect of the settlement. (Never) ③ have any requests been made to be excluded from the settlement. The Administrator suggests that the proposed settlement ④ be fair and reasonable.

**해설**
② oppose는 완전타동사이므로, 전치사 없이 목적어를 취한다. (have opposed to → have opposed)
① decide는 완전타동사로 to부정사를 목적어로 취할 수 있으므로 to mail이 목적어로 바르게 쓰였다. Point 06. 완전타동사와 동작의 목적어
③ 부정부사 Never가 문두에 와 문장이 「조동사 + 주어 + 동사원형」의 형태로 바르게 도치되었다. Point 50. 도치
④ 제안 동사 suggest 뒤에 오는 절은 「that + S + (should) 동사원형」의 형태로 와야 한다. should가 생략된 be가 바르게 쓰였다. Point 19. 당위의 조동사 should

**어휘** administrator 관리자   settlement 합의(안)   potential 잠재적인
class action 집단 소송

정답 ②

DAY 09  79

**133** 밑줄 친 부분에 들어갈 말로 가장 적절한 것은?

When I arrived at the party, I saw everyone _____.

① dances  ② is dancing
③ to dance  ④ dancing

**134** 밑줄 친 부분 중 어법상 옳지 않은 것은?

As soon as I wake up, I start my morning routine ① which includes stretching and preparing breakfast. I enjoy a peaceful moment with a cup of coffee before I begin checking emails and planning my schedule with the computer ② turning on. This morning ritual helps me ③ stay organized and focused throughout the day, ensuring I start each day on a productive note. It goes without saying that establishing this routine ④ sets a positive tone for the entire day ahead.

**135** 밑줄 친 부분 중 어법상 옳은 것은?

In biology class, the teacher ① explained to the students that in humans, the genes inherited from our father ② decides whether we will be boys or girls. Women have a perfect pair of sex chromosomes (XX), but men have a mismatched pair (XY). All children will inherit an X chromosome from their mother regardless of ③ that gender is a boy or a girl. Thus, the sex of the children will be determined by what they ④ are provided from their father.

## 133 문법포인트 | Point 10. 불완전타동사와 동작의 목적격보어

When I arrived at the party, I saw everyone dancing.

**해설** 지각동사의 목적격보어는 목적어와 능동의 관계이면 원형부정사(동사원형) 또는 현재분사가, 수동의 관계이면 과거분사가 되어야 한다. everyone이 목적어이며 빈칸은 목적격보어 자리이고 목적어와 의미상 능동의 관계이므로 ④ dancing이 들어가야 한다.

정답 ④

## 134 문법포인트 | Point 33. 분사구문

As soon as I wake up, I start my morning routine ① which includes stretching and preparing breakfast. I enjoy a peaceful moment with a cup of coffee before I begin checking emails and planning my schedule with the computer ② turning on. This morning ritual helps me ③ stay organized and focused throughout the day, ensuring I start each day on a productive note. It goes without saying that establishing this routine ④ sets a positive tone for the entire day ahead.

**해설**
② with 분사구문의 경우 목적어와 목적격보어의 관계가 수동이면 목적격보어에 과거분사를 써야 한다. 컴퓨터가 켜진다는 수동의 의미이므로 turning on은 turned on으로 고쳐야 한다. (turning on → turned on)
① 선행사가 routine으로 사물이며, 뒤에 주어가 빠진 불완전한 절이 왔으므로 관계대명사 which가 바르게 쓰였다. 이때 which 대신 that을 써도 된다. Point 43. 관계대명사의 선택
③ help는 목적격보어로 to부정사 또는 동사원형을 모두 취할 수 있다. 동사원형인 stay가 목적격보어로 바르게 쓰였다. Point 10. 불완전타동사와 동작의 목적격보어
④ 주어는 establishing으로, 동명사이다. 동명사는 단수 취급하므로 단수형인 sets가 바르게 쓰였다. Point 27. 주어 - 동사 수 일치

**어휘** routine 일과  ritual 의식  establish 확립하다
It goes without saying that ~은 두말할 나위가 없다  note 분위기

정답 ②

## 135 문법포인트 | Point 05. 완전타동사

In biology class, the teacher ① explained to the students that in humans, the genes (inherited from our father) ② decides whether we will be boys or girls. Women have a perfect pair of sex chromosomes (XX), but men have a mismatched pair (XY). All children will inherit an X chromosome from their mother regardless of ③ that gender is a boy or a girl. Thus, the sex of the children will be determined by what they ④ are provided from their father.

**해설**
① explain은 4형식 불가 완전타동사이다. 따라서 목적어 that절 앞에 놓인 의미상 간접목적어인 the students 앞에 전치사 to가 바르게 쓰였다.
② decides의 주어가 the genes이므로 복수 동사로 고쳐야 한다. (decides → decide) Point 27. 주어 - 동사 수 일치
③ 전치사 regardless of의 목적어가 될 수 있도록 or와 함께 '~인지 ...인지'를 뜻하는 명사절 접속사 whether가 와야 한다. (that → whether) Point 40. 명사절 접속사의 선택
④ provide는 4형식 불가 동사로 'A에게 B를 제공하다'는 「provide A with B」로 표현한다. 수동태가 될 경우 「A be provided with」가 되며 what이 with의 목적어에 해당한다. 따라서 전치사 with를 누락시키지 않고 be provided with라고 해야 한다. (are provided → are provided with) Point 17. 동사의 유형별 수동태

**어휘** biology 생물  gene 유전자  inherit 물려받다  sex 성  chromosome 염색체  mismatched 짝이 맞지 않는  regardless of ~에 상관없이  gender 성  thus 따라서  determine 결정하다

정답 ①

**136** 밑줄 친 부분에 들어갈 말로 가장 적절한 것은?

> We believe it is more _____ to revise the obsolete laws than abolish them.

① sensible   ② sensitive
③ sensory    ④ sensual

**138** 밑줄 친 부분에 들어갈 말로 가장 적절한 것은?

> Every teacher and every student _____ to contribute to the school's community service projects.

① expect      ② expecting
③ is expected ④ are expected

**137** 밑줄 친 부분 중 어법상 옳지 않은 것은?

> The police force ① is often referred to as "guardians of the peace" by the communities they serve, emphasizing their vital role in maintaining public safety and order. When ② deprived of sufficient resources, such as funding and personnel, police departments face challenges in fulfilling their duties effectively. So, officers undergo ongoing training sessions ③ aimed at improving their ability to handle diverse situations with tact and efficiency ④ every other weeks.

**139** 밑줄 친 부분 중 어법상 옳지 않은 것은?

> More than 95 percent of Crimeans voted for the Ukrainian region's accession to Russia in a controversial referendum, ① which was widely condemned by Western governments, who referred to it ② as 'illegal'. The European Union and the US threatened sanctions against Russia, ③ where they accused of ④ invading and annexing the Ukrainian territory.

## 136 문법포인트 | Point 35. 주의할 형용사와 부사

We believe it is more sensible to revise the obsolete laws than abolish them.

**해설** '시대에 뒤떨어진 법을 개정하는 것'에 대한 판단을 나타내는 형용사가 와야 한다. 따라서 문맥상 ① sensible(분별 있는)이 와야 알맞다.

**어휘** revise 개정하다　obsolete 시대에 뒤떨어지는　abolish 폐지하다
sensible 분별 있는　sensitive 민감한　sensory 감각의
sensual 관능적인

**정답** ①

## 137 문법포인트 | Point 25. 부정대명사

The police force ① is often referred to as "guardians of the peace" by the communities they serve, emphasizing their vital role in maintaining public safety and order. When ② deprived of sufficient resources, such as funding and personnel, police departments face challenges in fulfilling their duties effectively. So, officers undergo ongoing training sessions ③ aimed at improving their ability to handle diverse situations with tact and efficiency ④ every other weeks.
→ every other week

**해설**
④ '매 2주'를 뜻할 때 every other 다음에는 단수로 써야 한다. 따라서 weeks는 week로 고쳐야 한다. (every other weeks → every other week)
① 「refer to A as B」의 구문이 수동태가 될 때 전치사 as가 빠지지 않도록 주의해야 한다. is often referred to as가 바르게 쓰였다. Point 17. 동사의 유형별 수동태
② 의미를 강조하기 위해 접속사를 그대로 둔 분사구문으로 deprived의 의미상의 주어는 주절의 주어인 police departments이다. 경찰이 자원이 부족하게 된 수동의 의미이므로 deprived가 바르게 쓰였다. Point 33. 분사구문
③ 분사 aimed가 training sessions를 수식하고 있다. 문맥상 수동의 의미이므로 aimed가 바르게 쓰였다. Point 32. 현재분사 vs. 과거분사

**어휘** guardian 수호자　order 질서　deprive 부족하게 만들다
resource 자원　funding 기금　challenge 문제　undergo 받다
with tact 빈틈없이

**정답** ④

## 138 문법포인트 | Point 25. 부정대명사 / Point 16. 능동태 vs. 수동태 구분

Every teacher and every student is expected to contribute to the school's community service projects.

**해설** 「every + 단수 명사」는 항상 단수 취급하며 접속사 and로 연결되어도 단수로 취급한다. 또한 타동사 expect가 주어와 '기대되다'라는 수동의 관계이고 목적어가 없으므로 수동태가 되어야 한다. 따라서 정답은 ③ is expected이다.

**어휘** be expected to ~할 것으로 기대되다
contribute to ~에 기여하다

**정답** ③

## 139 문법포인트 | Point 43. 관계대명사의 선택

More than 95 percent of Crimeans voted for the Ukrainian region's accession to Russia in a controversial referendum, (① which was widely condemned by Western governments), who referred to it ② as 'illegal'. The European Union and the US threatened sanctions against Russia, ③ where they accused of ④ invading and annexing the Ukrainian territory.
→ which

**해설**
③ 선행사인 Russia를 수식하는 관계부사 where의 뒤에 accused의 목적어가 없는 불완전한 절이 왔으므로 where가 아닌 관계대명사 which가 적합하다. (where → which)
① 앞 문장 전체가 선행사이므로 단수 취급하여 관계대명사절의 동사는 단수인 was가 적합하다. Point 27. 주어 - 동사 수 일치
② refer to는 「refer to A as B」의 형태로 전치사구 목적격보어를 취하므로 as illegal이 바르게 쓰였다. Point 09. 불완전타동사의 목적격보어
④ 전치사 of의 목적어로 동명사 invading과 annexing이 and를 통해 병렬 구조로 바르게 연결되었다. Point 48. 전치사의 목적어 / Point 28. 동명사의 역할

**어휘** vote 투표하다　accession 편입　referendum 국민투표
condemn 비난하다　sanction 제재　annex 병합하다

**정답** ③

**140** 밑줄 친 부분에 들어갈 말로 가장 적절한 것은?

It was very nice _____ to forgive the man who had made false rumors to harm you.

① you
② your
③ for you
④ of you

**141** 밑줄 친 부분 중 어법상 옳은 것은?

Accurately reporting the news is the cornerstone of responsible journalism. ① A number of journalists in politically unstable regions were able to uncover critical information despite the dangers. Reporters mentioned ② their editor the difficulties faced in obtaining reliable sources. Although there is a possibility that many valuable stories ③ have almost been disappeared ④ because the challenges of reporting in such hostile environments, most reporters persist to ensure the truth is brought to light.

**142** 밑줄 친 부분 중 어법상 옳지 않은 것은?

Many people prefer summer ① to winter for vacations because the warm weather and long daylight hours offer abundant opportunities for outdoor activities. ② Planning for activities and family gatherings is as ③ important as choosing the right destination. Travel can be more enjoyable in this season ④ because the abundance of festivals, beach outings, and recreational events available.

**143** 밑줄 친 부분 중 어법상 옳은 것은?

More than 40 percent of households in the city ① have reported experiencing some form of financial hardship last year. Had it not been for government assistance programs, many families ② could be facing even more severe economic challenges today. Experts recommend that policymakers ③ would continue to prioritize economic relief measures to support vulnerable communities and ④ stabilizing the local economy.

## 140  문법포인트 | Point 30. 준동사의 형태 변화

It was very nice of you to forgive the man who had made false rumors to harm you.

**[해설]** nice는 인성형용사이므로 to forgive의 의미상의 주어는 「of + 목적격」의 형태로 써야 한다. 따라서 정답은 ④ of you이다.

**[어휘]** forgive 용서하다  false 거짓의  rumor 소문  harm 피해를 주다

**[정답]** ④

## 141  문법포인트 | Point 21. 명사의 이해

Accurately reporting the news is the cornerstone of responsible journalism. ① A number of journalists in politically unstable regions were able to uncover critical information despite the dangers. Reporters mentioned ② their editor the difficulties faced in obtaining reliable sources. Although there is a possibility that many valuable stories ③ have almost been disappeared ④ because the challenges of reporting in such hostile environments, most reporters persist to ensure the truth is brought to light.

**[해설]**
① a number of는 가산명사의 복수형을 수식하는 어구이다. 뒤에 journalists라는 가산명사 복수형을 수식하여 바르게 쓰였다.
② mention은 4형식이 불가한 완전타동사인데 뒤에 간접목적어와 직접목적어 두 개가 와서 맞지 않다. 간접목적어에 해당하는 their editor 앞에 전치사 to를 넣어주어야 한다. (their editor → to their editor) Point 05. 완전타동사
③ disappear는 자동사이므로 수동태로 쓸 수 없다. 따라서 능동태로 고쳐야 한다. (have almost been disappeared → have almost disappeared) Point 17. 동사의 유형별 수동태
④ because는 접속사이므로 뒤에 절 구조가 나와야 하는데 명사구만 나왔으므로 같은 의미의 전치사 because of 또는 due to로 고쳐야 한다. (because → because of/due to) Point 41. 부사절 접속사의 선택

**[어휘]** cornerstone 토대  unstable 불안정한  uncover 발굴하다  mention 언급하다  possibility 가능성  hostile 적대적인  persist 집요하게 계속하다  bring to light 밝히다

**[정답]** ①

## 142  문법포인트 | Point 41. 부사절 접속사의 선택

Many people prefer summer ① to winter for vacations because the warm weather and long daylight hours offer abundant opportunities for outdoor activities. ② Planning for activities and family gatherings is as ③ important as choosing the right destination. Travel can be more enjoyable in this season ④ because the abundance of festivals, beach outings, and recreational events available.

**[해설]**
④ 접속사 because 뒤에 절이 아닌 명사구가 나열되어 있으므로 전치사 because of로 고쳐야 한다. (because → because of)
① '더 선호하다'라는 의미의 prefer는 비교 대상 앞에 than이 아니라 to를 사용한다. Point 37. 비교 사용 표현
② 동명사가 문장의 주어로 바르게 쓰였다. Point 28. 동명사의 역할
③ 'A는 B만큼 ~하다'라는 원급 비교는 「A + as + 형용사·부사 원급 + as + B」로 나타내므로 형용사 important가 바르게 쓰였다. 동사 is의 보어 자리이므로 부사는 올 수 없다. Point 36. 비교 구문 / Point 04. 불완전 자동사의 보어

**[어휘]** gathering 모임  destination 행선지  abundance 풍부함  outing 소풍

**[정답]** ④

## 143  문법포인트 | Point 46. 기본 가정법

More than 40 percent of households in the city ① have reported experiencing some form of financial hardship last year. Had it not been for government assistance programs, many families ② could be facing even more severe economic challenges today. Experts recommend that policymakers ③ would continue to prioritize economic relief measures to support vulnerable communities and ④ stabilizing the local economy.

**[해설]**
② 「Had it not been for ~」은 '~이 없었다면'이라는 뜻의 가정법 과거완료이므로 과거 사실의 반대를 나타내지만, 주절은 시간 부사 today를 사용해 현재 사실의 반대를 나타내고 있으므로 가정법 과거로 could be가 왔다. 따라서 혼합 가정법이 바르게 쓰였다.
① last year라는 특정 과거 시간이 있으므로 완료 시제로 쓸 수 없고, 과거시제로 써야 한다. (have reported → reported) Point 13. 시제 사용 제한
③ 제안 동사 recommend는 종속절에 「(should) + 동사원형」의 형태를 취한다. 따라서 would를 should로 고쳐야 한다. should는 생략할 수 있다. (would → should) Point 19. 당위의 조동사 should
④ stabilizing은 등위접속사 and로 앞의 to support와 병렬되고 있으므로 to stabilize 또는 to가 생략된 형태인 stabilize로 고쳐야 한다. (stabilizing → (to) stabilize) Point 39. 등위접속사의 병렬 구조

**[어휘]** relief 구제  severe 심각한  prioritize 우선시하다  measures (pl.) 조치  vulnerable 취약한  stabilize 안정시키다

**[정답]** ②

**144** 밑줄 친 부분에 들어갈 말로 가장 적절한 것은?

> Sadly, the dog seems to _____ by his owners; he must have starved for days to be that skinny.

① abandon
② be abandoned
③ have abandoned
④ have been abandoned

**145** 밑줄 친 부분 중 어법상 옳은 것은?

> Recently, two paintings connected with the artwork *The Virgin of the Rocks* by da Vinci ① has found. There are two angels painted in them just like in *The Virgin of the Rocks*, each of whom plays a different instrument in one picture, but who look very solemn and ② which wings are dark in the both pictures. That is why there ③ arouse a great number of questions related with them and some experts assume that they ④ were painted by another painter.

**146** 밑줄 친 부분에 들어갈 말로 가장 적절한 것은?

> Hidden beneath the surface _____ layers of ancient rock formations.

① be    ② is
③ are    ④ was

**147** 밑줄 친 부분 중 어법상 옳지 않은 것은?

> Real estate markets ① are influenced by various factors, including location, economic conditions, and interest rates. Property values typically ② are risen in high-demand areas with good amenities and access to transportation. Buyers often seek properties that offer long-term investment potential and ③ appreciate in value over time. Market fluctuations can affect both residential and commercial real estate, ④ requiring investors to stay informed about economic shifts and property trends.

## 문장 분석 및 해설

### 144  문법포인트 | Point 30. 준동사의 형태 변화

Sadly, the dog seems to have been abandoned by his owners; he must have starved for days to be that skinny.

**[해설]** 동사 seems의 시제보다 이전의 시간에 주인에게서 버림받았다는 의미이므로 빈칸에는 완료부정사가 들어가야 하고 타동사 abandon 뒤에 목적어가 없으므로 수동형이어야 한다. 따라서 ④ have been abandoned가 정답이다.

**[어휘]** abandon 버리다  starve 굶다  skinny 마른

**[정답]** ④

### 146  문법포인트 | Point 50. 도치

(Hidden beneath the surface) are layers of ancient rock formations.

**[해설]** Hidden이라는 보어가 문장의 앞으로 이동하면서 주어와 동사가 도치된 문장이므로 동사가 들어가야 함을 알 수 있다. 주어가 layers로 복수이므로 빈칸에는 ③ are가 들어가야 한다.

**[어휘]** surface 표면  layer 층  rock formation 암반층

**[정답]** ③

### 145  문법포인트 | Point 14. 시제일치와 예외 / Point 16. 능동태 vs. 수동태 구분

Recently, two paintings (connected with the artwork *The Virgin of the Rocks* by da Vinci) ① has found. There are two angels painted in them just like in *The Virgin of the Rocks*, (each of whom plays a different instrument in one picture), but (who look very solemn) and ② (which wings are dark in the both pictures). That is why (there) ③ arouse a great number of questions (related with them) and some experts assume that they ④ were painted by another painter.

**[해설]**
④ they는 two paintings를 가리킨다. 타동사 paint와 수동의 관계이므로 수동태가 바르게 사용되었고 과거에 그려진 것이니 과거 시제가 바르게 사용되었다. 주어에 수 일치하여 복수형 동사 were가 바르게 쓰였다.
① 주어가 two paintings이고 동사가 has found이다. 주어와의 관계가 수동이므로 현재완료의 수동태로 고쳐야 한다. (has found → have been found) Point 16. 능동태 vs. 수동태 구분 / Point 27. 주어-동사 수 일치
② 선행사가 two angels로, wing에 대해 소유의 의미를 나타내야 하므로 관계대명사 소유격 whose로 고쳐야 한다. 관계절 each of whom, who도 모두 two angels를 선행사로 취하며 each of whom절은 두 천사의 행동을, who절은 두 천사의 표정을 각각 설명한다. 참고로 each of whom절과 who ~ and whose절이 but으로 연결되어 있다. (which → whose) Point 43. 관계대명사의 선택
③ there 다음에 동사가 먼저 나오고 주어가 나온 도치 구문이다. a great number of questions가 문장의 주어이고 목적어가 없으므로 타동사가 올 수 없다. 따라서 타동사인 arouse를 자동사인 arise로 고쳐야 한다. (arouse → arise) Point 11. 혼동하기 쉬운 동사의 불규칙 변화

**[어휘]** virgin 처녀  instrument 악기  solemn 엄숙한

**[정답]** ④

### 147  문법포인트 | Point 11. 혼동하기 쉬운 동사의 불규칙 변화 / Point 17. 동사의 유형별 수동태

Real estate markets ① are influenced by various factors, including location, economic conditions, and interest rates. Property values typically ② are risen in high-demand areas with good amenities and access to transportation. Buyers often seek properties that offer long-term investment potential and ③ appreciate in value over time. Market fluctuations can affect both residential and commercial real estate, ④ requiring investors to stay informed about economic shifts and property trends.

**[해설]**
② 자동사 rise는 수동태로 쓸 수 없으므로 are risen을 rise로 고쳐야 한다. (are risen → rise)
① 타동사 influence 뒤에 목적어가 없고 영향을 받는다는 수동의 의미로 쓰였으므로 수동태로 바르게 쓰였다. Point 16. 능동태 vs. 수동태 구분
③ appreciate는 '가치가 오르다'라는 뜻으로 앞의 offer와 병렬로 바르게 쓰였다. Point 39. 등위접속사의 병렬 구조
④ requiring은 분사구문으로 주절의 주어인 Market fluctuation과 의미상 능동의 관계이고 분사 뒤에 목적어 investors가 있으므로 현재분사형으로 바르게 쓰였다.

**[어휘]** amenity 편의 시설  potential 잠재력  appreciate 가치가 오르다  fluctuation 변동

**[정답]** ②

**148** 밑줄 친 부분에 들어갈 말로 가장 적절한 것은?

> The gymnast's flexibility enables her _____ complex routines with ease.

① perform  ② performing
③ to perform  ④ performed

**149** 밑줄 친 부분 중 어법상 옳지 않은 것은?

> Fanie Botha was ① brave enough to oppose the then Education Department. Nowhere ② did his will seem stronger than in the decision to build a dorm for the Grade 9 students. The education laws of that time forbade children ③ staying in a dorm after Grade 8, but nothing could stop him. ④ Hopeless as things might seem, he continued to fight without giving up.

**150** 밑줄 친 부분 중 어법상 옳지 않은 것은?

> The Chairperson ① mentioned about the issue about ② whether the observers possibly are involved in this process. He confirmed some observers ③ had already approached him to express interest in the discussions of the Working Group. One delegation, however, was ④ of the view that the Working Group should be limited to Member States only. He understood the sensitivities and for now the process would involve Member States only.

## 148 문법포인트 | Point 10. 불완전타동사와 동작의 목적격보어

The gymnast's flexibility enables her to perform complex routines with ease.

해설 enable은 목적격보어로 to부정사를 취한다. 목적어 her가 있으므로 빈칸은 목적격보어가 들어가야 한다. 따라서 정답은 ③ to perform 이다.

어휘 gymnast 체조선수  flexibility 유연성  complex 복잡한
routine 반복 동작  perform 수행하다

정답 ③

## 149 문법포인트 | Point 10. 불완전타동사와 동작의 목적격보어

Fanie Botha was ① brave enough to oppose the then Education Department. (Nowhere) ② did his will seem stronger than in the decision to build a dorm for the Grade 9 students. The education laws of that time forbade children ③ staying in a dorm after Grade 8, but nothing could stop him. ④ Hopeless as things might seem, he continued to fight without giving up.

해설
③ forbid는 목적격보어로 to부정사를 취하므로 staying을 to stay로 고쳐야 한다. (staying → to stay)
① enough는 부사일 때 항상 형용사나 부사를 뒤에서 수식하므로 형용사 brave 뒤에 바르게 쓰였다. Point 34. 형용사 vs. 부사
② 부정부사가 문두에 올 경우 주어와 동사가 도치되는데, 일반 동사가 쓰일 경우 do 조동사를 시제 일치와 수 일치하여 주어 앞으로 이동시켜야 한다. Point 50. 도치
④ 「형용사/부사/명사 + as/though + 주어 + 동사」 구문은 '비록 ~지만'이라는 양보의 의미를 나타낸다. 동사 seem의 보어로 형용사 Hopeless가 바르게 사용되었다. Point 42. 주요 양보구문

어휘 dorm 기숙사  forbid 금지하다  hopeless 절망적인

정답 ③

## 150 문법포인트 | Point 05. 완전타동사

The Chairperson ① mentioned about the issue about ② [whether the observers possibly are involved in this process]. He confirmed some observers ③ had already approached him to express interest in the discussions of the Working Group. One delegation, however, was ④ of the view that the Working Group should be limited to Member States only. He understood the sensitivities and for now the process would involve Member States only.

해설
① mention은 완전타동사로서 전치사 없이 목적어를 취하므로 about을 삭제해야 한다. (mentioned about → mentioned)
② 전치사 뒤에는 명사나 명사구 또는 일부 명사절이 올 수 있다. whether는 명사절을 이끌어 전치사 뒤에 올 수 있다. Point 40. 명사절 접속사의 선택
③ 주절의 동사가 과거 시제일 때 종속절에는 과거 또는 과거완료 시제가 올 수 있으므로 바르게 쓰였다. 이때 현재나 현재완료 시제는 올 수 없다. Point 12. 완료 시제
④ be동사 뒤에 「전치사 + 명사」가 보어로 바르게 쓰였다. 참고로, be of the view는 have the view와 같은 뜻이며 the view와 that절은 동격을 이룬다. Point 04. 불완전자동사의 보어

어휘 chairperson 의장  observer 참관인
be involved in ~에 참여하다  delegation 대표단

정답 ①

**151** 밑줄 친 부분에 들어갈 말로 가장 적절한 것은?

> We still feel so _____ even while we watch the famous comedy movie.

① bore　　　② boring
③ bored　　④ to be bored

**153** 밑줄 친 부분에 들어갈 말로 가장 적절한 것은?

> I wish I _____ more time with my grandparents before they passed away.

① spend　　　　② have spent
③ would spend　④ had spent

**152** 밑줄 친 부분 중 어법상 옳은 것은?

> It's so important to teach young people that they have rights, encourage them to understand those rights, and ① helping them to speak out when they aren't being upheld. They ② must empower by our giving them the knowledge they need to understand their rights and recognize ③ when have they been infringed. The government has proposed landmark legislation, if passed by the Parliament, ④ that will incorporate the United Nations Convention on the Rights of the Child (UNCRC) into the law.

**154** 밑줄 친 부분 중 어법상 옳지 않은 것은?

> The new community center project had ① been eagerly anticipated by local residents. After months of planning and securing necessary permits, construction was scheduled ② to complete by the end of the year. Construction crews were excited to start, ③ knowing that the state-of-the-art facility would offer a variety of activities and spaces for everyone. As the final completion ④ approached, the whole neighborhood looked forward to the grand opening, ready to enjoy their new community hub.

## 151 문법포인트 | Point 32. 현재분사 vs. 과거분사

We still feel so bored even while we watch the famous comedy movie.

**해설** 감정유발동사는 주체가 감정을 일으키면 현재분사로, 감정을 느끼면 과거분사로 써야 한다. 주체인 We가 지루함을 느낀다는 의미가 되어야 하므로 과거분사로 써야 한다. 따라서 ③ bored가 정답이다.

**정답** ③

## 152 문법포인트 | Point 43. 관계대명사의 선택

It's so important to teach young people that they have rights, encourage them to understand those rights, and ① helping them to speak out when they aren't being upheld. They ② must empower by our giving them the knowledge they need to understand their rights and recognize ③ [when have they been infringed]. The government has proposed landmark legislation, if passed by the Parliament, ④ (that will incorporate the United Nations Convention on the Rights of the Child (UNCRC) into the law).

**해설**
④ 관계대명사 that 앞에 콤마가 있지만 이는 계속적 용법이 아닌 삽입절을 의미하는 콤마이므로 관계대명사 that이 쓰일 수 있다.
① to teach ~, (to) encourage ~, and (to) helping이 병렬로 연결된 구조 이므로 helping을 help로 고쳐야 한다. (helping → help) Point 39. 등위접속사의 병렬 구조
② 주어인 They와 타동사 empower가 '그들이 힘을 얻는' 수동의 관계이며, 동사의 목적어가 없으므로 수동태로 고쳐야 한다. (must empower → must be empowered) Point 16. 능동태 vs. 수동태 구분
③ recognize의 목적어인 간접의문문으로 간접의문문은 「의문사 + 주어 + 동사」의 어순이 되어야 하므로 have는 주어인 they 뒤로 가야 한다. (when have they been infringed → when they have been infringed) Point 02. 의문문의 어순

**어휘** uphold 인정하다  empower 힘을 주다  infringe 침해하다  landmark 획기적인 일  legislation 법안  incorporate 통합하다  convention 협약

**정답** ④

## 153 문법포인트 | Point 47. 기타 가정법

I wish I had spent more time with my grandparents before they passed away.

**해설** I wish 가정법은 가정법 과거와 가정법 과거완료가 모두 가능하다. before they passed away를 통해 과거 시점임을 알 수 있으므로 빈칸에는 과거 상황에 대한 가정이므로 가정법 과거완료 동사가 들어가야 한다. 따라서 ④ had spent가 정답이다.

**어휘** pass away 죽다

**정답** ④

## 154 문법포인트 | Point 30. 준동사의 형태 변화

The new community center project had ① been (eagerly) anticipated by local residents. After months of planning and securing necessary permits, construction was scheduled ② to complete by the end of the year. Construction crews were excited to start, ③ knowing [that the state-of-the-art facility would offer a variety of activities and spaces for everyone]. As the final completion ④ approached, the whole neighborhood looked forward to the grand opening, ready to enjoy their new community hub.

**해설**
② 주어 construction과 to부정사로 사용된 complete는 수동의 관계이다. 따라서 to complete을 수동의 부정사 형태인 to be completed로 고쳐야 한다. (to complete → to be completed)
① 주어 project와 타동사인 anticipate는 '프로젝트가 기대를 받다'라는 수동의 관계이다. 따라서 수동태가 바르게 쓰였다. Point 16. 능동태 vs. 수동태 구분
③ know는 that절이라는 목적어가 있고, 문장의 주어 construction crew와 능동의 관계이므로 현재분사로 바르게 쓰였다. Point 33. 분사구문
④ approach는 '(시간이) 다가오다'를 의미할 때 완전자동사로 사용되므로 능동태로 시제에 맞게 과거형으로 바르게 쓰였다. Point 03. 완전자동사

**어휘** eagerly 열렬하게  anticipate 기대하다  secure 확보하다  permit 허가  construction 공사  state-of-the-art 첨단의  facility 시설  approach 다가오다  hub 허브: 중심이 되는 곳

**정답** ②

**155** 밑줄 친 부분에 들어갈 말로 가장 적절한 것은?

> Carbon is the element that diffuses the fastest _____.

① very  ② even
③ by far  ④ still

**156** 밑줄 친 부분 중 어법상 옳은 것은?

> As costs rise across the world, so ① does the rage. People spilled their anger onto the streets as they demanded economic justice, despite often being met with state violence. We can expect plenty more of this, and a rise in union activism, as governments fail ② to protecting citizens from the impacts of massive price hikes. Protests, which articulate wider demands or ③ demanding systemic changes, ④ is also evolving. Over 250 million more people are expected to be pushed into poverty in 2024.

**157** 밑줄 친 부분 중 어법상 옳지 않은 것은?

> The travel agency updated its policy after a series of complaints. Customers must ① be informed any changes to their bookings, and agents are required ② to provide clear explanations. Some staff members, however, claimed ③ that they were never notified about the new rules, and the manager promised ④ to review the communication process.

**158** 밑줄 친 부분 중 어법상 옳지 않은 것은?

> ① Recognizing the urgency of the situation, they immediately had the equipment in the laboratory ② fix to ensure smooth operations. This task was ③ of utmost importance as it directly impacted their ability to meet project deadlines. Under no circumstance ④ could they afford any further delays, and the prompt repair ensured minimal disruption to their research progress.

## 155 문법포인트 | Point 36. 비교 구문

Carbon is the element that diffuses the fastest by far.

[해설] 최상급을 수식할 수 있는 부사는 the very, by far 등인데, 최상급의 앞과 뒤 모두에서 수식이 가능한 것은 by far이다. 따라서 정답은 ③ by far이다.

[어휘] carbon 탄소  element 원소  diffuse 확산되다

[정답] ③

## 156 문법포인트 | Point 50. 도치 / Point 27. 주어 - 동사 수 일치

As costs rise across the world, so ① does the rage. People spilled their anger onto the streets as they demanded economic justice, despite often being met with state violence. We can expect plenty more of this, and a rise in union activism, as governments fail ② to protecting citizens (→ to protect) from the impacts of massive price hikes. Protests, (which articulate wider demands or ③ demanding systemic (→ demand) changes), ④ is also evolving. Over 250 million more (→ are) people are expected to be pushed into poverty in 2024.

[해설]
① '또한 그러하다'를 의미하는 so의 경우 도치를 해야 한다. 이때 앞 동사가 일반동사이면 조동사 do를 써서 도치해야 한다. 일반동사인 rise를 대신하고 주어가 단수이므로 does가 주어 앞에 바르게 도치되었다.
② fail은 to부정사를 목적어로 취하는 동사이다. 따라서 to protecting은 to protect로 고쳐야 한다. (to protecting → to protect) Point 06. 완전타동사와 동작의 목적어
③ demanding은 앞의 articulate와 등위접속사 or로 연결되어 두 요소는 병렬을 이루어야 한다. 따라서 demanding은 동사인 demand로 고쳐야 한다. (demanding → demand) Point 39. 등위접속사의 병렬 구조
④ 동사 is의 주어는 앞의 Protests이다. Protests가 복수형이므로 동사 is 역시 복수인 are로 고쳐야 한다. (is → are) Point 27. 주어 - 동사 수 일치

[어휘] rage 분노  activism 행동주의  hike 인상  protest 시위  articulate 분명히 표현하다

[정답] ①

## 157 문법포인트 | Point 17. 동사의 유형별 수동태

The travel agency updated its policy after a series of complaints. Customers must ① be informed any changes to (→ be informed of 목(X)) their bookings, and agents are required ② to provide clear explanations. Some staff members, however, claimed ③ [that they were never notified about the new rules], and the manager promised ④ to review the communication process.

[해설]
① inform 동사는 'A에게 B에 대해 알리다'라고 할 때 「inform A of B」의 구조를 취하고, 수동태로 사용되면 「A is informed of B」가 된다. 수동태로 전환될 때 전치사 of가 누락되지 않아야 한다. (be informed → be informed of)
② require는 5형식일 때 목적격보어에 to부정사를 취한다. require가 수동태가 되면 to부정사는 수동태 뒤에 이어서 써주어야 하므로 바르게 쓰였다. Point 17. 동사의 유형별 수동태
③ that 이후의 절이 완전하므로 claim의 목적어 역할을 하는 명사절을 이끄는 접속사 that이 바르게 쓰였다. Point 40. 명사절 접속사의 선택
④ promise는 to부정사를 목적어로 취하는 동사이므로 to review가 목적어로 바르게 쓰였다. Point 06. 완전타동사와 동작의 목적격보어

[어휘] travel agency 여행사  update 개정하다  policy 정책  a series of 일련의  complaint 불만  booking 예약  agent 직원  be required to ~해야 하다  explanation 설명  claim 주장하다  notify 통보하다  review 검토하다  process 과정

[정답] ①

## 158 문법포인트 | Point 10. 불완전타동사와 동작의 목적격보어

① Recognizing the urgency of the situation, they (능동) immediately had the equipment in the laboratory ② fix (→ fixed) to ensure smooth operations. This task was ③ of utmost importance as it directly impacted their ability to meet project deadlines. (Under no circumstance) ④ could they afford any further delays, and the prompt repair ensured minimal disruption to their research progress.

[해설]
② 사역동사 had의 목적어로 the equipment, 목적격보어로 fix가 쓰였다. 그러나 장비가 수리된다는 수동의 의미이므로 동사원형인 fix는 과거분사인 fixed로 고쳐야 한다. (fix → fixed)
① 분사구문인 Recognizing ~의 의미상의 주어는 주절의 they로 그들이 인식하는 능동의 관계이므로 Recognizing이 바르게 쓰였다. Point 33. 분사구문
③ 「전치사 + 추상명사」는 형용사적으로 쓰여 보어가 될 수 있다. of utmost importance가 was의 보어로 바르게 쓰였다. Point 04. 불완전자동사의 보어 / Point 48. 전치사의 목적어
④ 부정부사가 문두로 나오면 주어와 동사는 도치되어야 한다. Under no circumstance가 문장의 앞으로 나와 could와 they가 바르게 도치되었다. Point 50. 도치

[어휘] urgency 긴급  equipment 장비  laboratory 실험실  ensure 보장하다  smooth 원활한  operation 작동  delay 지연  prompt 신속한  repair 수리  disruption 차질

[정답] ②

**159** 밑줄 친 부분에 들어갈 말로 가장 적절한 것은?

> Please _____ the blanket over the bed when you're done.

① lie   ② lay
③ be laid   ④ have lied

**161** 밑줄 친 부분에 들어갈 말로 가장 적절한 것은?

> It is neither intelligence nor wealth _____ determines one's happiness.

① who   ② that
③ when   ④ what

**160** 밑줄 친 부분 중 어법상 옳지 않은 것은?

> Considering his current financial situation, he struggled to make ends meet with his part-time job. His minimal salary barely covered his rent, ① still more left him with any savings for unexpected expenses. His budget was stretched to its limits, ② leaving him with little room for any unexpected expenses or emergencies. ③ Whoever faces such challenges ④ understands the stress and uncertainty it brings.

**162** 밑줄 친 부분 중 어법상 옳은 것은?

> ① There is a number of challenges facing small businesses today, from navigating complex regulatory requirements ② to manage cash flow effectively. Small business owners often wish they ③ had been better prepared when they faced unexpected economic downturns or market shifts. This is not because they lack ambition, but because anticipating every fluctuation in consumer demand and economic conditions ④ are a daunting task.

## 159 문법포인트 | Point 11. 혼동하기 쉬운 동사의 불규칙 변화

Please lay the blanket over the bed when you're done.

**해설** 뒤에 blanket이라는 목적어가 있으므로 타동사가 와야 하며 주어가 없는 명령문이므로 동사원형이 와야 한다. lie는 자동사이므로 타동사인 ② lay가 들어가야 한다.

정답 ②

## 160 문법포인트 | Point 37. 비교 사용 표현

Considering his current financial situation, he struggled to make ends meet with his part-time job. His minimal salary barely covered his rent, ① still more left him with any savings for unexpected expenses. His budget was stretched to its limits, ② leaving him with little room for any unexpected expenses or emergencies. ③ [Whoever faces such challenges] ④ understands the stress and uncertainty it brings.

**해설**
① still more는 긍정을 강화하는 표현이다. 앞에 준부정사 barely를 사용한 부정의 절이 오고 문맥도 부정이므로 부정의 의미를 강화하는 still less로 고쳐야 한다. (still more → still less)
② 분사구문 leaving의 의미상의 주어는 주절의 주어인 His budget이다. 그의 예산이 남겨주는 능동의 의미라서 현재분사형이 바르게 쓰였다. Point 33. 분사구문
③ 복합관계사가 있는 명사절 안에 주어가 없으므로 주격인 Whoever가 바르게 쓰였다. Point 45. 복합관계사
④ Whoever faces such challenges의 복합관계사절이 주어로 쓰였다. 절은 단수로 취급하므로 단수형 동사 understands가 바르게 쓰였다. Point 27. 주어 - 동사 수 일치

**어휘** make ends meet 근근이 살아가다  cover 감당하다  rent 집세  unexpected 예상치 못한  expense 비용  budget 예산  uncertainty 불확실성

정답 ①

## 161 문법포인트 | Point 49. 강조

It is neither intelligence nor wealth that determines one's happiness.

**해설** 빈칸 뒤에 동사와 목적어가 나와 있고 앞에는 It이라는 주어가 나와 있다. 뒤가 불완전하므로 가주어 진주어 구문이 아닌 It~that 강조구문임을 파악할 수 있다. 따라서 빈칸에는 ② that이 들어가야 한다.

**어휘** intelligence 지능  wealth 재산  determine 결정하다

정답 ②

## 162 문법포인트 | Point 47. 기타 가정법

① There is a number of challenges facing small businesses today, from navigating complex regulatory requirements ② to manage cash flow effectively. Small business owners often wish they ③ had been better prepared when they faced unexpected economic downturns or market shifts. This is not because they lack ambition, but because anticipating every fluctuation in consumer demand and economic conditions ④ are a daunting task.

**해설**
③ 「I wish + 주어 + had p.p.」의 I wish 가정법 과거완료 구문으로, 과거에 이루지 못했던 것에 대한 아쉬움을 표현한다. when 절에 faced라는 과거동사가 있으므로 (과거에) 어땠다면 좋았을 것이라는 의미를 바르게 나타내고 있다.
① 「There + be동사」 구문은 주어가 뒤에 있으므로 a number of의 수식을 받는 challenges가 주어이다. 주어가 복수이므로 There is를 There are로 고쳐야 한다. (There is → There are) Point 27. 주어 - 동사 수 일치
② 「from A to B」는 'A에서 B까지'라는 뜻이고, 여기서 from과 to는 전치사이다. 전치사의 목적어 자리이므로 동명사 managing으로 고쳐야 한다. (to manage → to managing) Point 48. 전치사의 목적어
④ 주어가 anticipating ~ conditions로 동명사구이다. 동명사 주어는 단수 취급하므로 are를 단수 동사 is로 고쳐야 한다. (are → is) Point 27. 주어 - 동사 수 일치

**어휘** navigate 처리하다  regulatory 규제의  requirement 요구사항  downturn 침체  fluctuation 변동  daunting 버거운

정답 ③

**163** 밑줄 친 부분에 들어갈 말로 가장 적절한 것은?

> She patted her son _____ to congratulate him on his excellent performance in the school play.

① on the shoulder
② the shoulder
③ on shoulder
④ on a shoulder

**164** 밑줄 친 부분 중 어법상 옳지 않은 것은?

> At a recent political rally, the president referred to his opponents' efforts ① to politically smear him for coronavirus ② as the latest in a series of political hoaxes attempted against him. In a sign of how polarized we have become, some Democrats and some in the press accused the president ③ for saying the virus itself was a hoax. Any fair reading of his comments ④ shows this is preposterous.

**165** 밑줄 친 부분 중 어법상 옳은 것은?

> Early boat users, ① noticed that the wind sometimes helped their progress, stretched skins or matting between poles to make the most of it. Later came sails ② made of cloth. They first appeared in ancient Egyptian art from about 3300 BCE. Whatever they were made of, early sails worked only when the wind was behind them. Sails that could catch wind from the side, making sailors less ③ dependently on the weather, ④ was not invented for another 1,500 years.

## 163  문법포인트 | Point 22. 관사의 이해

She patted her son on the shoulder to congratulate him on his excellent performance in the school play.

**[해설]** 신체 부위에 대한 동작을 나타낼 때 「동사 + 목적어 + 전치사 + the + 신체 부위」로 나타낸다. '~의 어깨를 토닥이다'는 「pat + 목적어 + on the shoulder」로 나타낸다. 따라서 정답은 ① her son on the shoulder이다.

**[어휘]** pat 토닥이다  congratulate A on B B에 대해 A를 축하하다
excellent 우수한   performance 성적

**[정답]** ①

## 164  문법포인트 | Point 07. 완전타동사와 함께 사용되는 주요 전치사

At a recent political rally, the president referred to his opponents' efforts ① to politically smear him for coronavirus ② as the latest in a series of political hoaxes attempted against him. In a sign of how polarized we have become, some Democrats and some in the press accused the president ③ for saying (→ of saying) the virus itself was a hoax. Any fair reading (of his comments) ④ shows this is preposterous.

**[해설]**
③ 'A를 B하다고 비난하다'라는 말은 「accuse A of B」로 나타낸다. 따라서 for를 of로 고쳐야 한다. (for saying → of saying)
① 명사 efforts를 수식하는 형용사적 용법의 to부정사 to smear가 바르게 쓰였다. politically는 부사로 to부정사를 수식한다. Point 29. to부정사의 역할
② 「refer to A as B」는 'A를 B라고 하다'라는 뜻으로 A가 목적어이고 as B가 목적격보어에 해당한다. 목적어는 his opponents' efforts이고, as the latest가 목적격보어로 바르게 쓰였다. Point 09. 불완전타동사의 목적격보어
④ 단수인 Any fair reading이 주어이므로 단수형 동사 shows가 바르게 쓰였다. Point 27. 주어 - 동사 수 일치

**[어휘]** political 정치적인  rally 집회  opponent 반대자
smear 비방하다  hoax 거짓말  sign 징후  polarized 양극화된
Democrat 민주당원  press 언론  preposterous 터무니없는

**[정답]** ③

## 165  문법포인트 | Point 32. 현재분사 vs. 과거분사

Early boat users, ① noticed (→ noticing) that the wind sometimes helped their progress, stretched skins or matting between poles to make the most of it. Later came sails ② made of cloth. They first appeared in ancient Egyptian art from about 3300 BCE. Whatever they were made of, early sails worked only when the wind was behind them. Sails that could catch wind from the side, making sailors less ③ dependently (→ dependent) on the weather, ④ was (→ were) not invented for another 1,500 years.

**[해설]**
② made of는 과거분사로 앞의 명사 sails를 수식한다. sails가 '만들어진'이라는 수동의 의미이므로 과거분사로 바르게 수식했다.
① noticed의 주체는 문장의 주어인 Early boat users이고 목적어로 that절이 왔으므로 능동의 분사구문이 되어야 한다. 따라서 noticed는 noticing으로 고쳐야 한다. (noticed → noticing) Point 33. 분사구문
③ dependently는 불완전타동사인 make의 목적격보어로 쓰였다. 부사는 목적격보어로 쓸 수 없으므로 형용사인 dependent로 고쳐야 한다. (dependently → dependent) Point 09. 불완전타동사의 목적격보어
④ was의 주어는 앞의 Sails이다. Sails가 복수이므로 동사 역시 복수인 were로 고쳐야 한다. (was → were) Point 27. 주어 - 동사 수 일치

**[어휘]** stretch 펼쳐놓다  matting 매트
make the most of ~을 최대한 이용하다   sail 돛

**[정답]** ②

**166** 밑줄 친 부분에 들어갈 말로 가장 적절한 것은?

> They _____ each other for years before they got married.

① know
② have known
③ have been knowing
④ had known

**168** 밑줄 친 부분에 들어갈 말로 가장 적절한 것은?

> We'll discuss the project requirements again provided he _____ back to work tomorrow.

① comes
② will come
③ came
④ would come

**167** 밑줄 친 부분 중 어법상 옳지 않은 것은?

> The popularity of the patio makes a lot of sense. Canadians want low-maintenance, and there are few things that require less effort ① than stone. A properly ② installed patio with a good base and jointing sand can easily last 25 years. That's one important reason to make sure you pick a stone ③ what you will love the entire time you have the space. It also justifies the costs. Patios ④ are regarded as one of the highest expenses for outdoor renovations. However, if you average the cost over the lifespan, patios are a smart investment.

**169** 밑줄 친 부분 중 어법상 옳지 않은 것은?

> The community center ① has provided essential services since it opened five years ago. It offers various programs, ② of which the after-school tutoring is the most popular. Many parents enroll their children in these programs so as to relieve ③ them of the worry about their children's academic progress. The center continues to expand its services ④ to meet the growing needs of the neighborhood.

## 166 문법포인트 | Point 12. 완료 시제

They had known each other for years before they got married.

**해설** 빈칸은 동사의 자리로 before they got married로 보아 과거 이전의 일이므로 대과거인 ④ had known이 들어가야 한다. 참고로, know는 인식동사이므로 진행형으로 쓸 수 없다.

**정답** ④

## 168 문법포인트 | Point 14. 시제일치와 예외

We'll discuss the project requirements again provided he comes back to work tomorrow.

**해설** 시간과 조건의 부사절에서 미래를 표현할 때 will 대신 현재 시제를 사용해야 한다. provided가 조건의 부사절을 이끄므로 빈칸에는 ① comes가 들어가야 한다.

**어휘** discuss 논의하다  requirement 필요조건

**정답** ①

## 167 문법포인트 | Point 43. 관계대명사의 선택

The popularity of the patio makes a lot of sense. Canadians want low-maintenance, and there are few things that require less effort ① than stone. A properly ② installed patio with a good base and jointing sand can easily last 25 years. That's one important reason to make sure you pick a stone ③ (what you will love) the entire time you have the space. It also justifies the costs. Patios ④ are regarded as one of the highest expenses for outdoor renovations. However, if you average the cost over the lifespan, patios are a smart investment.

**해설**
③ 밑줄 앞에 선행사 a stone이 있고 문맥상 밑줄 이후의 절이 이것을 수식하는 관계절의 역할을 하므로 what을 관계대명사 that 또는 which로 고쳐야 한다. (what → that/which)
① 비교급인 less에 호응하여 비교급 전치사 than이 바르게 쓰였다. Point 36. 비교 구문
② installed는 과거분사로 명사 patio를 수식하고 있다. patio가 설치되는 수동의 의미이므로 과거분사 installed가 바르게 쓰였다. Point 32. 현재분사 vs. 과거분사
④ regard는 「regard A as B」의 구문으로 A에 해당하는 Patios가 주어가 된 수동태 구문이다. 수동태로 전환할 때 전치사 as를 빠트리지 않도록 주의해야 한다. Point 17. 동사의 유형별 수동태

**어휘** maintenance 유지  last 버티다  renovation 개보수  investment 투자

**정답** ③

## 169 문법포인트 | Point 24. 인칭대명사

The community center ① has provided essential services since it opened five years ago. It offers various programs, ② (of which the after-school tutoring is the most popular). Many parents enroll their children in these programs so as to relieve ③ them (→ themselves) of the worry about their children's academic progress. The center continues to expand its services ④ to meet the growing needs of the neighborhood.

**해설**
③ 동사의 목적어가 주어 자신인 경우 재귀대명사로 써야 한다. relieve의 목적어가 주어인 Many parents이므로 복수의 재귀대명사인 themselves로 써야 한다. (them → themselves)
① 「since + 과거시점」이 있으므로 주절은 현재완료로 써야 한다. 현재완료 has provided가 바르게 쓰였다. Point 12. 완료 시제
② 관계대명사 which 뒤에 완전한 절의 구조가 왔으므로 「전치사 + 관계대명사」의 형태인 of which가 바르게 쓰였다. Point 43. 관계대명사의 선택
④ to부정사의 부사적 용법 중 목적의 의미로 to meet이 바르게 쓰였다. Point 29. to부정사의 역할

**어휘** community center 주민센터
after-school tutoring 방과 후 학습  enroll 등록시키다
relieve 덜다  expand 확장하다

**정답** ③

**170** 밑줄 친 부분에 들어갈 말로 가장 적절한 것은?

Tom didn't take exercise that night because he was _____ tired to go to the gym.

① to
② so
③ such
④ too

**171** 밑줄 친 부분 중 어법상 옳은 것은?

Among the challenges facing the modern age ① are issues related to environmental sustainability. Most of the population is affected by climate change and its consequences. If there were no concerted global efforts to reduce carbon emissions, the future of our planet ② would have been at risk. It is crucial for governments and individuals alike ③ take action now to mitigate the impacts of climate change and ④ ensuring a sustainable future for generations to come.

**172** 밑줄 친 부분 중 어법상 옳은 것은?

The equipment malfunction ① was occurred unexpectedly during the production shift, causing a significant disruption. It was a serious issue, and ② by no means could it be ignored, as it affected the entire production line. The machinery had to ③ inspect thoroughly to identify and rectify the problem before operations could resume. The incident highlighted flaws in the maintenance schedule, ④ which regular checks were often overlooked.

**173** 밑줄 친 부분 중 어법상 옳지 않은 것은?

Nothing is more important than ① take care of your mental health in today's fast-paced world. Before making any major decisions, consider their long-term effects on your well-being. You'd be surprised at ② how much stress can impact your physical health. Many issues, the seeds ③ of which are planted by chronic stress, can ④ be prevented with proper self-care.

## 문장 분석 및 해설

**170** 문법포인트 | Point 29. to부정사의 역할

Tom didn't take exercise that night because he was too tired to go to the gym.

해설 '너무 ~해서 …할 수 없다'는 「too + 형용사/부사 + to부정사 …」로 나타낸다. 따라서 정답은 ④ too이다.

어휘 take exercise 운동하다  gym 체육관

정답 ④

**171** 문법포인트 | Point 27. 주어-동사 수 일치 / Point 50. 도치

(Among the challenges facing the modern age) ① are issues related to environmental sustainability. Most of the population is affected by climate change and its consequences. If there were no concerted global efforts to reduce carbon emissions, the future of our planet ② would have been (→ would be) at risk. It is crucial for governments and individuals alike ③ take (→ to take) action now to mitigate the impacts of climate change and ④ ensuring (→ (to) ensure) a sustainable future for generations to come.

해설
① among 전치사구는 위치를 나타내고, 위치를 나타내는 전치사구가 문장의 앞으로 나오면 주어와 동사는 도치되어야 한다. 주어 issues와 동사 are가 바르게 도치되었으며 주어가 issues로 복수이므로 동사 are도 바르게 쓰였다.
② 가정법 조건절의 동사가 were이므로 가정법 과거의 구문임을 알 수 있다. 따라서 주절의 동사도 가정법 과거인 would be로 고쳐야 한다. (would have been → would be) Point 46. 기본 가정법
③ It 뒤에 동사 is가 있어 다시 동사가 나올 수 없다. It이 가주어이므로 진주어인 to부정사로 고쳐야 한다. (take → to take) Point 01. 문장의 구성 / Point 29. to부정사의 역할
④ 문맥상 to mitigate와 병렬로 연결되어야 한다. 따라서 ensuring은 (to) ensure로 고쳐야 한다. (ensuring → (to) ensure) Point 39. 등위접속사의 병렬 구조

어휘 sustainability 지속 가능성  consequence 결과  concerted 일치단결된  carbon emission 탄소 배출  take action 행동을 취하다  mitigate 완화하다

정답 ①

**172** 문법포인트 | Point 49. 강조

The equipment malfunction ① was occurred (→ occurred) unexpectedly during the production shift, causing a significant disruption. It was a serious issue, and ② by no means could it be ignored, as it affected the entire production line. The machinery had to ③ inspect (→ be inspected) thoroughly to identify and rectify the problem before operations could resume. The incident highlighted flaws in the maintenance schedule, ④ (which (→ where/in which) regular checks were often overlooked.)

해설
② by no means는 '결코 ~가 아니다'라는 의미의 부정 강조 표현이며, 바르게 쓰였다. 부사구 by no means가 앞에 나와서 뒤의 절이 도치되어 「조동사 + 주어 + 동사원형」의 형태로 쓰였다.
① occur는 자동사이므로 수동태로 쓸 수 없다. 따라서 was occurred를 occurred로 고쳐야 한다. (was occurred → occurred) Point 17. 동사의 유형별 수동태
③ 주어 The machinery가 점검되는 수동의 의미이므로 수동태인 be inspected로 고쳐야 한다. (inspect → be inspected) Point 16. 능동태 vs. 수동태 구분
④ which 이하에 완전한 절이 왔고, 선행사가 maintenance schedule로 상황을 나타내므로 관계부사 where 또는 in which로 고쳐야 한다. (which → where/in which) Point 44. 관계부사

어휘 malfunction 오작동  unexpectedly 예기치 않게  disruption 혼란  machinery 기계류  inspect 점검하다  rectify 바로잡다  flaw 결함  maintenance 정비

정답 ②

**173** 문법포인트 | Point 38. 비교대상의 일치

Nothing is more important than ① take care of (→ taking care of) your mental health in today's fast-paced world. Before making any major decisions, consider their long-term effects on your well-being. You'd be surprised at ② [how much stress can impact your physical health]. Many issues, (the seeds ③ of which are planted by chronic stress), can ④ be prevented with proper self-care.

해설
① 「부정주어 + 비교급 비교 + A」 형태의 최상급 대용 표현이다. 비교되고 있는 대상이 주어인 명사 Nothing이다. 비교하는 대상이 명사인 경우 그 대상과 형태가 일치해야 하므로 take를 동명사 taking으로 고쳐야 한다. (take care of → taking care of)
② 간접의문문이 전치사 at의 목적어로 쓰여 「의문사 + 주어 + 동사」의 어순으로 바르게 쓰였다. Point 02. 의문문의 어순
③ 선행사 Many issues와 '그것들(그 많은 문제들)의 씨앗'이라는 소유의 관계이므로 소유격을 구성하는 관계대명사 of which가 바르게 왔다. Point 43. 관계대명사의 선택
④ 주어 Many issues와 prevent가 의미상 수동의 관계이므로 prevent의 수동태가 바르게 쓰였다. Point 16. 능동태 vs. 수동태 구분

어휘 fast-paced 빠르게 진행되는  well-being 건강  chronic 만성적인  prevent 예방하다  self-care 자기 관리

정답 ①

## DAY 12

**174** 밑줄 친 부분에 들어갈 말로 가장 적절한 것은?

> The new restaurant in town turned out _____ among the locals.

① to be a big hit   ② be a big hit
③ to being a big hit   ④ being a big hit

**176** 밑줄 친 부분에 들어갈 말로 가장 적절한 것은?

> The new software update will not be available _____ the end of the week.

① by   ② for
③ on   ④ until

**175** 밑줄 친 부분 중 어법상 옳지 않은 것은?

> She vividly remembered ① attending her first live concert with friends. It had taken considerable effort ② to save up for the tickets, but the anticipation and thrill of seeing her favorite band perform made it all worthwhile. The concert occurred on a hot summer night at an outdoor venue, with the music ③ echoing under a canopy of stars. She wouldn't be opposed to ④ relive such a magical event again in the future.

**177** 밑줄 친 부분 중 어법상 옳은 것은?

> The Lena Goldfield Strike was triggered by ① a great deal of factors such as the poor pay, long working hours and high accident rates in the gold mines. Tsar Nicholas II took action to end the strike, ② dispatched troops to arrest all participants. The next morning the public demanded ③ of the authorities the immediate release of the strike participants; however, the workers were met with soldiers who began to shoot at the crowd. ④ Hundred of people died and more were wounded.

## 문장 분석 및 해설

### 174 문법포인트 | Point 04. 불완전자동사의 보어

The new restaurant in town turned out to be a big hit among the locals.

해설 turn out은 불완전자동사로 to부정사를 보어로 취한다. 따라서 ① to be가 정답이다.

어휘 turn out ~으로 드러나다   hit 인기   local 현지인

정답 ①

### 175 문법포인트 | Point 48. 전치사의 목적어

She vividly remembered ① attending her first live concert with friends. It had taken considerable effort ② to save up for the tickets, but the anticipation and thrill of seeing her favorite band perform made it all worthwhile. The concert occurred on a hot summer night at an outdoor venue, with the music ③ echoing under a canopy of stars. She wouldn't be opposed to ④ relive such a magical event again in the future.
(→ reliving)

해설
④ be opposed to(~에 반대하다)에서 to는 전치사이다. 따라서 relive를 동명사 형태인 reliving으로 고쳐야 한다. (relive → reliving)
① 기억동사 remember의 목적어로 동명사가 사용되어 '(과거에) ~한 것을 잊었다'는 의미로 바르게 쓰였다. Point 06. 완전타동사와 동작의 목적어
② '~가 …하는 데 (시간/노력/돈)이 걸리다/들다'는 「It + take / cost + 목적어(시간/노력/돈) + (for ~) + to …」으로 나타낸다. 이때 가주어 It과 진주어인 to save up이 바르게 쓰였다. Point 08. 수여동사
③ with 분사구문으로, 목적어 the music과 목적격보어로 사용된 echo의 관계가 능동이므로 목적격보어가 현재분사인 echoing의 형태로 바르게 쓰였다. Point 33. 분사구문

어휘 vividly 생생하게   considerable 상당한
save up for ~을 위해 돈을 모으다   anticipation 기대   thrill 설렘
venue 장소   echo 울려 퍼지다   canopy 차양
relive 다시 경험하다

정답 ④

### 176 문법포인트 | Point 48. 전치사의 목적어

The new software update will not be available until the end of the week.

해설 상태가 계속되는 기간을 나타낼 때는 until을 쓴다. 업데이트가 불가능한 상태가 주말까지 계속되므로 정답은 ④ until이다.

어휘 available 이용 가능한

정답 ④

### 177 문법포인트 | Point 08. 수여동사

The Lena Goldfield Strike was triggered by ① a great deal of factors such as the poor pay, long working hours and high accident rates in the gold mines. Tsar Nicholas II took action to end the strike, ② dispatched troops to arrest all participants. The next morning the public demanded ③ of the authorities the immediate release of the strike participants; however, the workers were met with soldiers who began to shoot at the crowd. ④ Hundred of people died and more were wounded.
(① → a great number of)
(② → dispatching)
(④ → Hundreds of)

해설
③ ask, demand 등의 수여동사는 3형식으로 쓸 때 간접목적어 앞에 '~에게'를 의미하는 전치사 of를 써야 한다. 따라서 간접목적어 the authorities 앞에 of가 바르게 사용되었다.
① a great deal of는 '많은 양의'라는 뜻으로 불가산명사 앞에 사용된다. 따라서 가산명사의 복수형인 factors의 수식어는 '많은 수의'를 뜻하는 a great number of로 고쳐야 한다. (a great deal of → a great number of) Point 21. 명사의 이해
② 앞에 완전한 절이 왔으므로 부대 상황을 나타내기 위한 분사구문이 들어가야 한다. 타동사 dispatch의 목적어가 있고, 분사구문의 의미상 주어인 Tsar Nicholas II와 능동의 관계이므로 현재분사로 고쳐야 한다. (dispatched → dispatching) Point 33. 분사구문
④ 막연히 큰 수를 나타낼 때 수 단위명사를 복수형으로 써야 한다. 따라서 Hundred를 복수형인 Hundreds로 고쳐야 한다. (Hundred of → Hundreds of) Point 35. 주의할 형용사와 부사

어휘 strike 파업   trigger 촉발하다   gold mine 금광
Tsar (제정 러시아 시대의) 황제   take action 조치를 취하다
dispatch 파견하다   troop 군대   participant 참가자
authorities (pl.) 당국   release 석방   wounded 부상당한

정답 ③

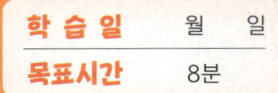

**178** 밑줄 친 부분에 들어갈 말로 가장 적절한 것은?

> She fondly remembers _____ under the stars during her last summer vacation.

① dance　　　② dancing
③ to dance　　④ danced

**179** 밑줄 친 부분 중 어법상 옳지 않은 것은?

> Remembering names and faces ① is probably the most common reason for people wanting to improve their memories, because it is the one case ② where written notes do not really help. You can write down a person's name, but how does that help you when you try to link ③ them with his face? Most of us recognize faces — it's the names that ④ cause us trouble. After all, have you ever heard someone say "I know your name, but I don't recognize your face."?

**180** 밑줄 친 부분 중 어법상 옳지 않은 것은?

> Former U.S. President Jimmy Carter, ① who promotes Habitat for Humanity, has toured various countries since 1994. In the summer of 2001, he ② has visited Asan, Korea, to participate in a housebuilding project. It was part of Habitat for Humanity International's campaign ③ to build houses for homeless people. He worked along with volunteers for the program, which is ④ named after him — the Jimmy Carter Work Project 2001.

## 178 문법포인트 | Point 06. 완전타동사와 동작의 목적어

She fondly remembers dancing under the stars during her last summer vacation.

[해설] 기억동사 remember는 동명사를 목적어로 취할 때 '(과거에) ~한 것을 기억하다'의 뜻이고, to부정사를 목적어로 취할 때는 '(미래에) ~할 것을 기억하다'의 의미이다. '지난 여름휴가' 때 일어난 일이므로 목적어로 동명사가 와야 한다. 따라서 정답은 ② dancing이다.

[어휘] fondly 애정을 담아

[정답] ②

## 179 문법포인트 | Point 24. 인칭대명사

Remembering names and faces ① is probably the most common reason for people wanting to improve their memories, because it is the one case ② (where written notes do not really help). You can write down a person's name, but how does that help you when you try to link ③ them with his face? Most of us recognize faces — it's the names that ④ cause us trouble. After all, have you ever heard someone say "I know your name, but I don't recognize your face."?

[해설]
③ 의미상 them이 a person's name을 지칭하므로 them을 it으로 고쳐야 한다. (them → it)
① 동명사 Remembering names and faces가 주어이고 동명사는 단수로 취급한다. Point 27. 주어 - 동사 수 일치
② 상황을 나타내는 one case가 선행사이고 관계사절이 완전하므로 관계부사 where는 바르게 쓰였다. Point 44. 관계부사
④ 「it ~ that」 강조구문으로 it과 that 사이에 위치한 the names를 강조하는 문장이다. the names가 주어이므로 복수형 동사 cause가 바르게 쓰였다. Point 27. 주어 - 동사 수 일치

[어휘] improve 향상시키다  recognize 알아보다

[정답] ③

## 180 문법포인트 | Point 13. 시제 사용 제한

Former U.S. President Jimmy Carter, ① (who promotes Habitat for Humanity), has toured various countries since 1994. In the summer of 2001, he ② has visited Asan, Korea, to participate in a housebuilding project. It was part of Habitat for Humanity International's campaign ③ (to build houses for homeless people). He worked along with volunteers for the program, which is ④ named after him — the Jimmy Carter Work Project 2001.

[해설]
② 전치사 in 뒤에 특정 과거 시간이 명시된 시간 표현 부사구가 있으므로 현재완료형인 has visited와 함께 쓸 수 없고 과거형인 visited로 고쳐야 한다. (has visited → visited)
① 선행사가 사람이고 관계사절의 동사인 promotes에 대한 주어가 빠져 있으므로 주격 관계대명사 who가 바르게 쓰였다. Point 43. 관계대명사의 선택
③ 「to build houses ~」가 to부정사의 형용사적 용법으로, campaign을 수식하며 바르게 쓰였다. Point 29. to부정사의 역할
④ 「name A after B」는 'B의 이름을 따서 A를 명명하다'라는 뜻이다. 여기서는 '~라고 이름 붙여지다'라는 수동의 의미이므로 is named after로 바르게 사용되었다. Point 16. 능동태 vs. 수동태 구분

[어휘] promote 홍보하다  name A after B B의 이름을 따서 A를 명명하다

[정답] ②

**181** 밑줄 친 부분에 들어갈 말로 가장 적절한 것은?

> Moving to a new country with a family requires dealing with _____, both physical and emotional.

① a variety of baggage
② a number of baggages
③ a large amount of baggage
④ a large amount of baggages

**182** 밑줄 친 부분 중 어법상 옳은 것은?

> Self-regulation is present in people's daily lives ① because of discrepancies between expectations and reality in situations ② where people encounter are inevitable. Successful adaptive functioning is based on effective self-regulation ③ by which people control their impulses, thoughts, and feelings ④ and adjusting their behaviour to close or minimize the gap between their expectations and present experiences.

**183** 밑줄 친 부분에 들어갈 말로 가장 적절한 것은?

> _____ his help, the project would not have been completed on time.

① Should it not be     ② Were it not to be
③ Were it not for      ④ Had it not been for

**184** 밑줄 친 부분 중 어법상 옳지 않은 것은?

> The earliest messages we get about ourselves come from our parents, so how they react to us and ① what they tell us have an enormous effect on the way we view ourselves as adults. Whether we feel good or bad about ourselves ② depend on how our parents reacted to us as young children. Praise is very important to a young child, and with encouragement and positive reinforcement she ③ will try harder and achieve more. A child who is constantly criticized or compared unfavourably to others will begin ④ to feel worthless, and those feelings can stay with her throughout her life.

## 181 문법포인트 | Point 21. 명사의 이해

Moving to a new country with a family requires dealing with a large amount of baggage, both physical and emotional.

**해설** baggage는 불가산명사이므로 복수형으로 만들 수 없고, 양으로 나타내며 수를 나타내는 말과 함께 쓸 수 없다. 따라서 정답은 ③ a large amount of baggage이다.

**어휘** deal with ~을 처리하다  a variety of 다양한  baggage 짐
a number of 수많은  a large amount of 많은 양의

**정답** ③

## 182 문법포인트 | Point 43. 관계대명사의 선택

Self-regulation is present in people's daily lives ① because of discrepancies (between expectations and reality in situations ② where people encounter) are inevitable. Successful adaptive functioning is based on effective self-regulation ③ by which people control their impulses, thoughts, and feelings ④ and adjusting their behaviour to close or minimize the gap between their expectations and present experiences.

**해설**
③ 관계대명사 which 이하의 절이 완전하므로 「전치사+관계대명사」의 형태가 바르다. 선행사가 effective self-regulation이며, 이러한 효율적인 자기 규제에 의해 사람들이 감정 등을 통제하고 행동을 조절한다는 의미이므로 전치사 by가 바르게 쓰였다.
① because of는 전치사구이므로 뒤에 목적어로 명사구를 취해야 한다. 그러나 주어가 discrepancies, 동사가 are인 절이 왔으므로 접속사로 고쳐야 한다. (because of → because) Point 41. 부사절 접속사의 선택
② where 뒤에 encounter의 목적어가 없는 불완전한 절이 왔으므로 관계부사 where는 올 수 없다. 따라서 encounter의 목적어 역할을 할 수 있는 목적격 관계대명사 which, 혹은 that으로 고쳐야 한다. 목적격 관계대명사이므로 생략할 수도 있다. (where → which/that/where 삭제) Point 43. 관계대명사의 선택
④ 「control ~ and adjust ~」의 병렬 구문이므로 adjusting을 adjust로 고쳐야 한다. (and adjusting → and adjust) Point 39. 등위접속사의 병렬 구조

**어휘** self-regulation 자기 규제  present 존재하는
discrepancy 불일치  expectation 기대  reality 현실
encounter 접하다  inevitable 피할 수 없는
adaptive 적응할 수 있는  functioning 작용  control 통제하다
impulse 충동  thought 생각  adjust 조절하다  close 메우다

**정답** ③

## 183 문법포인트 | Point 47. 기타 가정법

Had it not been for his help, the project would not have been completed on time.

**해설** 주절의 시제가 가정법 과거완료의 형태(would not have been completed)이므로 빈칸에도 가정법 과거완료의 조건절 시제가 들어가야 한다. 문맥상 '~이 없었더라면'이 가장 적절하므로 빈칸에는 ④ Had it not been for가 들어가야 한다.

**어휘** complete 완료하다  on time 제때

**정답** ④

## 184 문법포인트 | Point 27. 주어-동사 수 일치

The earliest messages we get about ourselves come from our parents, so [how they react to us] and ① [what they tell us] have an enormous effect on the way we view ourselves as adults. [Whether we feel good or bad about ourselves] ② depend on how our parents reacted to us as young children. Praise is very important to a young child, and with encouragement and positive reinforcement she ③ will try harder and achieve more. A child who is constantly criticized or compared unfavourably to others will begin ④ to feel worthless, and those feelings can stay with her throughout her life.

**해설**
② depend의 주어는 Whether we ~ ourselves라는 명사절인데, 명사절은 단수 취급하기 때문에 단수 동사가 와야 한다. (depend → depends)
① 동사인 have의 주어로 「how ~ us」와 「what ~ us」라는 두 개의 명사절이 왔다. what 이하의 절의 형태를 보면 tell의 직접목적어가 없는 불완전한 형태이므로 what이 바르게 쓰였다. Point 40. 명사절 접속사의 선택
③ 조동사 will 뒤에 동사원형 try와 achieve가 등위접속사 and에 의해 바르게 병렬되어 있다. Point 39. 등위접속사의 병렬 구조
④ begin의 목적어로 to부정사와 동명사가 모두 올 수 있으므로 to feel이 바르게 쓰였다. Point 06. 완전타동사와 동작의 목적어

**어휘** view 보다  depend on ~에 달려있다  reinforcement 강화
unfavourably 호의적이지 않게  worthless 가치 없는

**정답** ②

**185** 밑줄 친 부분에 들어갈 말로 가장 적절한 것은?

> It was regarded as inconsiderate for anyone _____ the room without permission during the emergency briefing, as that meant ignoring the speaker.

① leave　　② leaving
③ leaved　　④ to leave

**186** 밑줄 친 부분 중 어법상 옳지 않은 것은?

> More young people ① should have voted in the recent election, understanding the significant impact of civic engagement on shaping policies that affect daily life. Now, efforts should be made ② inform the public ③ of their rights and responsibilities as citizens, encouraging active participation in democratic processes. These actions are crucial for maintaining a healthy democracy and ④ ensuring that diverse voices are heard in government.

**187** 밑줄 친 부분 중 어법상 옳은 것은?

> It has been considered essential for individuals ① to maintain a healthy work-life balance to avoid burnout. Workplaces that prioritize employees' well-being ② makes people feel valued and appreciated. Studies have shown that these employees are twice ③ as more productive as those who feel unsupported by their employers. By fostering a positive work environment and providing adequate support, organizations can enhance productivity, ④ employee satisfactory, and company profit simultaneously.

**188** 밑줄 친 부분 중 어법상 옳은 것은?

> Unless there are ① not unforeseen circumstances, the project should be completed by next week. The current market conditions are more favorable than ② those in previous years. This indicates a potential increase in sales for the upcoming quarter, ③ that means higher revenue projections. Adjustments to marketing strategies may be necessary to capitalize on this opportunity and ④ maintaining competitive advantage.

### 185  문법포인트 | Point 29. to부정사의 역할

It was regarded as inconsiderate for anyone to leave the room without permission during the emergency briefing, as that meant ignoring the speaker.
(가S) (진S)

**해설** It이 가주어이고 for anyone이 의미상 주어이므로 빈칸에는 진주어 역할을 할 수 있는 ④ to leave가 들어가는 것이 적절하다.

**어휘** inconsiderate 배려 없는  permission 허락  ignore 무시하다

**정답** ④

### 186  문법포인트 | Point 17. 동사의 유형별 수동태

More young people ① should have voted in the recent election, understanding the significant impact of civic engagement on shaping policies that affect daily life. Now, efforts should be made ② inform the public ③ of their rights and responsibilities as citizens, encouraging active participation in democratic processes. These actions are crucial for maintaining a healthy democracy and ④ ensuring that diverse voices are heard in government.
(should have + p.p) (→ to inform)

**해설**
② 사역동사가 수동태로 전환될 때 능동태 문장의 원형부정사 목적격보어는 to부정사로 고쳐야 한다. (inform → to inform)
① 과거의 일을 「조동사 + have p.p.」의 형식으로 표현할 수 있다. 했어야 했는데 하지 않은 일에 대해서 「should have p.p.」로 바르게 표현했다. Point 20. 조동사 + have p.p.
③ inform은 대상을 먼저 쓰고 전하는 내용을 of 전치사구나 that절로 표현해야 하므로 of는 바르게 쓰였다. Point 07. 완전타동사와 함께 사용되는 주요 전치사
④ 문맥상 앞의 maintaining과 and로 병렬로 연결되어 전치사 for의 목적어 역할을 하고 있다. 따라서 동명사 ensuring은 바르게 쓰였다. Point 39. 등위접속사의 병렬 구조

**어휘** significant 상당한  civic 시민의  engagement 참여  encourage 권장하다  participation 참여  diverse 다양한

**정답** ②

### 187  문법포인트 | Point 29. to부정사의 역할 / Point 24. 인칭대명사

It has been considered essential for individuals ① to maintain a healthy work-life balance to avoid burnout. Workplaces (that prioritize employees' well-being) ② makes people feel valued and appreciated. Studies have shown that these employees are twice ③ as more productive as
(가S) (진S) (S) (V → make) (→ as productive as)

those who feel unsupported by their employers. By fostering a positive work environment and providing adequate support, organizations can enhance productivity, ④ employee satisfactory, and company profit simultaneously.
(→ employee satisfaction)

**해설**
① 문맥상 It은 가주어이고 to maintain은 진주어이다.
② makes의 주어는 Workplaces로 복수이다. 따라서 복수 동사인 make로 고쳐야 한다. (makes → make) Point 27. 주어 - 동사 수 일치
③ 「as 형용사/부사 as」는 원급 비교이다. 따라서 비교급인 more가 들어갈 수 없다. (as more productive as → as productive as) Point 36. 비교 구문
④ employee satisfactory는 명사 productivity, company profit과 병렬로 연결되어 있다. 병렬로 연결되려면 문법적 요소가 동일해야 하므로 명사인 satisfaction으로 고쳐야 한다. (employee satisfactory → employee satisfaction) Point 39. 등위접속사의 병렬 구조

**어휘** prioritize 우선순위를 두다  appreciate 진가를 알아보다  foster 조성하다  adequate 적절한  organization 조직  enhance 향상시키다  simultaneously 동시에

**정답** ①

### 188  문법포인트 | Point 38. 비교대상의 일치

Unless there are ① not unforeseen circumstances, the project should be completed by next week. The current market conditions are more favorable than ② those in previous years. This indicates a potential increase in sales for the upcoming quarter, ③ that means higher revenue projections. Adjustments to marketing strategies may be necessary to capitalize on this opportunity and ④ maintaining competitive advantage.
(→ unforeseen) (→ which) (→ (to) maintain)

**해설**
② 비교 대상이 market conditions로 복수이므로 those가 바르게 쓰였다.
① Unless는 부정의 의미를 내포한 접속사이므로 다시 부정어구를 사용하지 않아야 한다. 따라서 not unforeseen을 unforeseen으로 고쳐야 한다. (not unforeseen → unforeseen) Point 41. 부사절 접속사의 선택
③ 관계대명사 that은 계속적 용법으로 사용할 수 없다. 따라서 that을 which로 고쳐야 한다. (that → which) Point 43. 관계대명사의 선택
④ maintaining은 등위접속사 and로 to capitalize와 병렬되고 있으므로 to부정사인 to maintain으로 고쳐야 한다. 이때 to는 생략 가능하다. (maintaining → (to) maintain) Point 39. 등위접속사의 병렬 구조

**어휘** unforeseen 예상치 못한  circumstance 상황  indicate 나타내다  revenue 수익  projection 예측  adjustment 조정  capitalize 이용하다  competitive advantage 경쟁우위

**정답** ②

**189** 밑줄 친 부분에 들어갈 말로 가장 적절한 것은?

> Not until she had explored the winding paths, crossed over the ancient bridge, and climbed to the highest tower, _____ the full beauty and history of the castle.

① she grasped   ② she grasps
③ did she grasp   ④ does she grasp

**190** 밑줄 친 부분 중 어법상 옳지 않은 것은?

> She used to rely on traditional methods to manage projects, but ① others quickly adopted digital tools for greater efficiency. This shift enabled them ② to streamline tasks such as scheduling and communication ③ what were considered time-consuming before. The integration of technology has allowed for real-time updates and collaboration, significantly ④ enhancing team productivity.

**191** 밑줄 친 부분에 들어갈 말로 가장 적절한 것은?

> _____, the doctor arrived later than expected.

① As patiently he waited
② As patient he waited
③ Patient as he waited
④ Patiently as he waited

**192** 밑줄 친 부분 중 어법상 옳은 것은?

> Life has been anything but a bed of roses for Shirin Juwaley, a victim of an acid attack, which left her face ① disfiguring for life. As if it were not enough, she was exposed to ② be bullied by society in general due to the scars on her face. It took a great deal of courage ③ to stand up not just for herself but for several others like her. ④ Despite most victims might have been heart broken, Shirin was happy that she survived anyhow.

## 189　문법포인트 | Point 15. 시제 관련 표현

(Not until she had explored the winding paths, crossed over the ancient bridge, and climbed to the highest tower,) did she grasp the full beauty and history of the castle.

**해설** 'B가 되어서야 비로소 A하다'는 「Not until B A」로 나타낼 수 있다. 이때 Not until이라는 부정어가 문두에 있으므로 주절은 도치되어야 한다. 과거의 일을 설명하고 있으므로 주절에 과거 시제가 와야 한다. 따라서 ③ did she grasp이 정답이다.

**어휘** explore 탐색하다　winding 구불구불한　path 길
cross over ~을 건너다　ancient 아주 오래된　climb 오르다
castle 성　grasp 파악하다

정답 ③

## 190　문법포인트 | Point 43. 관계대명사의 선택

She used to rely on traditional methods to manage projects, but ① others quickly adopted digital tools for greater efficiency. This shift enabled them ② to streamline tasks such as scheduling and communication (③ what were considered time-consuming before). The integration of technology has allowed for real-time updates and collaboration, significantly ④ enhancing team productivity.

→ which/that

**해설**
③ 문맥상 선행사 task를 수식하는 형용사절이므로 관계대명사 which나 that으로 고쳐야 한다. (what → which/that)
① 문맥상 앞에 언급된 she를 제외한 막연한 다른 사람들을 지칭하는 것이므로 부정대명사 others가 바르게 쓰였다. Point 25. 부정대명사
② enable은 목적격보어로 to부정사를 써야 한다. streamline 뒤에 tasks라는 목적어가 있으므로 능동형 부정사인 to streamline이 바르게 쓰였다. Point 10. 불완전타동사와 동작의 목적격보어
④ 주절의 주어 The integration of technology와 enhance와의 관계가 능동이고, 목적어 team productivity가 있으므로 enhancing이 바르게 쓰였다. Point 33. 분사구문

**어휘** streamline 간소화하다　integration 통합
allow for ~을 가능하게 하다　real-time 실시간의

정답 ③

## 191　문법포인트 | Point 42. 주요 양보구문

Patiently as he waited, the doctor arrived later than expected.

**해설** 종속절과 주절의 내용이 서로 대립 혹은 대조되는 관계이고 종속절에 as가 있는 것으로 보아 빈칸은 양보구문이 되어야 함을 알 수 있다. wait는 완전자동사이므로 부사 patiently의 수식을 받아야 한다. 따라서 빈칸에는 ④ Patiently as he waited가 들어가야 한다.

**어휘** arrive 도착하다　patiently 끈기 있게

정답 ④

## 192　문법포인트 | Point 08. 수여동사

Life has been anything but a bed of roses for Shirin Juwaley, a victim of an acid attack, which left her face ① disfiguring for life. As if it were not enough, she was exposed to ② be bullied by society in general due to the scars on her face. It took a great deal of courage ③ to stand up not just for herself but for several others like her. ④ Despite most victims might have been heart broken, Shirin was happy that she survived anyhow.

→ disfigured
→ being bullied
→ Although / Though

**해설**
③ '~하는 데 ...의 노력/시간/돈이 들다'는 「It take/cost + (간목) + 직목 + to부정사」로 나타낸다. it이 가주어이고 to부정사가 진주어이다. 진주어로 to부정사가 바르게 쓰였다.
① 불완전타동사 leave는 목적격보어로 분사를 쓴다. 목적어와 목적격보어의 관계가 능동이면 현재분사를, 수동이면 과거분사를 쓴다. her face와 disfigure는 수동의 관계이므로 과거분사로 고쳐야 한다. (disfiguring → disfigured) Point 10. 불완전타동사와 동작의 목적격보어 / Point 32. 현재분사 vs. 과거분사
② be exposed to의 to는 전치사이므로 동명사가 목적어로 와야 한다. (be bullied → being bullied) Point 48. 전치사의 목적어
④ 전치사 despite는 명사(구/절)를 목적어로 취하는데 뒤에 완전한 절이 왔으므로 같은 뜻의 접속사 Although나 Though로 고쳐야 한다. (Despite → Although/Though) Point 41. 부사절 접속사의 선택

**어휘** anything but ~이 결코 아닌　bed of roses 장미꽃밭(안락한 삶)
victim 피해자　acid 산　disfigure 흉하게 만들다　bully 괴롭히다
society in general 사회 전반　scar 상처
stand up for ~을 지지하다　heart broken 비통해하는

정답 ③

**193** 밑줄 친 부분에 들어갈 말로 가장 적절한 것은?

> The museum displays artifacts that _____ ancient civilizations.

① belong to ② are belonged
③ are belonging to ④ have been belonging to

**194** 다음 글의 밑줄 친 부분 중 옳지 않은 것은?

> One of my patients was a busy self-employed man who was ① used to hurrying from one job site to another. One autumn afternoon a motorist ② cut him off as he rushed from one job site to another. Suddenly, he felt as though a red-hot poker ③ were being thrust into his chest. He barely managed to drive to the nearest hospital, ④ which he was admitted to the coronary care unit.

**195** 밑줄 친 부분 중 어법상 옳지 않은 것은?

> Reverse mortgages are loans against the equity in the home that provide cash advances to a homeowner and ① require no repayment until the loan term ends or the home is sold. The borrower can receive the cash in several ways: a lump sum or ② regular monthly payments. ③ Because of the borrower does not make payments, the amount of money ④ owed increases over the life of the loan. The borrower retains title to the home and must pay the property taxes and insurance.

### 193 〔문법포인트〕 Point 13. 시제 사용 제한

The museum displays artifacts (that belong to ancient civilizations).

**해설** that이 관계대명사이므로 동사가 들어가야 할 자리다. belong to는 소유의 상태를 의미하는 동사이므로 진행형으로 쓸 수 없으며, 수동태도 불가하다. 선행사 artifacts가 복수이므로 ① belong to가 들어가야 한다.

**어휘** display 전시하다  artifact 유물  ancient 고대의
civilization 문명  belong to ~에 속하다

**정답** ①

### 194 〔문법포인트〕 Point 44. 관계부사

One of my patients was a busy self-employed man who was ① used to hurrying from one job site to another. One autumn afternoon a motorist ② cut him off as he rushed from one job site to another. Suddenly, he felt as though a red-hot poker ③ were being thrust into his chest. He barely managed to drive to the nearest hospital, ④ (which he was admitted to the coronary care unit).
→ where / in which

**해설**
④ 뒤에 오는 절이 완전하므로 관계대명사를 쓸 수 없다. 선행사가 장소를 나타내는 the nearest hospital이므로 관계부사 where로 바꾸거나 전치사 in을 써서 in which로 고쳐야 한다. (which → where/in which)
① 「be used to -ing」는 '~하는 데 익숙하다'라는 뜻으로 hurrying이 바르게 쓰였다. Point 18. 조동사의 선택
② 「타동사+부사」의 목적어가 대명사일 때 목적어는 동사와 부사 사이에 위치해야 한다. Point 34. 형용사 vs. 부사
③ '마치 ~인 것처럼'을 의미하는 as though 가정법 표현이다. as though 뒤에 가정법 과거 시제가 와서 주절의 felt와 동일한 시점에 일어나는 일을 가정하는 것이므로 과거인 were가 맞다. Point 47. 기타 가정법

**어휘** self-employed 자영업을 하는  motorist 운전자
cut off ~을 가로막다  red-hot 뻘겋게 단  poker 부지깽이
admit 입원시키다  coronary 심장의  unit 병동

**정답** ④

### 195 〔문법포인트〕 Point 41. 부사절 접속사의 선택

Reverse mortgages are loans against the equity in the home that provide cash advances to a homeowner and ① require no repayment until the loan term ends or the home is sold. The borrower can receive the cash in several ways: a lump sum or ② regular monthly payments. ③ Because of the borrower does not make payments, the amount of money ④ owed increases over the life of the loan. The borrower retains title to the home and must pay the property taxes and insurance.

**해설**
③ Because of 뒤에 주어가 the borrower이고, 동사가 does not make인 절이 왔다. Because of는 전치사구이므로 절이 목적어로 올 수 없다. 따라서 부사절을 이끄는 부사절 접속사인 Because로 고쳐야 한다. (Because of → Because)
① 등위접속사인 and를 통해 관계대명사 that절의 동사인 provide와 require가 바르게 병렬되었다. Point 39. 등위접속사의 병렬 구조
② '월 지불금'을 의미하는 명사구인 monthly payments를 형용사인 regular가 바르게 수식한다. Point 34. 형용사 vs. 부사
④ owe는 '빚지다'는 뜻의 타동사이다. 이 동사가 수동의 의미인 과거분사로 앞의 명사를 수식하여 '빚진 돈(대출금)'이라는 의미로 바르게 쓰였다. Point 32. 현재분사 vs. 과거분사

**어휘** reverse mortgage 역 주택 담보 대출  equity (자산의) 순수 가치
cash advance 현금서비스  repayment 상환  term 기간
borrower 대출자  lump sum 일시금  retain 유지하다
title to ~의 소유권  property 재산  insurance 보험료

**정답** ③

**196** 밑줄 친 부분에 들어갈 말로 가장 적절한 것은?

Many campus protesters have taken down encampments after colleges agreed _____ ending investments in Israel.

① considering
② to consider
③ considering about
④ to consider about

**197** 밑줄 친 부분 중 어법상 옳지 않은 것은?

Martin Breeze is a visual artist and singer-songwriter ① who art is energetic and infectious. Bold and full of life, his canvasses are manifestations of flow and expression, without the inhibition of rules and boundaries. "I am ② fascinated by the abstract as I do not wish to replicate any fixed objects. Life has so many boundaries and restrictions, and abstract art allows me ③ to see where the flow takes me. I am in love with ④ not knowing what will become of the blank canvas!"

**198** 밑줄 친 부분 중 어법상 옳지 않은 것은?

Cultures use initiation ceremonies ① to mark the transition from childhood to adult status. Rites for males are usually more elaborate and dramatic than ② that for females. Boys' rites often involve seclusion from women, torment by older males, and ③ test of manliness. Actually, girls' rites are just as bad, with a part of a woman's sexual organs ④ removed.

**199** 밑줄 친 부분 중 어법상 옳지 않은 것은?

In the court where justice prevails, the prosecutor asks a question ① of the witness, hoping to clarify a critical point. The witness's response causes the jury ② to ponder the implications carefully. This pivotal exchange leaves jurors increasingly ③ convincing of the defendant's guilt. As the trial unfolds, each evidence and each testimony ④ strengthens their belief in the prosecution's case.

## 196　문법포인트 | Point 05. 완전타동사 / Point 06. 완전타동사와 동작의 목적어

Many campus protesters have taken down encampments after colleges agreed to consider ending investments in Israel.

**해설** agree는 완전타동사로 쓰일 때 목적어로 to부정사를 취하며 consider는 완전타동사로 전치사 없이 직접목적어를 취하므로 빈칸에는 ② to consider가 들어가야 한다.

**어휘** protester 시위자　take down ~을 해체하다
encampment 천막 농성장　investment 투자

정답 ②

## 197　문법포인트 | Point 43. 관계대명사의 선택

Martin Breeze is a visual artist and singer-songwriter ① who art is energetic and infectious. Bold and full of life, his canvasses are manifestations of flow and expression, without the inhibition of rules and boundaries. "I am ② fascinated by the abstract as I do not wish to replicate any fixed objects. Life has so many boundaries and restrictions, and abstract art allows me ③ to see where the flow takes me. I am in love with ④ not knowing what will become of the blank canvas!"

**해설**
① 문맥상 선행사와 art가 소유의 관계이므로 소유격 관계대명사 whose로 고쳐야 한다. (who → whose)
② 감정유발동사의 경우 주체가 감정을 일으키는 경우에는 현재분사로, 감정을 느끼는 것이면 과거분사로 쓴다. 주어인 I가 매료되는 감정을 느끼는 것이므로 과거분사가 바르게 쓰였다. Point 32. 현재분사 vs. 과거분사
③ allow는 to부정사를 목적격보어로 취하는 불완전타동사이다. to see가 목적격보어로 바르게 쓰였다. Point 10. 불완전타동사와 동작의 목적격보어
④ 동명사를 부정할 때는 부정어를 동명사 앞에 써야 한다. 동명사 knowing을 부정하는 not이 바로 앞에 바르게 쓰였다. Point 30. 준동사의 형태 변화

**어휘** manifestation 발현　inhibition 제약　boundary 경계
abstract 추상화　replicate 모사하다
become of ~은 어떻게 되는가

정답 ①

## 198　문법포인트 | Point 38. 비교대상의 일치

Cultures use initiation ceremonies ① to mark the transition from childhood to adult status. Rites for males are usually more elaborate and dramatic than ② that for females. Boys' rites often involve seclusion from women, torment by older males, and ③ test of manliness. Actually, girls' rites are just as bad, with a part of a woman's sexual organs ④ removed.

**해설**
② 비교 대상이 복수 명사인 Rites이므로 복수형인 those로 고쳐야 한다. (that → those)
① '~하기 위해'라는 목적의 의미인 to부정사의 부사적 용법으로 바르게 쓰였다. Point 29. to부정사의 역할
③ seclusion ~, torment ~, test의 세 명사가 and에 의해 병렬로 바르게 연결되었다. Point 39. 등위접속사의 병렬 구조
④ with 분사구문으로, 목적어인 a part of a woman's sexual organs와 목적격보어인 분사가 의미상 수동의 관계이므로 과거분사 removed가 바르게 쓰였다. Point 33. 분사구문

**어휘** initiation ceremony 성인식　transition 변화　elaborate 복잡한

정답 ②

## 199　문법포인트 | Point 10. 불완전타동사와 동작의 목적격보어

In the court where justice prevails, the prosecutor asks a question ① of the witness, hoping to clarify a critical point. The witness's response causes the jury ② to ponder the implications carefully. This pivotal exchange leaves jurors increasingly ③ convincing of the defendant's guilt. As the trial unfolds, each evidence and each testimony ④ strengthens their belief in the prosecution's case.

**해설**
③ leave는 목적어와 목적격보어의 관계가 능동이면 현재분사를 수동이면 과거분사를 목적격보어로 쓴다. 배심원들이 확신을 하게 되는 수동의 의미이므로 convincing은 convinced로 고쳐야 한다. (convincing → convinced)
① ask는 간접목적어에 해당하는 대상을 취할 때 직접목적어 뒤에 「of + 대상」으로 쓸 수 있다. '증인에게' 질문한다는 의미로 of the witness가 바르게 쓰였다. Point 08. 수여동사
② cause는 목적격보어로 to부정사를 취한다. to ponder가 목적격보어로 바르게 쓰였다. Point 10. 불완전타동사와 동작의 목적격보어
④ each는 and로 연결되어도 단수로 취급한다. 따라서 단수 동사인 strengthens가 바르게 쓰였다. Point 27. 주어 - 동사 수 일치

**어휘** prevail 지배하다　prosecutor 검사　witness 증인
clarify 명확히 하다　response 반응　ponder 숙고하다
implication 밀접한 관계　pivotal 중심이 되는
convince 확신시키다　defendant 피고　unfold 전개되다
testimony 증언　strengthen 강화하다　prosecution 기소

정답 ③

DAY 14　115

**200** 밑줄 친 부분에 들어갈 말로 가장 적절한 것은?

> The manager appreciated the suggestion that he _____ more tasks to his team members.

① delegate　　② delegates
③ is delegated　　④ be delegated

**201** 밑줄 친 부분 중 어법상 옳은 것은?

> A pencil is to writing ① what a paintbrush is to painting. The precision and control that each tool offers dictate the outcome of the creative process. The fact ② what they are essential instruments in their respective arts makes ③ do detailed work a big deal. Mastery of these tools ④ enhance artistic expression and craftsmanship.

**202** 밑줄 친 부분 중 어법상 옳은 것은?

> It was not because he lacked the necessary skills but because he didn't have enough experience ① that he was not selected for the job. ② Despite he was disappointed, he decided to use this feedback as motivation for improvement. By enrolling in additional training programs, he aimed ③ enhancing his qualifications and expertise. The more experience he gained, ④ the most confident he felt about reapplying and demonstrating his newfound abilities to the hiring committee.

**203** 밑줄 친 부분 중 어법상 옳지 않은 것은?

> The concept of sin has been present in many cultures throughout history, ① where it was usually equated with an individual's failure to live up to external standards of conduct or with his violation of taboos, laws, or moral codes. It was during the Ancient Greek era ② that people looked upon sin, in essence, ③ a failure on the part of a person to achieve his true self-expression and ④ preserve his due relation to the rest of the universe.

## 문장 분석 및 해설

**200** 문법포인트 | Point 19. 당위의 조동사 should / Point 16. 능동태 vs. 수동태 구분

The manager appreciated the suggestion [that he delegate more tasks to his team members].

**해설** 제안을 의미하는 suggestion 같은 명사의 동격절에서 동사는 「(should) + 동사원형」의 형태이어야 한다. delegate가 타동사인데 뒤에 목적어가 있으므로 능동태여야 한다. 따라서 정답은 ① delegate이다.

**어휘** appreciate 고마워하다 suggestion 제안 task 업무 team member 팀원 delegate 위임하다

정답 ①

**201** 문법포인트 | Point 40. 명사절 접속사의 선택

A pencil is to writing ① what a paintbrush is to painting. The precision and control that each tool offers dictate the outcome of the creative process. The fact ② [what they are essential instruments in their respective arts] makes ③ do detailed work a big deal. Mastery (of these tools) ④ enhance artistic expression and craftsmanship.

**해설**
① 'A와 B의 관계는 C와 D의 관계와 같다'는 「A is to B what C is to D」로 나타내므로 what이 바르게 쓰였다.
② 뒤에 완전한 절이 왔고, 앞에 나온 추상적 의미를 가진 the fact의 구체적인 내용을 설명해 주는 동격절이므로 what을 명사절 접속사 that으로 고쳐야 한다. (what → that) Point 40. 명사절 접속사의 선택
③ 5형식으로 사용된 동사 make의 목적어 자리에 do detailed work, 목적격보어 자리에 a big deal이 사용되었다. 명사 역할을 해서 목적어가 될 수 있도록 동명사 doing으로 고쳐야 한다. (do → doing) Point 28. 동명사의 역할
④ 주어가 Mastery로 단수이므로 단수 동사인 enhances로 고쳐야 한다. (enhance → enhances) Point 27. 주어 - 동사 수 일치

**어휘** paintbrush 그림 그리는 붓 precision 정밀함 dictate 좌우하다 outcome 결과 instrument 도구 respective 각각의 detailed 세심한 a big deal 대단한 것 mastery 숙달 enhance 향상시키다 expression 표현 craftsmanship 솜씨

정답 ①

**202** 문법포인트 | Point 49. 강조

It was not because he lacked the necessary skills but because he didn't have enough experience ① that he was not selected for the job. ② Despite he was disappointed, he decided to use this feedback as motivation for improvement. By enrolling in additional training programs, he aimed ③ enhancing his qualifications and expertise. The more experience he gained, ④ the most confident he felt about reapplying and demonstrating his newfound abilities to the hiring committee.

**해설**
① 주어 It과 that 사이에 강조 대상을 넣어 강조하는 It ~ that 강조 구문이다.
② Despite는 전치사인데, 뒤에 절이 왔으므로 동일한 의미의 접속사 Although로 고쳐야 한다. (Despite → Although) Point 41. 부사절 접속사의 선택
③ aim은 to부정사를 목적어로 취하는 완전타동사이므로 동명사 enhancing을 to enhance로 고쳐야 한다. (enhancing → to enhance) Point 06. 완전타동사와 동작의 목적어
④ 'S'가 V 하면 할수록, S는 더욱 V하다'는 「The 비교급 S' + V', the 비교급 S + V」으로 나타내므로 the most를 the more로 고쳐야 한다. (the most → the more) Point 37. 비교 사용 표현

**어휘** reapply 다시 지원하다 newfound 새롭게 얻은

정답 ①

**203** 문법포인트 | Point 09. 불완전타동사의 목적격보어

The concept of sin has been present in many cultures throughout history, ① where it was usually equated with an individual's failure to live up to external standards of conduct or with his violation of taboos, laws, or moral codes. It was during the Ancient Greek era ② that people looked upon sin, in essence, ③ a failure on the part of a person to achieve his true self-expression and ④ preserve his due relation to the rest of the universe.

**해설**
③ 'A를 B로 간주하다'는 「look upon A as B」라고 한다. 목적격보어 a failure 앞에 as가 있어야 하므로 a failure를 as a failure로 고쳐야 한다. (a failure → as a failure)
① where는 선행사인 many cultures에 대한 부연이다. 장소, 영역, 분야 등의 선행사 뒤에 where를 쓰므로 관계부사 where가 바르게 쓰였다. Point 44. 관계부사
② 강조 구문 It was ~ that 사이에 시간의 부사구(during the Ancient Greek era)가 바르게 강조되었다. Point 49. 강조
④ to achieve와 (to) preserve가 병렬 구조를 이루며 a failure를 수식하고 있다. 이때 두 번째 to부정사의 to는 생략이 가능하다. Point 39. 등위접속사의 병렬 구조

**어휘** equate 동일시하다 live up to ~에 부응하다 violation 위반 taboo 금기 moral code 도덕률 due 적절한

정답 ③

**204** 밑줄 친 부분에 들어갈 말로 가장 적절한 것은?

> Nothing is _____ a cool swim in the ocean on a hot summer day.

① as more refreshing as
② as refreshing than
③ more refreshing as
④ more refreshing than

**206** 밑줄 친 부분에 들어갈 말로 가장 적절한 것은?

> During the meeting, I noticed several colleagues _____ notes.

① takes      ② taken
③ taking     ④ to take

**205** 밑줄 친 부분 중 어법상 옳지 않은 것은?

> She spent every vacation ① exploring new destinations around the globe. Her camera was ② the most useful tool for capturing the beauty and essence of each place in which she visited. The girl ③ surrounding by the busy city streets or serene landscapes pursued her passion for travel and discovery. Every adventure enriched her with experiences and memories that shaped her worldview and ④ deepened her passion for exploration.

**207** 밑줄 친 부분 중 어법상 옳지 않은 것은?

> ① Having continued friendliness and peacefulness towards us, the Roman Empire suddenly changed our peace, and waged against us the most unjust war ever. Scarcely ② the second year of this war had passed when a revolution took place in the entire government, and it was ③ completely overturned. Constantius was attacked by an obstinate disease, ④ which led to his passing.

## 204  문법포인트 | Point 36. 비교 구문 / Point 37. 비교 사용 표현

Nothing is more refreshing than a cool swim in the ocean on a hot summer day.

**해설** 최상급 대용 표현으로 「부정 주어 + 원급 비교(as ~ as) / 비교급 비교(비교급 than) + A」가 사용되었다. 따라서 ④ more refreshing than이 정답이다.

**어휘** refreshing 상쾌한

**정답** ④

## 205  문법포인트 | Point 32 현재분사 vs. 과거분사

She spent every vacation ① exploring new destinations around the globe. Her camera was ② the most useful tool for capturing the beauty and essence of each place in which she visited. The girl ③ surrounding by the busy city streets or serene landscapes pursued her passion for travel and discovery. Every adventure enriched her with experiences and memories that shaped her worldview and ④ deepened her passion for exploration.

**해설**
③ 타동사 surround 뒤에 목적어가 없고 수식받는 명사 The girl과 의미상 수동의 관계이므로 과거분사가 되어야 한다. (surrounding → surrounded)
① '~하는 데 (돈/시간)을 쓰다'를 표현할 때 「spend + 시간/돈 + -ing」의 표현을 사용한다. Point 31. 준동사 주요 표현
② useful의 최상급은 most useful이고 최상급 앞에 the가 있으므로 바르게 쓰였다. Point 36. 비교 구문
④ 앞의 동사 shaped와 등위접속사 and를 통해 병렬 구조로 바르게 연결되었다. Point 39. 등위접속사의 병렬 구조

**어휘** explore 답사하다  destination 여행지  capture 포착하다  serene 고요한  discovery 발견  enrich 풍요롭게 하다  passion 열정  exploration 탐사

**정답** ③

## 206  문법포인트 | Point 10. 불완전타동사와 동작의 목적격보어

During the meeting, I noticed several colleagues taking notes.

**해설** 지각동사는 목적어와 목적격보어를 가지며 목적어와 목적격보어의 관계가 능동이면 원형부정사(동사원형) 또는 현재분사를, 수동의 관계이면 과거분사를 목적격보어로 취한다. colleagues가 목적어이며 빈칸은 목적격보어 자리이고 목적어와 능동의 관계이므로 현재분사인 ③ taking이 들어가야 한다.

**어휘** colleague 동료  take a note 필기하다

**정답** ③

## 207  문법포인트 | Point 15. 시제 관련 표현 / Point 50. 도치

① Having continued friendliness and peacefulness towards us, the Roman Empire suddenly changed our peace, and waged against us the most unjust war ever. Scarcely ② the second year of this war had passed when a revolution took place in the entire government, and it was ③ completely overturned. Constantius was attacked by an obstinate disease, ④ which led to his passing.

**해설**
② '~하자마자 ~했다'라는 말은 부정어가 문두에 있으므로 「Scarcely + had + 주어 + p.p. + when/before 주어 + 과거 동사」로 표현한다. 부정어 Scarcely 다음에 어순이 도치되고 주절에는 과거완료 시제가 되어야 하므로 had the second year of this war passed로 고쳐야 한다. (the second year of this war had passed → had the second year of this war passed)
① having p.p.의 완료 분사구문을 사용해 주절보다 앞선 시제를 바르게 표현했다. Point 33. 분사구문
③ 분사는 부사로 수식해야 하므로 부사 completely가 바르게 쓰였다. Point 34. 형용사 vs. 부사
④ an obstinate disease를 선행사로 하는 주격 관계대명사가 계속적 용법으로 바르게 쓰였다. Point 43. 관계대명사의 선택

**어휘** empire 제국  wage (전쟁을) 벌이다  unjust 부당한  scarcely 거의 (않다)  revolution 혁명  take place 일어나다  government 정부  overturn 뒤집다  obstinate (병이) 난치의  disease 병  passing 사망

**정답** ②

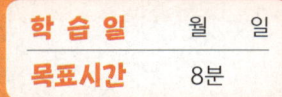

**208** 밑줄 친 부분에 들어갈 말로 가장 적절한 것은?

> The pizza sold in this shop is _____ than that of other shops.

① much tasty     ② more tastier
③ very tasty     ④ much tastier

**209** 밑줄 친 부분 중 어법상 옳지 않은 것은?

> Teachers are a fundamentally important part of our society's structure, ① educating our young and making them the leaders of tomorrow. Knowledge is power and without a good education system we ② are weakened as a nation. In many countries teaching is a profession highly ③ respecting by the nation. Teachers are seen as mentors. I ④ used to look on many of mine this way when I was at school.

**210** 밑줄 친 부분 중 어법상 옳지 않은 것은?

> ① Upon completing their tasks, students are encouraged to review their work for understanding. Children who diligently complete their homework or ② who actively participate in discussions often demonstrate higher academic achievement. Contrary to ③ that skeptics argue, consistent effort and engagement in learning activities ④ significantly contribute to students' overall educational development.

## 208  문법포인트 | Point 36. 비교 구문

The pizza sold in this shop is much tastier than that of other shops.

**해설** 비교급 비교는 「A + 형용사·부사의 비교급 + than + B」(A가 B보다 더 ~하다)로 나타낸다. 또한 비교급은 much, far, by far, still, even, a lot, rather, a little로 수식할 수 있다. 따라서 정답은 ④ much tastier이다.

**어휘** sell 팔다  tasty 맛있는

**정답** ④

## 209  문법포인트 | Point 32. 현재분사 vs. 과거분사

Teachers are a fundamentally important part of our society's structure, ① educating our young and making them the leaders of tomorrow. Knowledge is power and without a good education system we ② are weakened as a nation. In many countries teaching is a profession (highly ③ respecting by the nation). Teachers are seen as mentors. I ④ used to look on many of mine this way when I was at school.

**해설**
③ 수식받는 명사와 분사의 관계가 능동이면 현재분사, 수동이면 과거분사를 쓴다. profession과 respect의 관계를 보면, 직업이 존경하는 것이 아니고 존경받는 것이므로 수동의 관계임을 알 수 있다. 따라서 respecting을 과거분사 respected로 고쳐야 한다. (respecting → respected)
① 문맥상 분사구문의 의미상 주어가 주절의 주어인 Teachers와 동일하며 능동의 관계이므로 분사구문 educating이 바르게 쓰였다. Point 33. 분사구문
② 주어 we와 weaken의 관계가 수동이고, 뒤에 목적어가 없으므로 수동태 are weakened가 바르게 쓰였다. Point 16. 능동태 vs. 수동태 구분
④ 「used to + 동사원형」은 '~하곤 했다'라는 의미의 조동사 표현이다. used to 다음에 동사원형 look이 바르게 쓰였다. Point 18. 조동사의 선택

**어휘** fundamentally 근본적으로  young 젊은이들
weaken 약하게 하다  profession 직업
look on (~하다고) 보다[여기다]

**정답** ③

## 210  문법포인트 | Point 40. 명사절 접속사의 선택

① Upon completing their tasks, students are encouraged to review their work for understanding. Children (who diligently complete their homework) or ② (who actively participate in discussions) often demonstrate higher academic achievement. Contrary to ③ [that skeptics argue], consistent effort and engagement in learning activities ④ significantly contribute to students' overall educational development.

**해설**
③ 전치사의 목적어로 that절이 올 수 없다. 그리고 타동사 argue의 목적어가 없어 불완전한 절이므로 that을 what으로 고쳐야 한다. (that → what)
① Upon은 전치사이므로 동명사 completing이 목적어로 바르게 쓰였다. 「upon(on) -ing」는 '~하자마자'를 의미한다. Point 48. 전치사의 목적어
② 선행사가 Children이고 뒤에 주어가 없는 불완전한 절이 왔으므로 주격 관계대명사 who는 바르게 쓰였다. Point 43. 관계대명사의 선택
④ 동사 contribute를 수식하는 부사 significantly가 바르게 쓰였다. Point 34. 형용사 vs. 부사

**어휘** complete 끝내다  task 과제  encourage 권장하다
review 재검토하다  demonstrate 보이다  skeptic 회의론자
consistent 지속적인  engagement 관여  contribute 기여하다
overall 전반적인

**정답** ③

**211** 밑줄 친 부분에 들어갈 말로 가장 적절한 것은?

_____ she had little experience, she performed exceptionally well in the competition.

① Despite  ② Because
③ Although  ④ Because of

**212** 밑줄 친 부분 중 어법상 옳지 않은 것은?

My day begins with walks on the beach. It's a peaceful start ① that sets a positive tone for the day ahead. Without this start, I ② can hard gather the energy for the rest of the day. Afterward, I spend some time ③ reading the news and emails. Finally, I plan out the day's tasks ④ ensuring I stay productive and efficient.

**213** 밑줄 친 부분 중 어법상 옳지 않은 것은?

① Acknowledging the team's collaborative effort, stakeholders were impressed by ② what resulted in a successful project completion ahead of schedule. Stakeholders praised the team's communication skills, problem-solving abilities, and ③ resolute dedicate. This positive feedback underscores the importance of teamwork in achieving organizational goals. The project's success has bolstered team morale and ④ strengthened internal relationships.

**214** 밑줄 친 부분 중 어법상 옳지 않은 것은?

Between the guided tours and free exploration times ① were the most memorable experience ② that tourists cherished the most. While the guided tours provided valuable historical insights and cultural context, free exploration allowed tourists ③ to discover hidden gems at their own pace. Because of this flexibility, visitors could engage more deeply with the local culture and unique attractions. Consequently, the combination of structured learning and personal adventure created a ④ richly rewarding travel experience.

## 211 문법포인트 | Point 41. 부사절 접속사의 선택

Although she had little experience, she performed exceptionally well in the competition.

**해설** 빈칸 뒤에 절이 왔으므로 접속사인 ③ Although가 들어가야 한다. ② Because도 접속이지만 문맥상 적합치 않다.

**어휘** experience 경험   perform 해내다   exceptionally 특별히

정답 ③

## 212 문법포인트 | Point 35. 주의할 형용사와 부사

My day begins with walks on the beach. It's a peaceful start ① that sets a positive tone for the day ahead. Without this start, I ② can hard gather the energy for the rest of the day. Afterward, I spend some time ③ reading the news and emails. Finally, I plan out the day's tasks ④ ensuring I stay productive and efficient.

→ can hardly gather

**해설**
② hard는 부사로 '열심히'를, hardly는 '거의 ~하지 못한다'를 각각 의미한다. (can hard gather → can hardly gather)
① that이 앞의 start를 수식하는 주격 관계대명사로 뒤에 불완전한 절이 와서 바르게 쓰였다. Point 43. 관계대명사의 선택
③ '~을 하면서 …을 쓰다/보내다'를 의미할 때 「spend + 시간/돈 + (in) + -ing」의 구문을 이용한다. 구문이 바르게 쓰였다. Point 31. 준동사 주요 표현
④ ensuring의 의미상의 주어는 주절의 주어인 I이고 I가 유지하는 능동의 의미이므로 현재분사형인 ensuring이 바르게 쓰였다. Point 33. 분사구문

**어휘** brisk 활기찬   productive 생산적인   efficient 효율적인

정답 ②

## 213 문법포인트 | Point 39. 등위접속사의 병렬 구조

① Acknowledging the team's collaborative effort, stakeholders were impressed by ② [what resulted in a successful project completion ahead of schedule]. Stakeholders praised the team's communication skills, problem-solving abilities, and ③ resolute dedicate. This positive feedback underscores the importance of teamwork in achieving organizational goals. The project's success has bolstered team morale and ④ strengthened internal relationships.

→ resolute dedication

**해설**
③ 등위접속사 and로 resolute dedicate가 the team's communication, skills problem-solving abilities와 연결되고 있다. 따라서 명사구들과 병렬을 이루기 위해 resolute dedicate를 명사구인 resolute dedication으로 고쳐야 한다. (resolute dedicate → resolute dedication)
① 분사의 의미상 주어가 주절의 주어인 stakeholders인데, 이해 당사자들이 인정하는 능동의 관계이며 분사 뒤에 목적어가 있으므로 현재분사가 바르게 쓰였다. Point 33. 분사구문
② 앞에 선행사가 없고 what 이하에 주어가 없는 불완전한 절이 왔으므로 명사절 접속사 what이 바르게 쓰였다. Point 40. 명사절 접속사의 선택
④ strengthened와 bolstered는 and에 의해 과거 동사끼리 병렬되어 있으므로 바르게 쓰였다. Point 39. 등위접속사의 병렬 구조

**어휘** acknowledge 인정하다   collaborative 협력적인
stakeholder 이해 당사자   impress 깊은 인상을 주다
ahead of schedule 예정보다 빨리   resolute 불굴의
underscore 강조하다   bolster 북돋우다   morale 사기

정답 ③

## 214 문법포인트 | Point 50. 도치 / Point 27. 주어-동사 수 일치

(Between the guided tours and free exploration times) ① were the most memorable experience ② (that tourists cherished the most). While the guided tours provided valuable historical insights and cultural context, free exploration allowed tourists ③ to discover hidden gems at their own pace. Because of this flexibility, visitors could engage more deeply with the local culture and unique attractions. Consequently, the combination of structured learning and personal adventure created a ④ richly rewarding travel experience.

→ was

**해설**
① 부사구 Between ~ times가 강조되어 문장 맨 앞으로 나와 1형식 문장의 주어와 동사가 도치되었다. 주어는 the most memorable experience로 단수이므로 were를 was로 고쳐야 한다. (were → was)
② 선행사 the most memorable experience가 있고, that 이하에 cherished의 목적어가 없다. the most는 cherished의 목적어가 아니라 cherished를 수식하는 부사 much의 최상급이다. 따라서 목적격 관계대명사 that이 바르게 왔다. Point 43. 관계대명사의 선택
③ 목적어 tourists와 목적격보어가 능동의 관계이므로 목적격보어로 to discover가 바르게 쓰였다. Point 10. 불완전타동사와 동작의 목적격보어
④ 부사 richly(충분히)가 형용사 rewarding을 바르게 수식하고 있다. Point 34. 형용사 vs. 부사

**어휘** exploration 탐험   memorable 기억에 남는
cherish 소중히 여기다   insight 식견   flexibility 유연성
engage 참여하다   attraction 명소   consequently 결과적으로
structured 조직적인   richly 충분히   rewarding 보람 있는

정답 ①

### 215. 밑줄 친 부분에 들어갈 말로 가장 적절한 것은?

The restaurant is fully booked tonight, so we _____ try that new sushi place down the street.

① are used to  ② used to
③ may as well as  ④ may as well

### 216. 밑줄 친 부분 중 어법상 옳은 것은?

Two suspects were taken into custody on Wednesday morning at 3:56 AM after an officer on patrol noticed them ① to trespass on the railroad tracks near North Center Street. ② The 20-years-old New York women had a court order in effect prohibiting them ③ from making contact with anyone. In court, they were both scrambling to blame ④ one another.

### 217. 밑줄 친 부분에 들어갈 말로 가장 적절한 것은?

The flowers in the garden _____ after the rain.

① are smelling sweet  ② are smelling sweetly
③ smelled sweet  ④ smelled sweetly

### 218. 밑줄 친 부분 중 어법상 옳지 않은 것은?

The rainstorm was ① as an unexpected happening as a power outage during a sunny day. The poor ② are often the most affected by sudden changes in weather. At least, the roads ③ will have been cleared by the end of the day ④ for those people to travel safely.

## 215　문법포인트 | Point 18. 조동사의 선택

The restaurant is fully booked tonight, so we may as well try that new sushi place down the street.

**해설** 대안을 제시하는 상황이므로 '~하는 것이 좋겠다'라는 의미의 조동사 ④ may as well이 정답이다.

**어휘** book 예약하다　sushi place 초밥집

정답 ④

## 216　문법포인트 | Point 10. 불완전타동사와 동작의 목적격보어

Two suspects were taken into custody on Wednesday morning at 3:56 AM after an officer on patrol noticed them ① to trespass on the railroad tracks near North Center
→ trespass/trespassing
Street. ② The 20-years-old New York women had a court
→ The 20-year-old
order in effect prohibiting them ③ from making contact with anyone. In court, they were both scrambling to blame ④ one another.
→ each other

**해설**
③ 「prohibit A from -ing」는 'A가 하는 것을 금지하다'라는 뜻으로 쓴다. prohibit의 목적어 뒤에 금지하는 내용이 「from + 동명사」의 형태로 바르게 쓰였다. Point 07. 완전타동사와 함께 사용되는 주요 전치사
① 지각동사인 notice는 목적어와 목적격보어가 능동의 관계일 때 목적격보어로 동사원형 또는 현재분사를 쓸 수 있다. 목적어인 them이 목적격보어인 trespass와 능동의 관계이므로, 목적격보어를 동사원형 trespass나 현재분사인 trespassing으로 고쳐야 한다. (to trespass → trespass/trespassing)
② 단위명사가 명사를 수식할 때는 반드시 단수 명사로 쓴다. 따라서 years를 year로 고쳐야 한다. (The 20-years-old → The 20-year-old) Point 35. 주의할 형용사와 부사
④ 두 명 사이의 '서로서로'는 each other이고, 세 명 이상은 one another이다. Two suspects에 관한 이야기이므로 each other로 고쳐야 한다. (one another → each other) Point 25. 부정대명사

**어휘** take ~ into custody ~를 구금시키다　on patrol 순찰 중인
trespass 무단침입하다　scramble 앞다투다

정답 ③

## 217　문법포인트 | Point 04. 불완전자동사의 보어 / Point 13. 시제 사용 제한

The flowers in the garden smelled sweet after the rain.

**해설** 감각동사인 smell은 불완전자동사로 쓰이며 형용사를 보어로 취한다. 또한 감각동사로 사용할 때 진행형이 불가하다. 따라서 ③ smelled sweet가 정답이다.

**어휘** smell 냄새가 나다　sweetly 달콤하게

정답 ③

## 218　문법포인트 | Point 23. 관사의 위치

The rainstorm was ① as an unexpected happening as
→ as unexpected a happening
a power outage during a sunny day. The poor ② are often the most affected by sudden changes in weather.
목(X)
At least, the roads ③ will have been cleared by the end of the day ④ for those people to travel safely.

**해설**
① 원급 비교에 사용되는 부사인 so나 as는 「so/as + 형용사 + a/an + 명사」의 어순을 취하므로 as unexpected a happening으로 고쳐야 한다. (as an unexpected happening → as unexpected a happening)
② 「정관사 + 형용사/분사」는 복수 보통명사로 쓰이므로 복수 동사인 are가 바르게 쓰였다. Point 27. 주어 - 동사 수 일치
③ 도로가 치워진다는 수동의 의미이므로 수동태로 바르게 쓰였다. 또한 미래의 어떤 시점까지 완료된다는 의미로 미래완료 시제 역시 바르게 쓰였다. Point 16. 능동태 vs. 수동태 구분 / Point 12. 완료 시제
④ to부정사에 대한 의미상의 주어로 for those people이 바르게 쓰였다. Point 30. 준동사의 형태 변화

**어휘** unexpected 예상치 못한　power outage 정전

정답 ①

**219** 밑줄 친 부분에 들어갈 말로 가장 적절한 것은?

> The purpose of this study is to direct drama activities for _____ children.

① 10-year-old's   ② 10-year-olds
③ 10-years-old    ④ 10-year-old

**220** 밑줄 친 부분 중 어법상 옳지 않은 것은?

> ① Though his reservations, John decided to accept the job offer from the prestigious law firm. The salary, benefits, and location of the office were also factors that ② influenced his decision. John, ③ having reviewed the contract thoroughly, signed it confidently, ④ knowing it's a step towards his career goals.

**221** 밑줄 친 부분 중 어법상 옳지 않은 것은?

> As floodwaters recede across the country, ① millions of people who ② survived the deluge are finding that they have nowhere to live and their fields have turned into swamps and lakes. For many of them, the worst is not over. The lack of clean water, as well as poor food, sleeping in the open and the collapse of any healthcare provision ③ mean the very young, the elderly and the weak ④ are starting to die off.

**222** 밑줄 친 부분 중 어법상 옳지 않은 것은?

> Heidelberg is a university town in the German state of Baden-Württemberg, ① situated on the river Neckar. It is rightly regarded as one of Germany's most beautiful towns. Not only ② does Heidelberg offer a world-famous castle, romantic alleys in the old town and Germany's oldest university, ③ but also a modern scientific and economic infrastructure of international acclaim and a very lively and multifaceted culture scene. The town has ④ over 8 hundreds years of history and is a lively center of the metropolitan Rhine-Neckar region today.

## 219 문법포인트 | Point 35. 주의할 형용사와 부사

The purpose of this study is to direct drama activities for 10-year-old children.

해설 수량형용사가 측정 단위명사와 사용될 때 측정 단위명사를 단수로 쓰므로 ④ 10-year-old가 정답이다.

어휘 purpose 목적   direct 연출하다

정답 ④

## 220 문법포인트 | Point 41. 부사절 접속사의 선택

① Though his reservations, John decided to accept the job offer from the prestigious law firm. The salary, benefits, and location of the office were also factors (that ② influenced his decision). John, ③ having reviewed the contract thoroughly, signed it confidently, ④ knowing it's a step towards his career goals.

해설
① 뒤에 절이 아니라 명사구가 왔으므로 접속사가 아닌 전치사를 써야 한다. 접속사 Though를 비슷한 의미의 전치사 Despite이나 In spite of로 고쳐야 한다. (Though → Despite/In spite of)
② 관계사절의 동사이며, 선행사는 factors이다. factors와 동사의 관계가 능동이고, 뒤에 his decision이라는 목적어가 있으므로 능동태로 바르게 쓰였다. Point 16. 능동태 vs. 수동태 구분
③ 계약서를 검토한(having reviewed) 사실이 주절의 사인을 한 (signed) 사실보다 시제가 앞서기 때문에 완료 분사구문이 바르게 쓰였다. Point 33. 분사구문
④ 문장의 동사가 signed이므로 분사구문을 만드는 분사가 와야 하는 자리이다. 분사구문의 의미상의 주어는 문장의 주어인 John이고, John과 know의 관계가 능동이며 뒤에 목적어로 it's ~ goals라는 절을 취했으므로 현재분사 knowing이 바르게 쓰였다. Point 33. 분사구문 / Point 01. 문장의 구성

어휘 reservation 의구심   prestigious 명망 있는   benefit 복리후생
contract 계약서   thoroughly 철저히   confidently 자신 있게

정답 ①

## 221 문법포인트 | Point 27. 주어 - 동사 수 일치

As floodwaters recede across the country, ① millions of people who ② survived the deluge are finding that they have nowhere to live and their fields have turned into swamps and lakes. For many of them, the worst is not over. The lack (of clean water), as well as poor food, sleeping in the open and the collapse of any healthcare provision ③ mean the very young, the elderly and the weak ④ are starting to die off.

해설
③ 「B as well as A」의 구문이 주어가 되는 경우 동사의 수를 B에 맞추어야 하므로 mean의 주어는 The lack이다. 주어가 3인칭 단수이고 시제는 현재이므로 동사 mean은 means가 되어야 한다. (mean → means)
① 막연하게 많은 수를 의미할 때는 수단위명사의 복수형을 써서 표현한다. '수백만 명'이라는 뜻이므로 millions of people이 바르게 쓰였다. Point 35. 주의할 형용사와 부사
② survive는 '(사고나 병으로부터) 살아남다'라는 뜻일 때는 완전타동사로 쓰여 전치사 없이 목적어를 바로 취할 수 있다. Point 05. 완전타동사
④ 주어가 the very young, the elderly and the weak로 복수 명사이므로 are가 바르게 쓰였다. Point 27. 주어 - 동사 수 일치

어휘 recede 물러나다   deluge 대홍수   swamp 늪
die off 하나하나씩 죽어 가다   collapse 붕괴   provision 공급

정답 ③

## 222 문법포인트 | Point 35. 주의할 형용사와 부사

Heidelberg is a university town in the German state of Baden-Württemberg, ① situated on the river Neckar. It is rightly regarded as one of Germany's most beautiful towns. (Not only) ② does Heidelberg offer a world-famous castle, romantic alleys in the old town and Germany's oldest university, ③ but also a modern scientific and economic infrastructure of international acclaim and a very lively and multifaceted culture scene. The town has ④ over 8 hundreds years of history and is a lively center of the metropolitan Rhine-Neckar region today.

해설
④ 수량형용사와 수단위명사가 함께 사용될 때 수단위명사는 단수가 된다. 수단위명사 hundreds가 수량형용사 8과 함께 쓰였으므로 단수인 hundred로 고쳐야 한다. (over 8 hundreds → over 8 hundred)
① situated의 의미상의 주어는 문장의 주어인 Heidelberg이다. situate는 '위치시키다'라는 타동사이고, 의미상의 주어와 수동의 관계이므로 과거분사가 바르게 쓰였다. Point 33. 분사구문
② 부정부사 Not only가 문장의 앞으로 나와 주어와 동사가 도치되었다. offer가 일반동사이므로 조동사 do를 사용한 것 역시 바르다. Point 50. 도치
③ 「Not only A but (also) B」는 등위상관접속사로 'A뿐만 아니라 B도'의 의미이다. Not only에 호응하여 but also가 바르게 쓰였다. Point 39. 등위접속사의 병렬 구조

어휘 situate 위치시키다   infrastructure 기반   acclaim 찬사
multifaceted 다면적인   metropolitan 대도시

정답 ④

## DAY 15

**223** 밑줄 친 부분에 들어갈 말로 가장 적절한 것은?

> The rescue operation _____ for weeks before it was finally executed by the emergency response team.

① will plan  ② will be planned
③ had planned  ④ had been planned

**225** 밑줄 친 부분 중 어법상 옳지 않은 것은?

> I noticed a fluffy gray cat with a collar ① sitting comfortably on my neighbor's porch this morning. Hoping to encourage it ② to feel safe and cared for, I left the food and water nearby and spoke soothingly to it. The heartening aspect of ③ showing kindness to animals is ④ what it not only benefits them but also fosters a sense of empathy and community among people.

**224** 밑줄 친 부분 중 어법상 옳지 않은 것은?

> ① The most challenging part of the job interview process is the final round, where candidates face rigorous assessments and tough questions. Yesterday, an applicant ② whose phone rang during the interview had to quickly apologize and ③ turn it off. It was generous ④ for the hiring manager to overlook the interruption and continue the interview. Despite the unexpected disruption, the applicant managed to leave a positive impression.

## 223 문법포인트 | Point 16. 능동태 vs. 수동태 구분 / Point 12. 완료 시제

The rescue operation had been planned for weeks before it was finally executed by the emergency response team.

**해설** 구조 활동이 계획되는 수동의 의미이므로 수동태가 적절하다. 종속절의 과거보다 더 먼저 일어난 과거의 일을 나타내므로 과거완료 시제가 적절하다. 따라서 정답은 ④ had been planned이다.

**어휘** rescue 구조  operation 활동  execute 실행하다
emergency 긴급  response 대응

정답 ④

## 224 문법포인트 | Point 30. 준동사의 형태 변화

① The most challenging part of the job interview process is the final round, where candidates face rigorous assessments and tough questions. Yesterday, an applicant ② whose phone rang during the interview had to quickly apologize and ③ turn it off. It was generous ④ for the hiring manager to overlook the interruption and continue the interview. Despite the unexpected disruption, the applicant managed to leave a positive impression.

**해설**
④ to부정사의 의미상의 주어는 주로 「for + 목적격」으로 to부정사 앞에 쓰지만 인성형용사가 사용되는 경우에는 「of + 목적격」으로 쓴다. generous라는 인성형용사가 있으므로 for는 of로 고쳐야 한다. (for the hiring manager → of the hiring manager)
① 최상급 앞에는 정관사 the가 쓰여야 한다. The most challenging의 최상급이 바르게 쓰였다. Point 36. 비교 구문
② 선행사 an applicant와 관계절의 주어인 phone이 소유의 관계이고, whose 뒤에 완전한 절이 와서 바르게 쓰였다. Point 43. 관계대명사의 선택
③ 「타동사 + 부사」의 동사구에서 목적어가 대명사이면 타동사와 부사 사이에 와야 한다. turn off의 목적어인 대명사 it이 이 사이에 바르게 쓰였다. Point 34. 형용사 vs. 부사

**어휘** challenging 힘든  rigorous 엄격한  assessment 평가
overlook 눈감아주다  interruption 중단  disruption 붕괴

정답 ④

## 225 문법포인트 | Point 40. 명사절 접속사의 선택

I noticed a fluffy gray cat with a collar ① sitting comfortably on my neighbor's porch this morning. Hoping to encourage it ② to feel safe and cared for, I left the food and water nearby and spoke soothingly to it. The heartening aspect of ③ showing kindness to animals is ④ what it not only benefits them but also fosters a sense of empathy and community among people.

**해설**
④ what 이하의 절이 완전하므로 what을 명사절 접속사 that으로 고쳐야 한다. (what → that)
① 지각동사는 목적어와 목적격보어가 능동이면 현재분사나 동사원형을, 수동이면 과거분사를 쓴다. notice의 목적어 a fluffy gray cat with a collar가 목적격보어인 분사와 능동의 관계이므로 현재분사 sitting이 바르게 쓰였다. 동사원형 sit도 가능하다. Point 10. 불완전타동사와 동작의 목적격보어
② encourage는 목적격보어에 to부정사를 써야 한다. 따라서 목적격보어에 to부정사인 to feel이 바르게 사용되었다. Point 10. 불완전타동사와 동작의 목적격보어
③ 전치사 of의 목적어로 동명사인 showing이 올바르게 쓰였다. Point 48. 전치사의 목적어

**어휘** fluffy 솜털이 보송보송한  collar 목걸이  comfortably 편안하게
porch 현관  nearby 근처에  soothingly 달래듯이
heartening 고무적인  aspect 측면  foster 조성하다
empathy 공감

정답 ④

**226** 밑줄 친 부분에 들어갈 말로 가장 적절한 것은?

Disappointed with the attraction they were currently visiting, they decided _____ the next destination right away.

① to leave
② leaving
③ to leave for
④ leaving for

**227** 밑줄 친 부분 중 어법상 옳지 않은 것은?

The first impression one gets from listening to Sylvia Plath ① read her poetry is that she ② was possessing the most haunting of voices. Her voice echoes throughout ③ whatever chamber it is played in, filling the space. ④ Fierce though they are on the page, Sylvia's words become even more so as they come from the mouth of the poet herself.

**228** 밑줄 친 부분 중 어법상 옳지 않은 것은?

Our goal is the total prevention of job related injuries and illness. Thus, all employees are requested to ① participate in the further development and implementation of our safety and health program. ② Every employee is expected to observe established safe practices, to use the ③ safety equipments and devices provided, and to conduct the task in a manner ④ that will ensure their own safety as well as the safety of their fellow employees.

**229** 밑줄 친 부분 중 어법상 옳지 않은 것은?

Six months ① have passed since the office implemented its new remote work policy. ② However subjectively employees' opinions may be, the flexibility has led to increased job satisfaction. Staff members should ③ be offered regular virtual meetings to maintain communication and collaboration. This new arrangement has proven ④ to be effective and beneficial for the company's productivity.

## 226 문법포인트 | Point. 06 완전타동사와 동작의 목적어 / Point 03. 완전자동사

Disappointed with the attraction they were currently visiting, they decided to leave for the next destination right away.

**해설** decide는 to부정사를 목적어로 취하는 완전타동사이고, leave는 완전타동사일 때는 '~을 떠나다,' 완전자동사일 때는 전치사 for와 함께 써서 '~로 출발하다'라는 의미를 각각 나타낸다. 따라서 정답은 ③ leave for이다.

**어휘** attraction 관광지   currently 지금   destination 목적지

**정답** ③

## 227 문법포인트 | Point 13. 시제 사용 제한

The first impression one gets from listening to Sylvia Plath ① read her poetry is that she ② was possessing (→ possessed) the most haunting of voices. Her voice echoes throughout ③ [whatever chamber it is played in], filling the space. ④ Fierce though they are on the page, Sylvia's words become even more so as they come from the mouth of the poet herself.

**해설**
② '소유하다'를 의미하는 possess는 진행형 불가 동사다. 따라서 was possessing을 possessed로 고쳐야 한다. (was possessing → possessed)
① 지각동사는 목적어와 능동의 관계일 때 목적격보어에 동사원형 또는 현재분사를 사용한다. listen to의 목적격보어로 동사원형인 read가 바르게 쓰였다. Point 10. 불완전타동사와 동작의 목적격보어
③ 전치사 throughout 뒤에 명사(구/절)가 와야 한다. 명사절을 이끌면서 명사 chamber를 수식할 수 있는 형용사 역할의 복합관계사 whatever가 바르게 쓰였다. 또한 whatever chamber가 전치사 in의 목적어로 쓰였다. Point 45. 복합관계사
④ 「(As) +무관사 명사/형용사/부사/분사 + as/though + 주어 + 동사」 구문은 '비록 ~이지만'이라는 양보의 의미를 갖는다. Fierce가 are의 보어이므로 어순과 형태가 바르게 사용되었다. Point 42. 주요 양보구문

**어휘** haunting 잊히지 않는   echo 울려 퍼지다   chamber 방   fierce 강렬한

**정답** ②

## 228 문법포인트 | Point 21. 명사의 이해

Our goal is the total prevention of job related injuries and illness. Thus, all employees are requested to ① participate in the further development and implementation of our safety and health program. ② Every employee is expected to observe established safe practices, to use the ③ safety equipments (→ equipment) and devices provided, and to conduct the task in a manner ④ (that will ensure their own safety as well as the safety of their fellow employees).

**해설**
③ equipment는 절대 불가산명사로 반드시 단수로 사용된다. 따라서 equipment가 되어야 한다. (equipments → equipment)
① participate는 자동사로 뒤에 목적어가 오기 위해서는 반드시 전치사 in과 함께 사용되어야 한다. Point 03. 완전자동사
② 「every+단수 명사+단수 동사」이므로 employee, is 모두 바르게 사용되었다. Point 25. 부정대명사 / Point 27. 주어 - 동사 수 일치
④ that은 선행사인 a manner를 수식하는 관계대명사로 뒤에 will ensure가 나와 주어가 없으므로 주어 역할을 하는 주격 관계대명사로 바르게 쓰였다. Point 43. 관계대명사의 선택

**어휘** implementation 실행   observe 따르다   established 확립된

**정답** ③

## 229 문법포인트 | Point 42. 주요 양보구문

Six months ① have passed since the office implemented its new remote work policy. ② However subjectively (→ However subjective) employees' opinions may be, the flexibility has led to increased job satisfaction. Staff members should ③ be offered regular virtual meetings to maintain communication and collaboration. This new arrangement has proven ④ to be effective and beneficial for the company's productivity.

**해설**
② However 뒤에는 형용사나 부사가 올 수 있는데, be동사의 보어 역할을 할 수 있는 것은 형용사이므로 부사 subjectively를 subjective로 고쳐야 한다. (subjectively → subjective)
① 「since + 과거(시점)」은 완료 시제와 주로 사용된다. 따라서 현재완료 have passed가 바르게 쓰였다. 또한 주어가 복수이므로 동사도 복수형인 have가 바르게 쓰였다. Point 12. 완료 시제 / Point 27. 주어 - 동사 수 일치
③ offer는 두 개의 목적어를 취할 수 있는데 그 중 간접목적어를 주어로 전환한 수동태 문장이므로 동사의 뒤에 직접 목적어가 올 수 있다. should가 조동사이므로 be offered가 바르게 쓰였다. Point 17. 동사의 유형별 수동태
④ 불완전자동사 prove의 보어로 to부정사가 바르게 쓰였다. Point 04. 불완전자동사의 보어

**어휘** implement 시행하다   subjectively 주관적으로   virtual 가상의   collaboration 협력   arrangement 방식

**정답** ②

**230** 밑줄 친 부분에 들어갈 말로 가장 적절한 것은?

> After years of traveling for work, she became accustomed to _____ out of a suitcase.

① live
② have lived
③ living
④ being lived

**231** 밑줄 친 부분 중 어법상 옳지 않은 것은?

> She left the meeting ① disappointed due to the lack of progress on important issues. Despite her efforts, she ② was not given the opportunity to present her ideas. To avoid ③ to feel excluded in the future, she now plans to speak up more assertively in upcoming discussions. By taking proactive steps, she aims to ensure her contributions ④ are valued.

**232** 밑줄 친 부분에 들어갈 말로 가장 적절한 것은?

> Nothing in the world is worth _____ unless it means effort, pain, or difficulty.

① to do
② do
③ doing
④ done

**233** 밑줄 친 부분 중 어법상 옳은 것은?

> Because Soviet bench scientists had only limited opportunities to influence the often-unrealistic goals ① setting by the highest officials of the Soviet hierarchy, they resorted to secretly ② using coping mechanisms that created a distorted picture of the work performed in the bio-weapons program. These coping mechanisms included faking scientific results, ③ to establish research in view of achieving negative results, or defining tasks so ④ narrow that the procedures needed to accomplish an experiment became more important than the results.

## 230 | 문법포인트 | Point 48. 전치사의 목적어 / Point 31. 준동사 주요 표현

After years of traveling for work, she became accustomed to living out of a suitcase.

**해설** be/become accustomed to의 to는 전치사이므로 동명사인 living이 들어가야 한다.

**어휘** become accustomed to ~에 익숙해지다
live out of a suitcase (짐도 제대로 못 풀고 여기저기) 여행 다니다

정답 ③

## 231 | 문법포인트 | Point 06. 완전타동사와 동작의 목적어

She left the meeting ① disappointed due to the lack of progress on important issues. Despite her efforts, she ② was not given the opportunity to present her ideas. To avoid ③ to feel excluded in the future, she now plans to speak up more assertively in upcoming discussions. By taking proactive steps, she aims to ensure her contributions ④ are valued.

**해설**
③ avoid는 동명사를 목적어로 취한다. 따라서 to feel은 feeling으로 고쳐야 한다. (to feel → feeling)
① 감정유발동사 disappoint는 주어가 감정을 일으키는 주체이면 능동으로, 그 감정을 느끼는 사람이면 수동으로 표현한다. 주절의 주어와 수동의 관계이므로 분사구문은 (being) p.p. 형태가 되어야 한다. Point 33. 분사구문
② give는 4형식 동사로 목적어 두 개를 취하므로 수동태가 되어도 목적어가 뒤에 올 수 있다. 간접목적어가 주어가 되고 직접목적어가 동사 뒤에 남은 수동태 문장이 바르게 쓰였다. Point 17. 동사의 유형별 수동태
④ 타동사 value 뒤에 목적어가 없고 주어인 her contributions와 수동의 관계이므로 수동태가 바르게 쓰였다. Point 16. 능동태 vs. 수동태 구분

**어휘** exclude 소외시키다  assertively 단호히  proactive 적극적인

정답 ③

## 232 | 문법포인트 | Point 31. 준동사 주요 표현

Nothing in the world is worth doing unless it means effort, pain, or difficulty.

**해설** '~할 만한 가치가 있다'는 「be worth -ing」 또는 「be worthy of -ing」로 나타내므로 답은 ③ doing이다.

**어휘** worth 가치가 있는  unless ~하지 않으면  effort 노력
pain 고통  difficulty 어려움

정답 ③

## 233 | 문법포인트 | Point 48. 전치사의 목적어

Because Soviet bench scientists had only limited opportunities to influence the often-unrealistic goals ① setting by the highest officials of the Soviet hierarchy, they resorted to secretly ② using coping mechanisms that created a distorted picture of the work performed in the bio-weapons program. These coping mechanisms included faking scientific results, ③ to establish research in view of achieving negative results, or defining tasks so ④ narrow that the procedures needed to accomplish an experiment became more important than the results.

**해설**
② resort to는 '~에 의존하다'라는 의미로 이때 to는 전치사이다. 동명사 using이 전치사 to의 목적어로 바르게 쓰였다.
① setting은 goals를 수식하고 있다. 목표가 소련의 최고위 계층에 의해 설정되는 것으로 수동의 의미이므로 과거분사 set으로 고쳐야 한다. (setting → set) Point 32. 현재분사 vs. 과거분사
③ include는 동명사를 목적어로 취하는 동사다. faking ~, to establish ~, defining ~이 병렬로 연결되었다. 따라서 to establish는 동명사 establishing으로 고쳐야 한다. (to establish → establishing) Point 39. 등위접속사의 병렬 구조
④ narrow는 문맥상 동명사 defining을 수식해야 한다. 동명사는 동사의 의미를 강조할 때 부사의 수식을 받으므로 부사인 narrowly로 고쳐야 한다. (narrow → narrowly) Point 34. 형용사 vs. 부사

**어휘** bench scientist 과학 연구원  official 관리  hierarchy 지배층
resort to ~에 의존하다  coping mechanism 대처 방법
distorted 왜곡된  bio-weapon 생물 무기  fake 조작하다
in view of ~을 고려하여

정답 ②

**234** 밑줄 친 부분에 들어갈 말로 가장 적절한 것은?

> How can I feel relaxed, with you _____ me like that?

① watch  ② watching
③ watched  ④ being watched

**236** 밑줄 친 부분에 들어갈 말로 가장 적절한 것은?

> He says the day will not be far away when all the poor will be _____ happy.

① economy  ② economical
③ economic  ④ economically

**235** 밑줄 친 부분 중 어법상 옳지 않은 것은?

> The house is composed of a series of concrete slabs that ① lean slightly on each level. From street view, the concrete roof ② is folded down to create a sculptural element while also protecting the home from the western sun and ③ providing privacy for the overlooked site. Internally, the visible concrete construction is contrasted with refined and polished materials. Openings, recesses, doors, stairs and wall panels are made of warm timber finishes, ④ complementing by pockets of soft, natural light from skylights, as well as full-height glazing.

**237** 밑줄 친 부분 중 어법상 옳지 않은 것은?

> Despite his reservations, John decided ① to accept the job offer from the prestigious law firm. The salary, benefits, and location of the office ② were also factors that influenced his decision. John, ③ having reviewed the contract thoroughly, signed it confidently, ④ know it was a step towards his career goals.

## 234 문법포인트 | Point 33. 분사구문

How can I feel relaxed, with you watching me like that?

**해설** 「with + 목적어 + 분사」는 '목적어가 ~한 채'로의 의미를 나타내는 with 분사구문이다. 목적어 you와 watch의 관계가 능동이고, watch의 목적어 me가 있으므로 현재분사로 써야 한다. 따라서 정답은 ② watching이다.

**어휘** relaxed 마음이 편한

**정답** ②

## 235 문법포인트 | Point 33. 분사구문

The house is composed of a series of concrete slabs that ① lean slightly on each level. From street view, the concrete roof ② is folded down to create a sculptural element while also protecting the home from the western sun and ③ providing privacy for the overlooked site. Internally, the visible concrete construction is contrasted with refined and polished materials. Openings, recesses, doors, stairs and wall panels are made of warm timber finishes, ④ complementing by pockets of soft, natural light from skylights, as well as full-height glazing.

**해설**
④ 분사 complementing의 의미상의 주어는 주절의 주어인 Openings, recesses, doors, stairs and wall panels이다. 이 주어가 보완되는 수동의 의미이며, complement는 타동사인데 뒤에 목적어가 없으므로 과거분사인 complemented가 되어야 한다. (complementing → complemented)
① 관계대명사 that의 선행사가 slabs로 복수 명사이므로 동사 lean 역시 복수형으로 바르게 쓰였다. Point 27. 주어 - 동사 수 일치
② 주어인 the concrete roof가 접히는 수동의 의미이므로 수동태로 바르게 쓰였다. 타동사 fold의 목적어가 없는 것으로도 수동태가 되어야 함을 알 수 있다. Point 16. 능동태 vs. 수동태 구분
③ providing은 앞의 protecting과 등위접속사 and로 바르게 병렬되었다. Point 39. 등위접속사의 병렬 구조

**어휘** slab 판  refined 고상한  polished 세련된  opening 창
recess 우묵한 곳  timber 목재  finish 마감재  pocket 작은 공간
skylight 천창  glazing 창유리

**정답** ④

## 236 문법포인트 | Point 34. 형용사 vs. 부사

He says the day will not be far away when all the poor will be economically happy.

**해설** 형용사 happy를 수식하기 위해서는 부사가 와야 하므로 정답은 ④ economically이다.

**어휘** far away 멀리에  economy 경제  economical 경제적인
economic 경제의  economically 경제적으로

**정답** ④

## 237 문법포인트 | Point 01. 문장의 구성 / Point 33. 분사구문

Despite his reservations, John decided ① to accept the job offer from the prestigious law firm. The salary, benefits, and location of the office ② were also factors that influenced his decision. John, ③ having reviewed the contract thoroughly, signed it confidently, ④ know it was a step towards his career goals.

**해설**
④ 문장의 동사는 signed이므로 접속사 없이 다시 동사가 나올 수 없다. 문맥상 분사구문이 적절하다. 문장의 주어인 John과 능동의 관계이므로 현재분사형인 knowing으로 고쳐야 한다. (know → knowing)
① decide는 to부정사를 목적어로 취하는 완전타동사이므로 to accept가 바르게 쓰였다. Point 06. 완전타동사와 동작의 목적어
② 주어가 The salary, benefits, and location으로 복수이므로 동사 역시 복수형인 were가 바르게 쓰였다. Point 27. 주어 - 동사 수 일치
③ 기준 시제는 signed로 과거이고, 의미상의 주어가 John이고 John이 sign하기 이전에 재검토를 마쳤다는 의미이므로 완료 분사구문이 바르게 쓰였다. Point 33. 분사구문

**어휘** reservation 의구심  prestigious 명망 있는  benefit 수당
location 위치  contract 계약서  thoroughly 철저하게
confidently 확신을 가지고

**정답** ④

## DAY 16

**238** 밑줄 친 부분에 들어갈 말로 가장 적절한 것은?

> The new smartphone battery lasts _____ the original model's battery.

① as four times long as
② as long as four times
③ four times as long as
④ four times longer as

**239** 밑줄 친 부분 중 어법상 옳지 않은 것은?

> A cash register records every sale and prevents store clerks ① from putting money into their own pockets. The first one ② invented by US tavern keeper James Ritty in 1879, displaying the money paid on a dial and ③ recording it by punching a paper roll. It wasn't easy to use, and cash registers caught on only after coal merchant John Patterson bought the idea. As well as improving it, he set up the world's first professional sales force ④ to sell it.

**240** 밑줄 친 부분 중 어법상 옳지 않은 것은?

> It seems to me ① that I can hardly pick up a magazine nowadays ② without encountering someone's view on our colleges. ③ Most of the writer are critical; they contend that the colleges are not doing a good job, and they question the value of a college education. Less often, a champion ④ arises to argue that a college degree is worthwhile.

## 238 　문법포인트 | Point 37. 비교 사용 표현

The new smartphone battery lasts four times as long as the original model's battery.

[해설] '몇 배만큼 ~하다'라는 의미를 전달하기 위해서는 배수사를 앞에 넣고 뒤에 원급 비교 또는 비교급 비교를 넣는다. 따라서 배수사 뒤에 원급이 쓰인 ③ four times as long as가 정답이다.

[어휘] last 지속되다 　 original 원래의

[정답] ③

## 239 　문법포인트 | Point 01. 문장의 구성 / Point 16. 능동태 vs. 수동태 구분

A cash register records every sale and prevents store clerks ① from putting money into their own pockets. The first one ② invented by US tavern keeper James Ritty in 1879, displaying the money paid on a dial and ③ recording it by punching a paper roll. It wasn't easy to use, and cash registers caught on only after coal merchant John Patterson bought the idea. As well as improving it, he set up the world's first professional sales force ④ to sell it.

[해설]
② one은 앞의 cash register를 가리키는 부정대명사이다. 이 cash register가 발명하는 것이 아니라 발명된 것이고 뒤에 목적어가 없이 수동태 행위자를 의미하는 by 전치사구가 왔으므로 수동태인 was invented로 고쳐야 한다. (invented → was invented)
① from putting은 앞의 prevent 동사와 함께 「prevent + 목적어 + from -ing」의 형태로 '목적어가 ~하는 것을 막다, 저지하다'라는 의미를 바르게 표현하였다. Point 07. 완전타동사와 함께 사용되는 주요 전치사
③ 두 개의 분사구문 displaying ~과 recording ~이 등위접속사 and로 바르게 병렬되었다. 금전 등록기가 거래를 기록한다는 능동의 의미이므로 현재분사형 분사구문이 바르게 쓰였다. Point 39. 등위접속사의 병렬 구조 / Point 33. 분사구문
④ '그것을 팔기 위해'라는 뜻의 목적을 나타내는 to부정사의 부사적 용법이 바르게 쓰였다. Point 29. to부정사의 역할

[어휘] cash register 금전 등록기 　 prevent 막다 　 store clerk 점원
　 tavern 선술집 　 keeper 주인 　 punch 구멍을 뚫다
　 catch on 인기를 얻다 　 coal 석탄 　 merchant 상인 　 set up 꾸리다
　 sales force 영업 인력

[정답] ②

## 240 　문법포인트 | Point 27. 주어 - 동사 수 일치

It seems to me ① that I can hardly pick up a magazine nowadays ② without encountering someone's views on our colleges. ③ Most of the writer are critical; they contend that the colleges are not doing a good job, and they question the value of a college education. Less often, a champion ④ arises to argue that a college degree is worthwhile.

[해설]
③ Most는 부분사로 of 뒤에 나오는 명사에 따라 단수, 복수가 결정된다. 뒤에 복수 동사(are)가 사용되고 있으므로, most of 뒤에 명사의 복수형이 쓰여야 함을 알 수 있다. 따라서 Most of the writer가 아니라 Most of the writers가 되어야 옳다. (Most of the writer → Most of the writers)
① It은 가주어이고, that절이 진주어로 바르게 쓰였다. Point 24. 인칭대명사
② 「hardly ~ without -ing」 구문으로 '~하면 거의 언제나 …하게 된다'의 뜻이다. 「never ~ without -ing」로도 쓸 수 있다. 타동사인 encounter가 동명사 형태로 without 뒤에 바르게 쓰였다. Point 31. 준동사 주요 표현
④ '일어나다'를 의미하는 자동사 arise의 단수 형태가 옳게 쓰였다. Point 11. 혼동하기 쉬운 동사의 불규칙 변화

[어휘] hardly 거의 ~ 않는 　 pick up ~을 집어들다
　 encounter 맞닥뜨리다 　 view 견해 　 critical 비판적인
　 contend 주장하다 　 question 의문을 제기하다 　 champion 옹호자
　 arise 나타나다 　 argue 주장하다 　 worthwhile 가치 있는

[정답] ③

**241** 밑줄 친 부분에 들어갈 말로 가장 적절한 것은?

> The concert tickets _____ to lucky winners of the radio contest last Sunday.

① handed out  ② will hand out
③ were handed out  ④ will be handed out

**242** 밑줄 친 부분 중 어법상 옳지 않은 것은?

> The first question that most people considering radiation therapy ask ① is "How can radiation kill cancer cells and not kill normal cells?" The answer is surprisingly simple. Although we imagine cancer cells are ② deadly and ③ dangerously, they are actually sick and weak. When pathologists state a cell is malignant, they have identified some abnormal features. Although cancer cells can grow out of control and spread, they are also unable to tolerate radiation ④ as well as normal cells can.

**243** 밑줄 친 부분에 들어갈 말로 가장 적절한 것은?

> These questions need _____ in preparation for the entrance examination.

① solve  ② solving
③ to solve  ④ solved

**244** 밑줄 친 부분 중 어법상 옳은 것은?

> The brand message can be short, but make sure it gives ① all the vital informations. ② Kept this in mind, you should leave the readers ③ impressing, not clueless. Let them know who they are buying from, what they will be buying, and ④ why they should buy it from you. And let them know all this within seconds or a few minutes. This makes your content a powerful tool in the long run.

**241** 문법포인트 | Point 16. 능동태 vs. 수동태 구분 / Point 14. 시제일치와 예외

The concert tickets were handed out to lucky winners of the radio contest last Sunday.

**해설** 사물이 주어이고, 타동사구인 hand out이 목적어 없이 쓰였으므로 수동태가 되어야 한다. last Sunday라는 과거 표현이 있으므로 과거 시제인 ③ were handed out이 정답이다.

**어휘** winner 우승자  hand out 배부하다

정답 ③

**242** 문법포인트 | Point 39. 등위접속사의 병렬 구조 / Point 04. 불완전자동사의 보어

The first question (that most people considering radiation therapy ask) ① is "How can radiation kill cancer cells and not kill normal cells?" The answer is surprisingly simple. Although we imagine cancer cells are ② deadly and ③ dangerously, they are actually sick and weak. When pathologists state a cell is malignant, they have identified some abnormal features. Although cancer cells can grow out of control and spread, they are also unable to tolerate radiation ④ as well as normal cells can.

**해설**
③ cancer cells가 치명적이고 위험하다는 의미로 are의 보어인 deadly와 dangerously가 등위접속사 and로 연결된 병렬 구조이다. be동사의 보어이므로 둘 다 형용사가 와야 한다. dangerously는 부사이므로 dangerous로 고쳐야 한다. (dangerously → dangerous)
① that most people ~ ask는 앞의 The first question을 꾸미는 관계대명사절이며, is는 단수 주어인 The first question의 동사로, 단수형으로 바르게 쓰였다. Point 27. 주어 - 동사 수 일치
② deadly는 '치명적인'이라는 뜻을 가진 형용사이므로 보어로 쓰일 수 있다. Point 35. 주의할 형용사와 부사
④ 「as + 형용사/부사 원급 + as」의 원급 비교 구문으로 동사 tolerate를 수식하므로 부사인 well이 원급으로 바르게 쓰였다. as well as normal cells can (tolerate radiation)의 구문이다. '암세포는 또한 정상 세포가 방사선을 견뎌내는 만큼 잘(훌륭하게) 방사선을 견뎌내지 못한다'라는 의미이다. Point 36. 비교 구문

**어휘** radiation 방사선  therapy 치료  pathologist 병리학자  malignant 악성의  tolerate 견디다

정답 ③

**243** 문법포인트 | Point 30. 준동사의 형태 변화

These questions need solving in preparation for the entrance examination.

**해설** need, want, require는 목적어로 동작의 수동 의미를 표현할 때 to be p.p. 또는 동명사(-ing)로 쓸 수 있다. These questions와 동사 solve의 관계는 수동이므로 빈칸에 ② solving이 와야 한다.

**어휘** in preparation for ~에 대비해  entrance 입학  examination 시험

정답 ②

**244** 문법포인트 | Point 39. 등위접속사의 병렬 구조 / Point 02. 의문문의 어순

The brand message can be short, but make sure it gives ① all the vital informations. ② Kept this in mind, you should leave the readers ③ impressing, not clueless. Let them know [who they are buying from], [what they will be buying], and ④ [why they should buy it from you]. And let them know all this within seconds or a few minutes. This makes your content a powerful tool in the long run.

**해설**
④ Let them know ~에서 know의 목적어로 who ~, what ~ and why ~라는 세 개의 간접의문문이 병렬 구조로 바르게 사용되었다. 또한 간접의문문의 어순도 바르다.
① information은 절대 불가산명사이므로 단수로 사용되어야 한다. (informations → information) Point 21. 명사의 이해
② Kept this in mind는 분사구문인데, 의미상의 주어가 you이며 you가 '기억한다'는 능동의 의미이므로 현재분사가 되어야 한다. (Kept → Keeping) Point 33. 분사구문
③ leave는 분사를 목적격보어로 취하는 동사로 목적어와 목적격보어의 관계가 능동이면 목적격보어로 현재분사를, 수동이면 과거분사를 쓴다. 목적어인 readers가 인상을 받는 수동의 의미이므로 목적격보어 impressing을 impressed로 고쳐야 한다. (impressing → impressed) Point 10. 불완전타동사와 동작의 목적격보어 / Point 32. 현재분사 vs. 과거분사

**어휘** clueless 혼란한  in the long run 결국에는

정답 ④

**245** 밑줄 친 부분에 들어갈 말로 가장 적절한 것은?

> I think that if she had known about the meeting earlier, she would have been able to attend it, _____?

① does she  ② doesn't she
③ would she  ④ wouldn't she

**246** 밑줄 친 부분 중 어법상 옳지 않은 것은?

> The data ① has to be pulled from multiple sources, which can be time-consuming. Therefore, team members have to organize the information themselves to ensure consistency. It's worth ② getting accurate results for the report to maintain credibility. The more precise the data, ③ better the analysis will be, leading to more informed decisions. This thorough process ④ ultimately enhances the overall quality of the project.

**247** 밑줄 친 부분 중 어법상 옳지 않은 것은?

> The committee ① were divided on the proposed changes to the education policy. More members supported integrating technology in classrooms ② than supported sticking with traditional teaching methods. The implications of this ③ highlights the challenges in reaching a consensus on educational reforms. Ultimately, a decision must balance the use of much new ④ equipment with proven instructional practices to benefit students.

**248** 밑줄 친 부분 중 어법상 옳지 않은 것은?

> Addiction is a widespread problem ① that affects people from all walks of life. It often starts with behaviors that may seem no different from ② ours. However, as addiction deepens, its effects become ③ increasingly apparent. Addicts cannot predict the full extent of its impact on their lives and relationships, and neither ④ cannot their family.

## 245 문법포인트 | Point 02. 의문문의 어순

I think that if she had known about the meeting earlier, she would have been able to attend it, wouldn't she?

**해설** 「I think [believe / guess / imagine / suppose / presume] that S+V」의 경우, '내가 생각하기에'를 의미하는 I think는 중요한 의미가 없으므로 that절의 주어와 동사를 기준으로 부가의문문을 만든다. 따라서 주절의 주어 she를 사용하고, 긍정형이므로 조동사 would를 부정형으로 바꾸어 wouldn't로 나타내야 한다. 따라서 정답은 ④ wouldn't she이다.

**어휘** attend 참석하다

**정답** ④

## 246 문법포인트 | Point 37. 비교 사용 표현

The data ① has to be pulled from multiple sources, which can be time-consuming. Therefore, team members have to organize the information themselves to ensure consistency. It's worth ② getting accurate results for the report to maintain credibility. The more precise the data, ③ better the analysis will be, leading to more informed decisions. This thorough process ④ ultimately enhances the overall quality of the project.

**해설**
③ 'S'가 V하면 할수록, S는 더욱 V하다'는 「The 비교급 S' + V', the 비교급 S + V」으로 나타내므로 better를 the better로 고쳐야 한다. (better → the better)
① 주어 The data와 pull의 관계가 수동이고, 목적어가 없으므로 수동 부정사로 써야 한다. 따라서 to부정사의 수동형인 to be p.p.의 형태로 바르게 쓰였다. Point 30. 준동사의 형태 변화
② '~할 만한 가치가 있다'는 「be worth -ing」로 나타내므로 바르게 쓰였다. Point 31. 준동사 주요 표현
④ 부사 ultimately가 동사 enhances를 바르게 수식하고 있다. 참고로 부사는 동사, 형용사, 분사, 부사, 문장 전체를 수식할 수 있다. Point 34. 형용사 vs. 부사

**어휘** ensure 보장하다  consistency 일관성  accurate 정확한  credibility 신뢰성  precise 정확한  analysis 분석  informed 정보에 근거한  thorough 철저한  enhance 높이다  overall 전반적인

**정답** ③

## 247 문법포인트 | Point 27. 주어-동사 수 일치

The committee ① were divided on the proposed changes to the education policy. More members supported integrating technology in classrooms ② than supported sticking with traditional teaching methods. The implications (of this) ③ highlights the challenges in reaching a consensus on educational reforms. Ultimately, a decision must balance the use of much new ④ equipment with proven instructional practices to benefit students.

**해설**
③ 복수형 주어 The implications에 동사의 수를 일치시켜야 하므로 highlights를 highlight로 고쳐야 한다. (highlights → highlight)
① 집합명사 The committee가 위원회의 위원들을 나타낼 수 있고 이때 복수 취급해야 한다. 복수형 동사 were가 바르게 쓰였다. Point 21. 명사의 이해
② 주어(More members)가 비교급으로 쓰였고, 비교 대상을 도입하는 than이 나와서 기술을 통합하는 방식과 전통적 방법 고수를 비교하고 있으므로 than이 바르게 쓰였다. Point 36. 비교 구문
④ equipment는 절대 불가산명사이므로 복수형으로 나타낼 수 없다. 따라서 단수형이 바르게 쓰였다. Point 21. 명사의 이해

**어휘** integrate 통합하다  stick with ~을 고수하다  implication 의미  consensus 합의

**정답** ③

## 248 문법포인트 | Point 35. 주의할 형용사와 부사

Addiction is a widespread problem ① (that affects people from all walks of life). It often starts with behaviors that may seem no different from ② ours. However, as addiction deepens, its effects become ③ increasingly apparent. Addicts cannot predict the full extent of its impact on their lives and neither ④ cannot their family.

**해설**
④ 부정부사는 중복해서 쓰지 않는다. neither와 not이 중복되므로 not을 삭제해야 한다. (neither cannot → neither can)
① that은 problem을 선행사로 하는 주격 관계대명사로 뒤에 불완전한 절이 와서 바르게 쓰였다. Point 43. 관계대명사의 선택
② ours는 our behaviors를 지칭하는 소유대명사이다. Point 24. 인칭대명사
③ 형용사는 부사로 수식해야 한다. 부사 increasingly가 형용사 apparent를 바르게 수식하고 있다. Point 34. 형용사 vs. 부사

**어휘** addiction 중독  apparent 분명한

**정답** ④

**249** 밑줄 친 부분에 들어갈 말로 가장 적절한 것은?

> After the team won the championship, they celebrated by treating _____ to a luxurious dinner.

① itself ② themselves
③ them ④ it

**251** 밑줄 친 부분에 들어갈 말로 가장 적절한 것은?

> As the storm was approaching, they decided to keep _____.

① close the windows
② to close the windows
③ the windows closed
④ the windows closing

**250** 밑줄 친 부분 중 어법상 옳지 않은 것은?

> Through her essay, ① published in *XOJANE*, an online magazine for women, she explained ② how difficult the process of recovering from addiction was. ③ Described herself as having been "miserable" for her entire adolescence, she concluded ④ that she finally got to learn the way to change herself.

**252** 밑줄 친 부분 중 어법상 옳은 것은?

> Colonial apologists often argue that India's ① densely and intricately railway network, one of the largest networks in the world, was built thanks to the British. But the opponents' simple rejoinder, after reiterating that the railways and roads were built ② only to serve British interests, ③ is what "many independent countries have built railways and roads without ④ having to colonize in order to do so."

## 249 문법포인트 | Point 24. 인칭대명사

After the team won the championship, they celebrated by treating themselves to a luxurious dinner.

**해설** treating의 의미상의 주어는 they이다. 그런데 목적어도 they이므로 주어와 목적어가 동일할 때는 목적어로 재귀대명사를 써야 한다. 따라서 ② themselves가 정답이다.

**어휘** championship 선수권 대회   treat 대접하다
luxurious 호화로운

정답 ②

## 250 문법포인트 | Point 33. 분사구문

Through her essay, (① published in *XOJANE*, an online magazine for women,) she explained ② [how difficult the process of recovering from addiction was]. ③ Described herself as having been "miserable" for her entire adolescence, she concluded ④ [that she finally got to learn the way to change herself].

**해설**
③ 의미상 while she described herself as ~의 부사절에서 접속사인 while을 생략하고 동사를 분사로 고쳐 분사구문을 만든 형태이다. 주절의 주어가 she이며 분사구문에서 herself가 목적어인 것을 보아 그녀가 묘사한다는 능동의 분사구문이 되어야 한다. 따라서 과거분사 described가 아니라 현재분사 describing으로 고쳐야 한다. (Described → Describing)

① 분사구문의 분사의 의미상의 주어는 her essay이다. essay가 실렸다는 수동의 의미가 되어야 하므로 과거분사인 published가 바르게 쓰였다. Point 33. 분사구문

② explain의 목적어로 간접의문문이 쓰였다. 주어가 the process of recovering from addiction이며 동사가 was이다. 불완전자동사인 was의 보어로 형용사가 올 수 있으므로 how difficult의 형용사 형태가 바르다. how는 의문부사로 형용사 difficult를 수식하고 있다. Point 02. 의문의 어순

④ that절이 concluded의 목적어 역할을 하는 명사절이다. that 이하가 완전하므로 명사절 접속사 that이 바르게 사용되었다. Point 40. 명사절 접속사의 선택

**어휘** publish (기사를) 싣다   process 과정   recover 회복하다
addiction 중독   describe 묘사하다   miserable 비참한
adolescence 사춘기   conclude 끝맺다

정답 ③

## 251 문법포인트 | Point 10. 불완전타동사와 동작의 목적격보어

As the storm was approaching, they decided to keep the windows closed.

**해설** keep은 목적어와 목적격보어의 관계가 능동이면 현재분사를, 수동이면 과거분사를 목적격보어로 취한다. 창문이 닫혀지는 수동의 의미이므로 ③ the windows closed이 정답이다.

**어휘** storm 폭풍   approach 다가오다

정답 ③

## 252 문법포인트 | Point 29. to부정사의 역할

Colonial apologists often argue that India's ① densely and intricately railway network (→ dense and intricate), one of the largest networks in the world, was built thanks to the British. But the opponents' simple rejoinder, after reiterating that the railways and roads were built ② only to serve British interests, ③ is what (→ that) "many independent countries have built railways and roads without ④ having to colonize (→ having to be colonized) in order to do so]."

**해설**
② 「only to+동사원형」은 '~했으나 결국 …하다'의 의미로, to부정사의 부사적 용법 중 '결과'의 의미로 바르게 쓰였다.

① densely와 intricately는 명사인 railway network를 수식한다. 따라서 형용사가 되어야 한다. (densely and intricately → dense and intricate) Point 34. 형용사 vs. 부사

③ is 뒤의 what ~은 be동사의 보어 역할을 하는 명사절이다. 그러나 what의 뒤에 위치한 절의 형태가 완전하므로 that이 되어야 한다. (what → that) Point 40. 명사절 접속사의 선택

④ 의미상 '그렇게 하기 위해 식민지화되지 않고도 많은 철로와 도로를 건설했다'는 것이므로 colonize는 절의 주어와 수동 관계이므로 능동의 부정사 to colonize를 수동의 부정사로 고쳐야 한다. (having to colonize → having to be colonized) Point 30. 준동사의 형태 변화

**어휘** colonial 식민지의   apologist 옹호론자   argue 주장하다
densely 촘촘하게   intricately 복잡하게   British 영국인들
opponent 반대자   rejoinder 응수   reiterate 반복해서 말하다
serve ~에 도움이 되다   interest 이익   colonize 식민지화하다

정답 ②

**253** 밑줄 친 부분에 들어갈 말로 가장 적절한 것은?

If my friend hadn't pointed out the landmarks, I _____ them.

① would recognize
② would have recognized
③ wouldn't recognize
④ wouldn't have recognized

**254** 밑줄 친 부분 중 어법상 옳은 것은?

The plays I have discussed so far as examples of the new realism actually ① contains elements of two important 19th-century theatrical forms: melodrama and the well-made play. Melodramas involved stock characters such as the young ingenue, the hero, the villain, and ② a great deal of suspense as well as breathtaking stage scenery ③ what included full-scale train crashes, waterfalls, burning forests, and watery caves. In the early 1850s, stage versions of *Uncle Tom's Cabin* sensationally depicted Eva's escape ④ pursuing by Legree and his yapping hounds on the ice floes.

\* ingenue: 순진한 처녀

**255** 밑줄 친 부분 중 어법상 옳지 않은 것은?

She graduated from university with a degree in computer science, ① specializing in artificial intelligence. Her academic achievements and practical skills were enough ② securing a coveted position at a prestigious tech firm known for cutting-edge innovation. Her dedication and expertise were ③ so profound that she quickly became ④ instrumental in developing advanced software solutions for complex problems. Undoubtedly, she earned a reputation for excellence and leadership in her field, contributing significantly to the company's success and technological advancements.

## 253 문법포인트 | Point 46. 기본 가정법

If my friend hadn't pointed out the landmarks, I wouldn't have recognized them.

**해설** If절의 had p.p.로 가정법 과거완료 문장임을 알 수 있으므로 정답은 ④ wouldn't have recognized이다. ②는 긍정으로 문맥상 맞지 않는다.

**어휘** point out 언급하다  landmark 명소  recognize 알아보다

**정답** ④

## 254 문법포인트 | Point 21. 명사의 이해

The plays (I have discussed so far as examples of the new realism) actually ① contains (→ contain) elements of two important 19th-century theatrical forms: melodrama and the well-made play. Melodramas involved stock characters such as the young ingenue, the hero, the villain, and ② a great deal of suspense as well as breathtaking stage scenery ③ what (→ which/that) included full-scale train crashes, waterfalls, burning forests, and watery caves). In the early 1850s, stage versions of *Uncle Tom's Cabin* sensationally depicted Eva's escape (④ pursuing (→ pursued) by Legree and his yapping hounds on the ice floes).

**해설**
② suspense가 불가산명사이므로 양을 의미하는 a great deal of가 바르게 수식하고 있다.
① contains의 주어는 The plays로 복수이므로 복수형인 contain이 되어야 한다. (contains → contain) Point 27. 주어 - 동사 수 일치
③ what은 명사절을 이끄는 접속사이므로 선행사가 있어서는 안 된다. 앞에 선행사 breathtaking stage scenery가 있으므로 what을 which나 that으로 고쳐야 한다. (what → which/that) Point 43. 관계대명사의 선택
④ pursue는 '뒤쫓다'라는 의미로 타동사 pursue의 목적어도 없고 문맥상 '쫓기는'으로 수동의 의미이므로 과거분사인 pursued로 고쳐야 한다. (pursuing → pursued) Point 32. 현재분사 vs. 과거분사

**어휘** stock 상투적인  breathtaking 숨 막힐 정도로 아름다운  full-scale 실물 크기의  sensationally 매우 훌륭하게  yap 요란하게 짖어대다  hound 사냥개  ice floe 부빙

**정답** ②

## 255 문법포인트 | Point 29. to부정사의 역할

She graduated from university with a degree in computer science, ① specializing in artificial intelligence. Her academic achievements and practical skills were enough ② securing (→ to secure) a coveted position at a prestigious tech firm known for cutting-edge innovation. Her dedication and expertise were ③ so profound that she quickly became ④ instrumental in developing advanced software solutions for complex problems. Undoubtedly, she earned a reputation for excellence and leadership in her field, contributing significantly to the company's success and technological advancements.

**해설**
② to부정사의 부사적 용법으로 앞선 형용사인 enough를 수식한다. (securing → to secure)
① specializing의 의미상의 주어가 주절의 주어인 She이고 그녀가 전공했다는 능동의 의미이므로 specializing이 바르게 쓰였다. Point 33. 분사구문
③ '너무 ~해서 …하다'를 의미하는 「so ~ that」의 부사절 접속사가 바르게 쓰였다. Point 41. 부사절 접속사의 선택
④ 불완전자동사인 become의 보어로 형용사 instrumental이 바르게 쓰였다. Point 04. 불완전자동사의 보어

**어휘** secure 얻다  coveted 갈망하는  prestigious 일류의  cutting-edge 최첨단의  dedication 헌신  expertise 전문 지식  profound 심오한  instrumental 중요한  reputation 명성  excellence 우수함  advancement 진보

**정답** ②

**256** 밑줄 친 부분에 들어갈 말로 가장 적절한 것은?

> We suggest _____ all the options before making a decision.

① considering　　② to consider
③ considered　　④ consider

**257** 밑줄 친 부분 중 어법상 옳은 것은?

> The team was busy ① to prepare for the upcoming conference to ensure that every detail was meticulously planned. Anyone with questions should ② contact to the project manager for clarification to avoid any confusion. The preparations ③ are consisted of organizing materials, scheduling sessions, coordinating with speakers, and setting up the venue. For any urgent issues, the office hotline is the primary resource ④ to turn to, providing immediate assistance and support.

**258** 밑줄 친 부분 중 어법상 옳지 않은 것은?

> The recent market trends have shown a significant shift towards sustainable products. Analysts suggested that companies ① should invest more in eco-friendly technologies to stay ② competitive. This recommendation aligns with the growing consumer demand for greener options. However, the guidelines ③ provided are ④ enough ambiguous to allow for various interpretations and implementations.

**259** 밑줄 친 부분 중 어법상 옳지 않은 것은?

> Even after a person recovers from COVID-19, the test results may be positive if the virus is still present in the body in lower concentrations for a ① three-month period after illness onset. Replication-competent virus ② has not been isolated at all from the patient, but it is highly unlikely he/she is infectious. The PCR test is extremely ③ sensitive at detecting the presence of the virus proteins. Hence, the results of COVID-19 PCR tests for the patient who has recovered remain ④ positively for 3 months.

## 256 문법포인트 | Point 06. 완전타동사와 동작의 목적어

We suggest considering all the options before making a decision.

**해설** suggest, recommend, advise 등의 동사는 동명사를 목적어로 취하는 동사이다. 따라서 동명사인 ① considering이 정답이다.

정답 ①

## 257 문법포인트 | Point 29. to부정사의 역할

The team was busy ① to prepare (→ preparing) for the upcoming conference to ensure that every detail was meticulously planned. Anyone with questions should ② contact to (→ contact) the project manager for clarification to avoid any confusion. The preparations ③ are consisted of (→ consist of) organizing materials, scheduling sessions, coordinating with speakers, and setting up the venue. For any urgent issues, the office hotline is the primary resource ④ to turn to, providing immediate assistance and support.

**해설**
④ to부정사의 형용사적 용법으로, 앞의 명사구 the primary resource를 바르게 수식하고 있다. turn to는 '~에 의지하다'라는 뜻이다.
① '~하느라 바쁘다'는 「be busy -ing」로 나타낸다. 따라서 to prepare를 동명사 형태인 preparing으로 고쳐야 한다. (to prepare → preparing) Point 31. 준동사 주요 표현
② contact는 완전타동사이므로 전치사 없이 목적어를 취할 수 있다. 따라서 contact to를 contact로 고쳐야 바르다. (contact to → contact) Point 05. 완전타동사
③ consist는 완전자동사로, 전치사 of와 함께 목적어를 취하지만 수동태로는 나타낼 수 없으므로 are consisted of를 consist of로 고쳐야 한다. (are consisted of → consist of) Point 17. 동사의 유형별 수동태

**어휘** upcoming 다가오는  meticulously 면밀하게  clarification 명확한 설명  confusion 혼란  session 모임  coordinate 조율하다  venue 장소  urgent 긴급한  immediate 즉각적인  assistance 도움

정답 ④

## 258 문법포인트 | Point 34. 형용사 vs. 부사

The recent market trends have shown a significant shift towards sustainable products. Analysts suggested that companies ① should invest more in eco-friendly technologies to stay ② competitive. This recommendation aligns with the growing consumer demand for greener options. However, the guidelines ③ provided are ④ enough ambiguous (→ ambiguous enough) to allow for various interpretations and implementations.

**해설**
④ enough는 형용사나 부사를 뒤에서 수식해야 한다. (enough ambiguous → ambiguous enough)
① 요구, 제안 동사의 목적어가 되는 that절의 동사는 「(should) + 동사원형」의 형태가 되어야 한다. suggest의 목적어가 되는 that절의 동사가 바르게 쓰였다. Point 19. 당위의 조동사 should
② stay는 보어를 취하는 2형식 동사이다. 형용사인 competitive가 보어로 바르게 쓰였다. Point 04. 불완전자동사의 보어
③ guidelines와 이를 수식하는 provided가 제공된다는 수동의 관계이므로 과거분사가 바르게 쓰였다. Point 32. 현재분사 vs. 과거분사

**어휘** significant 상당한  sustainable 지속 가능한  analyst 분석가  competitive 경쟁력 있는  align 일치하다  ambiguous 모호한  interpretation 해석  implementation 실행

정답 ④

## 259 문법포인트 | Point 04. 불완전자동사의 보어

Even after a person recovers from COVID-19, the test results may be positive if the virus is still present in the body in lower concentrations for a ① three-month period after illness onset. Replication-competent virus ② has not been isolated at all from the patient, but it is highly unlikely he/she is infectious. The PCR test is extremely ③ sensitive at detecting the presence of the virus proteins. Hence, the results of COVID-19 PCR tests for the patient who has recovered remain ④ positively (→ positive) for 3 months.

**해설**
④ 불완전자동사 remain은 형용사를 보어로 취하므로 부사인 positively를 형용사 positive로 고쳐야 한다. (positively → positive)
① 명사를 수식하는 측정단위 명사는 단수 취급하므로 period를 수식하는 측정단위 명사 month가 단수로 바르게 쓰였다. Point 35. 주의할 형용사와 부사
② 타동사 isolate가 목적어가 없이 쓰였고 주어인 virus가 '고립되다'라는 의미이므로 수동태가 바르게 쓰였다. Point 16. 능동태 vs. 수동태 구분
③ sensitive는 '민감한'이라는 뜻의 보어로 바르게 쓰였다. 비슷한 단어인 sensible(지각 있는), sensational(선풍적인), sensory(감각의)와 혼동하지 말아야 한다. Point 35. 주의할 형용사와 부사

**어휘** concentration 농도  onset 발병  replication-competent 복제 가능한  isolate 격리시키다  infectious 전염력이 있는  detect 탐지하다  presence 존재

정답 ④

DAY 18　147

**260** 밑줄 친 부분에 들어갈 말로 가장 적절한 것은?

_____ they arrived earlier, they could have seen the beginning of the movie.

① Would  ② Should
③ Were  ④ Had

**261** 밑줄 친 부분 중 어법상 옳은 것은?

Among the best historical sites in Spain ① are the stunning and impressive Mezquita. Most of historians assume the Mosque-Cathedral, a former Islamic mosque ② has converted into a Christian cathedral in the 13th century, ③ was built in 785 CE. ④ Were it not for the alteration of its use, this beautiful building would have been a testament of the religious tolerance in Spain.

**262** 밑줄 친 부분 중 어법상 옳지 않은 것은?

Mistakes can occur at any time, ① whether in personal or professional settings. Handling potentially ② embarrassing situations is essential for maintaining reputation. Neither ignoring mistakes nor ③ overreact to them helps in resolving issues. Addressing them and learning from them will foster growth, ④ whatever challenges may arise.

**263** 밑줄 친 부분 중 어법상 옳지 않은 것은?

Regarding the shooting spree, the fact that 72 percent of innocent victims of the rampage ① were minors was ② the worst part of the incident. We were reminded ③ for the tragic impact of gun violence. Sadly, it is ④ regrettable that gun violence is made all the more deadly with the proliferation of firearms.

## 260 문법포인트 | Point 46. 기본 가정법

Had they arrived earlier, they could have seen the beginning of the movie.

**해설** 주절에 가정법 과거완료 시제인 「조동사 과거형 + have p.p.」가 사용되었다. 과거에 관한 것이므로 조건절도 가정법 과거완료가 되어야 한다. 조건절에서 if가 생략될 경우 「Had + 주어 + p.p.」의 어순이 되어야 하므로 정답은 ④ Had이다.

**정답** ④

## 261 문법포인트 | Point 14. 시제일치와 예외 / Point 16. 능동태 vs. 수동태 구분

(Among the best historical sites in Spain) ① are the stunning and impressive Mezquita. Most of historians assume the Mosque-Cathedral, a former Islamic mosque (② has converted into a Christian cathedral in the 13th century), ③ was built in 785 CE. ④ Were it not for the alteration of its use, this beautiful building would have been a testament of the religious tolerance in Spain.

(→ is)
(→ converted)
(→ Had it not been for)

**해설**
③ 구체적인 연도가 있는 역사적 사실을 언급하므로 과거 시제로 바르게 사용되었다. 또한 주어와 수동 관계이므로 수동태 역시 바르다.
① 장소, 범위의 전치사구가 문두에 와서 1형식 문장의 주어와 동사가 도치되었다. 주어가 단수이므로 are를 is로 고쳐야 한다. (are → is) Point 27. 주어 - 동사 수 일치
② 이 문장의 동사는 was built이므로 has converted는 a former Islamic mosque를 수식하는 분사가 되어야 한다. 수식하는 명사와 수동 관계이므로 과거분사인 converted로 고쳐야 한다. (has converted → converted) Point 01. 문장의 구성
④ '~이 없었다면'을 의미하는 과거 사실에 대해 가정을 하므로 가정법 과거완료 시제가 와야 한다. (Were it not for → Had it not been for) Point 47. 기타 가정법

**어휘** stunning 굉장히 아름다운  mosque 사원  cathedral 성당
assume 추정하다  convert 바꾸다
alteration 변경  testament 증거  tolerance 관용

**정답** ③

## 262 문법포인트 | Point 39. 등위접속사의 병렬 구조

Mistakes can occur at any time, ① whether in personal or professional settings. Handling potentially ② embarrassing situations is essential for maintaining and reputation. Neither ignoring mistakes nor ③ overreact to them helps in resolving issues. Addressing them and learning from them will foster growth, ④ whatever challenges may arise.

(→ overreacting)

**해설**
③ 「neither A nor B」는 'A도 B도 아닌'이라는 뜻의 등위상관접속사이다. overreact는 ignoring과 병렬되어야 하므로 동명사 형태인 overreacting으로 고쳐야 한다. (overreact → overreacting)
① 'A이든 B이든'은 부사절 접속사 「whether A or B」로 나타내므로 바르게 쓰였다. Point 41. 부사절 접속사의 선택
② 감정유발동사 embarrass가 분사 형태로 situations를 수식하고 있다. '당황스러운 감정을 느끼게 하는 상황'의 의미이므로 현재분사로 바르게 쓰였다. Point 32. 현재분사 vs. 과거분사
④ 복합관계형용사 whatever가 명사 challenges를 수식하며 양보의 부사절을 바르게 이끌고 있다. Point 45. 복합관계사

**어휘** potentially 잠재적으로 일어날 수 있는  embarrassing 당혹스러운
reputation 평판  overreact 과민하게 반응하다  foster 촉진하다

**정답** ③

## 263 문법포인트 | Point 17. 동사의 유형별 수동태

Regarding the shooting spree, the fact that 72 percent of innocent victims of the rampage ① were minors was ② the worst part of the incident. We were reminded ③ for the tragic impact of gun violence. Sadly, it is ④ regrettable that gun violence is made all the more deadly with the proliferation of firearms.

(→ of)
(가주어 / 진주어)

**해설**
③ 「remind A of B」는 수동태 전환 시 「A be reminded of B」의 구조가 된다. 따라서 for가 아니라 of로 고쳐야 한다. (for → of)
① percent는 부분사이므로 「percent of + 명사」의 경우 명사에 수 일치하므로 주어인 victims에 맞게 복수형 동사가 바르게 쓰였다. Point 27. 주어 - 동사 수 일치
② 최상급에는 the를 붙여야 한다. Point 36. 비교 구문
④ regrettable은 '유감스러운'이고, regretful은 '후회하는'의 뜻인데, 여기서는 문맥상 유감을 의미하므로 regrettable이 옳다. Point 35. 주의할 형용사와 부사

**어휘** shooting spree 총기 난사  innocent 무고한  rampage 광란
incident 사건  violence 폭력  regrettable 유감스러운
deadly 치명적인  proliferation 확산  firearms (pl.)총기

**정답** ③

**264** 밑줄 친 부분에 들어갈 말로 가장 적절한 것은?

> I wish we _____ the opportunity when it was offered.

① seize
② will seize
③ have seized
④ had seized

**265** 밑줄 친 부분 중 옳지 않은 것은?

> All complaints must be acknowledged in writing ① no later than three working days after receiving it. The acknowledgement will give the name and contact details of the person who will deal with the complaint. Complaints will usually ② investigate either by the staff who have been dealing with the complainant or by the local manager with direct responsibility for the case or service in question. If this is not appropriate, ③ they will be ④ referred to the Designated Complaints Officer.

**266** 밑줄 친 부분 중 어법상 옳지 않은 것은?

> The National Museum of Korea displays ① 115 pieces of earthenware from many Asian countries. The exhibits not only reflect a typical Asian style of living but also ② reveals the different characteristics of diverse Asian ethnic groups; Southeast Asian potteries ③ were suitable for hot and humid weather; South Asian potteries ④ were made for folk customs such as marriage and burial.

**267** 밑줄 친 부분 중 어법상 옳지 않은 것은?

> Almost 20% of the Amazon rainforest ① has been disappeared since the 1970s. Last year, deforestation exceeded 2.47 million acres. We are now in a do-or-die moment when it comes to ② protecting this precious ecosystem. Brazil is a large country spanning 3.2 million square miles, and has plenty of biodiversity. The rich way the climate, plants, animals and people are tied to the lands ③ has always given me a sense of purpose. As a plant ecologist I have spent a lot of time ④ carrying out plant inventories deep in the Amazon.

## 문장 분석 및 해설

**264** 문법포인트 | Point 47. 기타 가정법

I wish we had seized the opportunity when it was offered.

[해설] I wish 가정법 문장에서 과거 시점을 나타내는 when it was offered 절이 있으므로 I wish 가정법 과거완료 시제인 「I wish + 주어 + had p.p.」가 되어야 한다. 따라서 정답은 ④ had seized이다.

[어휘] seize 잡다

[정답] ④

**265** 문법포인트 | Point 16. 능동태 vs. 수동태 구분

All complaints must be acknowledged in writing ① no later than three working days after receiving it. The acknowledgement will give the name and contact details of the person who will deal with the complaint. Complaints will usually ② investigate either by the staff who have been dealing with the complainant or by the local manager with direct responsibility for the case or service in question. If this is not appropriate, ③ they will be ④ referred to the Designated Complaints Officer.

(→ be investigated)

[해설]
② 주어 Complaints와 investigate는 민원이 조사되는 수동의 관계이므로 수동태가 되어야 한다. 또한 타동사인 investigate가 목적어 없이 쓸 수 없는 것으로도 수동태가 되어야 함을 알 수 있다. 따라서 investigate를 be investigated로 고쳐야 한다. (investigate → be investigated)
① 「no later than ~」은 '늦어도 ~까지는'을 의미하는 표현으로 시점 명사 앞에 바르게 쓰였다. Point 37. 비교 사용 표현
③ they는 앞의 Complaints를 지칭하는 대명사이므로 복수형이 바르다. Point 24. 인칭대명사
④ 'A를 B에게 위탁하다'를 의미하는 「refer A to B」의 표현이 수동태로 사용된 경우이므로 「A be referred to B」의 형태로 바르게 쓰였다. Point 17. 동사의 유형별 수동태

[어휘] acknowledge ~의 접수를 알리다   receive 접수하다
acknowledgement 접수 확인(서)   complainant 민원인
direct 직접적인   investigate 조사하다

[정답] ②

**266** 문법포인트 | Point 39. 등위접속사의 병렬 구조

The National Museum of Korea displays ① 115 pieces of earthenware from many Asian countries. The exhibits not only reflect a typical Asian style of living but also ② reveals the different characteristics of diverse Asian ethnic groups; Southeast Asian potteries ③ were suitable for hot and humid weather; South Asian potteries ④ were made for folk customs such as marriage and burial.

(→ reveal)

[해설]
② 「not only A but also B」에서 A와 B의 문법적 구조는 같아야 한다. not only 다음이 동사인 reflect이므로 but also 뒤에도 동사인 reveals가 나왔다. 그러나 주어가 The exhibits로 복수이므로 reveals는 복수 형태인 reveal로 고쳐야 한다. (reveals → reveal)
① earthenware는 흙으로 만들어진 그릇, 즉 토기를 의미하며 불가산명사인 물질명사이므로 단위명사인 piece를 사용하여 수를 바르게 표기하였다. Point 21. 명사의 이해
③ 「be suitable for + 명사」는 '~에 적합하다'를 의미한다. 주어가 potteries이므로 동사 were가 바르게 쓰였다. Point 27. 주어-동사 수 일치
④ potteries가 민속 풍습을 위해 '만들어지는' 것을 의미하므로 were made라는 수동태가 바르게 쓰였다. Point 16. 능동태 vs. 수동태 구분

[어휘] earthenware 토기

[정답] ②

**267** 문법포인트 | Point 17. 동사의 유형별 수동태

Almost 20% of the Amazon rainforest ① has been disappeared since the 1970s. Last year, deforestation exceeded 2.47 million acres. We are now in a do-or-die moment when it comes to ② protecting this precious ecosystem. Brazil is a large country spanning 3.2 million square miles, and has plenty of biodiversity. The rich way (the climate, plants, animals and people are tied to the lands) ③ has always given me a sense of purpose. As a plant ecologist I have spent a lot of time ④ carrying out plant inventories deep in the Amazon.

(→ has disappeared)

[해설]
① disappear는 자동사로 수동태로 쓸 수 없다. 따라서 능동태로 고쳐야 한다. 뒤에 since가 나와 현재완료 시제는 바르게 사용되었다. (has been disappeared → has disappeared)
② when it comes to의 to는 전치사이므로 목적어로 동명사 protecting이 바르게 쓰였다. Point 48. 전치사의 목적어
③ 동사 has의 주어는 The rich way로 단수이다. 따라서 단수 동사인 has가 바르게 쓰였다. Point 27. 주어 - 동사 수 일치
④ '~하는 데 (돈/시간)을 쓰다'의 준동사 주요 표현인 「spend + 시간/돈 + (in) -ing」가 바르게 쓰였다. Point 31. 준동사 주요 표현

[어휘] deforestation 삼림벌채   do-or-die 중대한
span ~에 걸쳐 이어지다   ecologist 생태학자   inventory 목록

[정답] ①

**268** 밑줄 친 부분에 들어갈 말로 가장 적절한 것은?

> A number of books _____ recently, each of them exploring different aspects of the topic.

① has published  ② have published
③ has been published  ④ have been published

**270** 밑줄 친 부분 중 어법상 옳은 것은?

> It's truly generous ① for people to offer their time and resources to help others in need. Whether it's volunteering at a local shelter or ② assist a neighbor with yard work, these acts of kindness make a difference in communities. Getting a job ③ doing with dedication and compassion shows the power of collective effort. ④ Seeing that everyone benefits from such selfless actions, it reinforces the importance of empathy and community support.

**269** 밑줄 친 부분 중 어법상 옳지 않은 것은?

> The future of renewable energy development ① presents significant challenges, as they ② are highlighted in two recent articles. Scientists have noted promising trends that ③ underscore the ongoing importance of renewable energy sources. Both articles stress the crucial role of innovation and supportive policies in advancing green technologies. Governments and industries alike face complex issues ④ to deal in transitioning to a cleaner and more efficient energy landscape.

## 268 문법포인트 | Point 27. 주어-동사 수 일치 / Point 16. 능동태 vs. 수동태 구분

A number of books have been published recently, each of them exploring different aspects of the topic.

**해설** 주어가 복수이므로 복수 동사가 필요하다. A number of는 복수 명사를 수식하고 복수 취급한다. 또한 publish는 타동사인데 목적어가 없이 쓰였고, 주어와의 관계가 책이 출판되는 것이므로 수동태가 되어야 한다. 따라서 ④ have been published가 정답이다.

**어휘** a number of 수많은  explore 탐구하다  aspect 측면  publish 출판하다

**정답** ④

## 269 문법포인트 | Point 29. to부정사의 역할

The future of renewable energy development ① presents significant challenges, as they ② are highlighted in two recent articles. Scientists have noted promising trends that ③ underscore the ongoing importance of renewable energy sources. Both articles stress the crucial role of innovation and supportive policies in advancing green technologies. Governments and industries alike face complex issues ④ to deal in transitioning to a cleaner and more efficient energy landscape.

**해설**
④ to부정사가 수식하는 명사가 to부정사의 의미상의 목적어이고 to부정사의 동사가 자동사인 경우 의미에 맞는 전치사를 써 주어야 한다. issues가 to deal의 의미상의 목적어이고 deal이 자동사이며 '~을 다루다'는 뜻으로 with와 함께 쓰이므로 with를 써 주어야 한다. (to deal → to deal with)
① presents의 주어는 The future로 단수이다. 따라서 단수 동사가 바르게 쓰였다. Point 27. 주어 - 동사 수 일치
② they는 앞의 significant challenges를 가리키며 이것이 강조된다는 수동의 의미이므로 수동태로 바르게 쓰였다. Point 16. 능동태 vs. 수동태 구분
③ 선행사인 trends가 복수이므로 관계절의 동사인 underscore도 복수 형태로 잘 쓰였다. Point 27. 주어 - 동사 수 일치

**어휘** renewable energy 재생 가능 에너지  significant 중요한  challenge 어려움  highlight 강조하다  article 기사  promising 유망한  underscore 강조하다  crucial 중요한  innovation 혁신  deal with ~을 다루다  transition 이행하다  efficient 효율적인

**정답** ④

## 270 문법포인트 | Point 41. 부사절 접속사의 선택

It's truly generous ① for people to offer their time and resources to help others in need. Whether it's volunteering at a local shelter or ② assist a neighbor with yard work, these acts of kindness make a difference in communities. Getting a job ③ doing with dedication and compassion shows the power of collective effort. ④ Seeing that everyone benefits from such selfless actions, it reinforces the importance of empathy and community support.

**해설**
④ Seeing that은 '~인 것으로 보아'의 뜻으로 이유를 나타내는 부사절 접속사이며, 문장에서 바르게 쓰였다.
① for people은 to부정사 to offer의 의미상의 주어이다. 앞에 인성형용사 generous가 있으므로 for people을 of people로 고쳐야 바르다. (for people → of people) Point 30. 준동사의 형태 변화
② assist가 volunteering과 A or B(A이든 B이든)의 형태로 병렬되었으므로 동명사 형태인 assisting으로 고쳐야 한다. (assist → assisting) Point 39. 등위접속사의 병렬 구조
③ 불완전타동사 get은 목적어와 목적격보어의 관계가 수동이면 목적격보어에 과거분사를 쓴다. 목적어 a job과 목적격보어가 수동의 관계이므로 doing을 과거분사 형태인 done으로 고쳐야 한다. (doing → done) Point 10. 불완전타동사와 동작의 목적격보어

**어휘** shelter 보호소  dedication 헌신  compassion 동정심  selfless 이타적인

**정답** ④

**271** 밑줄 친 부분에 들어갈 말로 가장 적절한 것은?

> She donated _____ money to the charity organization to support their humanitarian efforts.

① few
② a few
③ a number of
④ a large amount of

**273** 밑줄 친 부분에 들어갈 말로 가장 적절한 것은?

> The company, _____ CEO is known for his innovative ideas, has seen significant growth this year.

① whose
② that
③ which
④ of which

**272** 밑줄 친 부분 중 어법상 옳지 않은 것은?

> It was ① quite amazing an achievement for the team to complete the project ahead of schedule. The challenging requirements did not discourage them ② from putting in extra hours to ensure quality. Some members focused on the technical aspects, ③ while others handled the project management and client communication. ④ What distinguished this project from others was its innovative approach and collaborative effort.

**274** 밑줄 친 부분 중 어법상 옳지 않은 것은?

> If ① there were more awareness about how noise affects productivity, workplaces would be more efficient. Understanding different preferences for background noise is crucial for creating a harmonious environment. ② Essentially though music is for relaxation, it should not be too loud when others are working nearby. Some people need silence to concentrate, and loud music can be a major distraction. The audience ③ don't always appreciate background noise, so it's important ④ to consider everyone's needs.

## 271 문법포인트 | Point 21. 명사의 이해

She donated a large amount of money to the charity organization to support their humanitarian efforts.

**[해설]** money는 불가산명사이므로 수를 나타내는 few, a few, a number of 등의 수식을 받을 수 없다. 양을 의미하는 단어가 들어가야 하므로 ④ a large amount of가 정답이다.

**[어휘]** donate 기부하다  charity 자선  organization 단체
humanitarian 인도주의적인

**[정답]** ④

## 272 문법포인트 | Point 23. 관사의 위치

It was ① quite amazing an achievement for the team to complete the project ahead of schedule. The challenging requirements did not discourage them ② from putting in extra hours to ensure quality. Some members focused on the technical aspects, ③ while others handled the project management and client communication. ④ [What distinguished this project from others] was its innovative approach and collaborative effort.
→ quite an amazing achievement

**[해설]**
① 부사 quite와 함께 쓸 때 관사의 위치는 「quite + a/an + 형용사 + 명사」의 순으로 써야 한다. 따라서 quite an amazing achievement로 고쳐야 바르다. (quite amazing an achievement → quite an amazing achievement)
② 'A가 ~하는 것을 막다'는 「discourage A from -ing」로 나타낸다. 따라서 from putting이 바르게 쓰였다. Point 07. 완전타동사와 함께 사용되는 주요 전치사
③ while이 완전한 절을 이끌고 있으므로 부사절 접속사 while이 바르게 쓰였다. Point 41. 부사절 접속사의 선택
④ 문장의 동사는 was이고, 주어절을 이끌 수 있는 명사절 접속사가 필요하다. What 뒤에 불완전한 절이 왔고, 선행사가 없으므로 명사절 접속사 what이 바르게 쓰였다. Point 40. 명사절 접속사의 선택

**[어휘]** achievement 성과  complete 완료하다
ahead of schedule 예정보다 빨리  challenging 어려운
discourage A from B A가 B하는 것을 막다
put in (시간, 노력을) 들이다  distinguish 구별하다
innovative 혁신적인  collaborative 협력적인

**[정답]** ①

## 273 문법포인트 | Point 43. 관계대명사의 선택

The company, (whose CEO is known for his innovative ideas,) has seen significant growth this year.

**[해설]** 주어 뒤에 완전한 절이 삽입되었다. 주어인 The company와 삽입절의 주어 CEO는 문맥상 소유의 관계가 성립하므로 소유격 관계대명사인 ① whose가 들어가야 한다.

**[어휘]** innovative 획기적인  significant 상당한

**[정답]** ①

## 274 문법포인트 | Point 42. 주요 양보구문

If ① there were more awareness about how noise affects productivity, workplaces would be more efficient. Understanding different preferences for background noise is crucial for creating a harmonious environment. ② Essentially though music is for relaxation, it should not be too loud when others are working nearby. Some people need silence to concentrate, and loud music can be a major distraction. The audience ③ don't always appreciate background noise, so it's important ④ to consider everyone's needs.
→ Essential

**[해설]**
② 「(As) 명사(무관사)/형용사/부사/분사 + as / though +S+V」 형태의 양보구문으로, '비록 ~이지만'을 뜻한다. 동사 is의 보어가 되어야 하므로 부사 Essentially를 형용사 Essential로 고쳐야 한다. (Essentially → Essential)
① 주절이 가정법 과거 시제이므로 가정법 과거의 if절에 be동사가 쓰일 경우 인칭과 수에 관계없이 were가 쓰이므로 there were가 바르게 쓰였다. Point 46. 기본 가정법
③ 집합명사 audience가 '청중들'을 지칭해 복수 취급할 수 있으므로 복수형 조동사 don't가 바르게 쓰였다. Point 21. 명사의 이해 / Point 27. 주어-동사 수 일치
④ it이 가주어이고 to부정사인 to consider가 진주어로 사용되었다. to부정사는 명사 역할을 하여 주어로 사용될 수 있으므로 바르게 쓰였다. Point 29. to부정사의 역할

**[어휘]** awareness 인식  productivity 생산성  efficient 효율적인
preference 선호  harmonious 조화로운  relaxation 휴식
concentrate 집중하다  distraction 방해 요소
appreciate 고마워하다

**[정답]** ②

**275** 밑줄 친 부분에 들어갈 말로 가장 적절한 것은?

> She referred to him _____ her mentor, acknowledging his guidance and support throughout her career.

① of  ② for
③ as  ④ so

**276** 밑줄 친 부분 중 어법상 옳지 않은 것은?

> ① Being unexpectedly warm for this time of the year, people should remember ② to enjoy outdoor activities while they can. It's ③ such a good chance to go for a hike, have a picnic in the park, or simply soak up the sunshine. Taking advantage of these pleasant conditions allows everyone ④ to recharge and appreciate nature's beauty.

**277** 밑줄 친 부분 중 어법상 옳은 것은?

> While a defendant was in jail, her landlord called the police because rent ① had not been paid and he detected a disagreeable odor from the defendant's apartment. The police thought of the stench from the defendant's apartment ② for that of decomposing flesh and, without waiting to obtain a warrant and using the landlord's passkey, ③ entering the apartment. The police found a large trunk in the bedroom, ④ which they assumed there was a dead body.

**278** 밑줄 친 부분 중 어법상 옳은 것은?

> Cold temperatures can reduce our perception of taste, for our taste buds like many other parts of our body ① doesn't function as well in colder conditions. Cold food or drink can numb the taste buds, ② what makes your food taste ③ like a metal spoon, for example. Additionally, the sense of smell is actually affected by cold temperatures as much as ④ those of taste, and they can be said to be correlated.

**275** 문법포인트 | Point 09. 불완전타동사의 목적격보어

She referred to him as her mentor, acknowledging his guidance and support throughout her career.

해설 '~을 …라고 부르다'는 「refer to + 목적어 + as + 목적격보어」로 나타내므로 정답은 ③ as이다.

어휘 acknowledge 인정하다   guidance 지도

정답 ③

**276** 문법포인트 | Point 33. 분사구문

① Being unexpectedly warm for this time of the year, people should remember ② to enjoy outdoor activities while they can. It's ③ such a good chance to go for a hike, have a picnic in the park, or simply soak up the sunshine. Taking advantage of these pleasant conditions allows everyone ④ to recharge and appreciate nature's beauty.

해설
① 분사구문의 의미상의 주어와 주절의 주어가 다르므로 의미상의 주어를 써 주어야 한다. 문맥상 날씨를 말하므로 It을 써 주어야 한다. (Being → It being)
② 기억동사의 목적어로 to부정사가 오면 미래에 할 일을 의미한다. 야외활동을 즐기는 일을 기억한다는 뜻이므로 to부정사가 remember의 목적어로 바르게 쓰였다. Point 06. 완전타동사와 동작의 목적어
③ such 뒤에 명사가 오는 경우 「such + 부정관사 + 형용사 + 명사」의 어순을 써야 한다. such a good chance가 바른 어순으로 쓰였다. Point 23. 관사의 위치
④ allow는 목적격보어로 to부정사를 취한다. 목적격보어로 to부정사인 to recharge and appreciate가 바르게 쓰였다. Point 10. 불완전타동사와 동작의 목적격보어

어휘 unexpectedly 예상치 못하게   soak up 흡수하다
take advantage of ~을 이용하다   conditions (pl.) 날씨
appreciate 감상하다

정답 ①

**277** 문법포인트 | Point 16. 능동태 vs. 수동태 구분 / Point 12. 완료 시제

While a defendant was in jail, her landlord called the police because rent ① had not been paid and he detected a disagreeable odor from the defendant's apartment. The police thought of the stench from the defendant's apartment ② for that of decomposing flesh and, (without waiting to obtain a warrant and using the landlord's passkey), ③ entering the apartment. The police found a large trunk in the bedroom, ④ which they assumed there was a dead body).

해설
① rent와 pay는 수동의 관계이므로 수동태로 써야 한다. 또한 경찰을 부른 것보다 집세가 지불되지 않은 상태가 더 이전이므로 과거완료 수동태가 바르게 사용되었다.
② 「think of A as B」는 'A를 B로 간주하다'라는 뜻이므로 for를 as로 고쳐야 한다. (for → as) Point 09. 불완전타동사의 목적격보어
③ and를 통해 thought of와 병렬 구조를 이루고 있으므로 과거 동사 entered로 고쳐야 한다. (entering → entered) Point 39. 등위접속사의 병렬 구조
④ the bedroom이라는 장소를 부연 설명하는 관계절이 올 수 있다. 뒤에 완전한 절이 왔으므로 which를 장소의 관계부사로 고쳐야 한다. (which → where) Point 44. 관계부사

어휘 defendant 피고   landlord 집주인   disagreeable 불쾌한
stench 악취   decompose 부패하다

정답 ①

**278** 문법포인트 | Point 04. 불완전자동사의 보어

Cold temperatures can reduce our perception of taste, for our taste buds like many other parts of our body ① doesn't function as well in colder conditions. Cold food or drink can numb the taste buds, ② what makes your food taste ③ like a metal spoon, for example. Additionally, the sense of smell is actually affected by cold temperatures as much as ④ those of taste, and they can be said to be correlated.

해설
③ 감각동사의 보어로 명사가 올 때는 전치사 like를 써야 한다. taste의 보어로 like a metal spoon이 바르게 쓰였다.
① 주어가 our taste buds로 복수이므로 doesn't를 복수형인 don't로 고쳐야 한다. (doesn't function → don't function) Point 27. 주어 - 동사 수 일치
② 완전한 절 뒤에 what이 이끄는 명사절이 올 수 없고, 문맥상 앞 절을 which로 받는 관계대명사의 계속적 용법이 오는 것이 적절하다. (what → which) Point 43. 관계대명사의 선택
④ the sense of smell과 the sense of taste를 비교하고 있는데 뒤에서 반복되는 the sense는 단수이므로 단수 대명사인 that으로 받아야 한다. (those → that) Point 38. 비교대상의 일치

어휘 temperature 온도   perception 지각   taste bud 미뢰
function 작동하다   numb 마비시키다
correlated 상관관계가 있는

정답 ③

DAY 19   157

**279** 밑줄 친 부분에 들어갈 말로 가장 적절한 것은?

> The ancient manuscript is as _____ any other artifact in the museum's collection.

① significant
② significant as
③ more significant as
④ more significant than

**280** 밑줄 친 부분 중 어법상 옳지 않은 것은?

> Since the company's recent restructuring, there ① has been a strong insistence on exploring new opportunities for growth and innovation, urging my team ② to embrace these changes and adapt to our dynamic environment. By staying proactive and open to innovation, we ensure our relevance in an ever-evolving market landscape. Belonging to a forward-thinking team not only keeps us competitive but also ③ positions us to lead in our industry with ④ innovatively solutions and approaches.

**281** 밑줄 친 부분 중 어법상 옳은 것은?

> The elephants, ① the largest mammal of all the land creatures, is known for their remarkable intelligence and intricate social behaviors. Sadly, many elephant habitats have been lost ② because human encroachment and habitat destruction, resulting in significant declines in wild populations. ③ Protect elephants from the illegal ivory trade remains ④ crucially for their conservation efforts in Africa and Asia.

**282** 밑줄 친 부분 중 어법상 옳지 않은 것은?

> No sooner ① did the exploratory team launch the craft than it hit a rock and was shattered. All of the baggage save the pack containing food and drinking water ② was lost. One of them must have clung unconsciously to the pack ③ whose loss they would have felt ④ most severely.

## 문장 분석 및 해설

**279** 문법포인트 | Point 36. 비교 구문

The ancient manuscript is as significant as any other artifact in the museum's collection.

**[해설]** 두 개의 대상이 서로 동등함을 표현할 때 사용하는 원급 비교는 「A + as + 형용사·부사 원급 + as + B」로 나타내며, 'A는 B만큼 ~하다'의 뜻이다. 따라서 정답은 ② significant as이다.

**[어휘]** manuscript 사본   artifact 유물   collection 수집품

[정답] ②

**280** 문법포인트 | Point 34. 형용사 vs. 부사

Since the company's recent restructuring, there ① has been a strong insistence on exploring new opportunities for growth and innovation, urging my team ② to embrace these changes and adapt to our dynamic environment. By staying proactive and open to innovation, we ensure our relevance in an ever-evolving market landscape. Belonging to a forward-thinking team not only keeps us competitive but also ③ positions us to lead in our industry with ④ innovatively solutions and approaches.
→ innovative

**[해설]**
④ innovatively가 뒤의 solutions and approaches를 수식하고 있다. 그러나 명사를 수식할 수 있는 것은 형용사이므로 형용사인 innovative로 고쳐야 한다. (innovatively → innovative)
① 「since + 과거시점」이 와서 주절에 현재완료 시제가 바르게 사용되었다. Point 12. 완료 시제
② urge는 목적격보어에 to부정사를 취한다. to embrace가 urge의 목적격보어로 바르게 쓰였다. Point 10. 불완전타동사와 동작의 목적격보어
③ 등위상관접속사로 연결되는 요소는 문법적으로 같아야 한다. 「not only A but also B」의 등위상관접속사로 두 개의 동사 keeps와 positions가 바르게 연결되었다. Point 39. 등위접속사의 병렬 구조

**[어휘]** restructuring 구조조정   insistence 주장   embrace 수용하다   adapt 적응하다   dynamic 역동적인   proactive 적극적인   relevance 관련성(존재 가치)   forward-thinking 미래지향적인   competitive 경쟁력 있는   innovative 혁신적인

[정답] ④

**281** 문법포인트 | Point 36. 비교 구문

The elephants, ① the largest mammal of all the land creatures, is known for their remarkable intelligence and intricate social behaviors. Sadly, many elephant habitats have been lost ② because human encroachment and
→ due to/because of
habitat destruction, resulting in significant declines in wild populations. ③ Protect elephants from the illegal ivory
→ Protecting/To protect
trade remains ④ crucially for their conservation efforts in
→ crucial
Africa and Asia.

**[해설]**
① 최상급은 정관사 the와 함께 써야 한다. the largest의 최상급이 바르게 쓰였다.
② because는 접속사이므로 뒤에 절이 와야 하는데 명사구가 왔으므로 같은 의미의 전치사로 고쳐야 한다. (because → due to/because of) Point 41. 부사절 접속사의 선택
③ 문장 안에 remains라는 동사가 있으므로 다시 동사가 올 수 없다. 문맥상 문장의 주어가 코끼리를 보호하는 것이므로 Protect는 동명사나 to부정사로 고쳐야 한다. (Protect → Protecting/To protect) Point 01. 문장의 구성 / Point 28. 동명사의 역할
④ 불완전자동사 remain은 보어가 필요하다. 부사 crucially는 보어가 될 수 없으므로 형용사인 crucial로 고쳐야 한다. (crucially → crucial) Point 04. 불완전자동사의 보어

**[어휘]** intricate 복잡한   habitat 서식지   encroachment 침입   destruction 파괴   population 개체수   conservation 보존

[정답] ①

**282** 문법포인트 | Point 15. 시제 관련 표현

No sooner ① did the explorer team launch the craft than
→ had the exploratory team launched
it hit a rock and was shattered. All of the baggage (save the pack containing food and drinking water) ② was lost. One of them must have clung unconsciously to the pack ③ whose loss they would have felt ④ most severely.

**[해설]**
① 「No sooner + had + 주어 + p.p. + than 주어 + 과거 동사」는 '~하자마자 ~했다'는 뜻으로 than 앞의 주절에는 과거완료 시제가 쓰인다. (did the exploratory team launch → had the exploratory team launched)
② all은 부분사로 뒤에 오는 명사에 의해 수가 결정된다. all 뒤의 baggage는 불가산명사이므로 단수 취급해야 한다. 따라서 단수 동사 was가 바르게 쓰였다. save는 전치사로 쓰일 때는 '~을 제외한'의 의미이다. Point 27. 주어 - 동사 수 일치
③ 선행사 the pack을 수식하며 관계절의 목적어인 loss를 수식하는 소유격 관계대명사가 필요하다. Point 43. 관계대명사의 선택
④ 동사 have felt를 수식하는 부사가 필요하므로 severely가 바르다. 부사의 최상급에는 the가 생략될 수 있다. Point 34. 형용사 vs. 부사

**[어휘]** exploratory 탐사의   launch (배를) 물에 띄우다   craft 배   shatter 산산이 부수다   baggage 짐   save ~외에   cling to ~을 꼭 붙잡다

[정답] ①

**283** 밑줄 친 부분에 들어갈 말로 가장 적절한 것은?

> He _____ sincerely instead of making excuses for his mistake. It would have shown genuine remorse and helped rebuild trust with his colleagues.

① shouldn't have apologized
② should have apologized
③ must have apologized
④ need not have apologized

**284** 밑줄 친 부분 중 어법상 옳지 않은 것은?

> For the student ① who academic grades were affected by personal challenges, ② receiving extra support and guidance from academic advisors has proven crucial in navigating the semester successfully. This situation underscores the importance of having flexibility and robust support systems in place to help students ③ achieve their academic and professional goals. Such supportive measures not only enhance learning outcomes, foster a conducive environment for growth and achievement, but also ④ promote resilience and well-being among students facing difficulties.

**285** 밑줄 친 부분 중 어법상 옳은 것은?

> A true friend is someone ① to depend through life's ups and downs. To forge such a bond, you must share countless experiences and support each other through thick and thin. Friendships thrive when ② driven by mutual respect, trust, and shared values ③ what bind you together. Also, overcoming hardships together can cause you ④ appreciate each other's presence even more.

## 283 [문법포인트 | Point 20. 조동사+have p.p.]

He should have apologized sincerely instead of making excuses for his mistake. It would have shown genuine remorse and helped rebuild trust with his colleagues.

**[해설]** 과거에 '~했어야 했는데' 하지 않은 아쉬움은 should have p.p.로 나타낸다. 따라서 정답은 ② should have apologized이다.

**[어휘]** sincerely 진심으로  make an excuse 변명하다
genuine 진정한  remorse 반성  rebuild 재건하다

[정답] ②

## 284 [문법포인트 | Point 43. 관계대명사의 선택]

For the student ① who (→ whose) academic grades were affected by personal challenges, ② receiving extra support and guidance from academic advisors has proven crucial in navigating the semester successfully. This situation underscores the importance of having flexibility and robust support systems in place to help students ③ achieve their academic and professional goals. Such supportive measures not only enhance learning outcomes, foster a conducive environment for growth and achievement, but also ④ promote resilience and well-being among students facing difficulties.

**[해설]**
① 선행사 the student가 academic grades에 대해 소유의 의미를 나타내야 하므로 who를 소유격 관계대명사 whose로 고쳐야 한다. (who → whose)
② 동명사 receiving이 문장의 주어로 바르게 쓰였다. Point 28. 동명사의 역할
③ 준사역동사 help는 목적격보어로 to부정사 또는 동사원형을 모두 취할 수 있으므로 동사원형 achieve가 바르게 쓰였다. Point 10. 불완전타동사와 동작의 목적격보어
④ 「not only A but (also) B」(A뿐만 아니라 B도) 구문으로 enhance, foster, 그리고 promote가 바르게 병렬되었다. Point 39. 등위접속사의 병렬 구조

**[어휘]** academic 학업의  guidance 지도  flexibility 유연성
robust 강력한  in place 준비된  supportive 지원적인
measure 조치  conducive 도움이 되는  promote 증진하다
resilience 회복력  well-being 삶의 질

[정답] ①

## 285 [문법포인트 | Point 33. 분사구문]

A true friend is someone ① to depend (→ to depend on) through life's ups and downs. To forge such a bond, you must share countless experiences and support each other through thick and thin. Friendships thrive when ② driven by mutual respect, trust, and shared values ③ what (→ which/that) bind you together. Also, overcoming hardships together can cause you ④ appreciate (→ to appreciate) each other's presence even more.

**[해설]**
② 접속사가 생략되지 않은 분사구문으로, 분사의 의미상의 주어는 주절의 주어인 Friendships이다. Friendships와 drive의 관계가 수동이고, 분사 뒤에 목적어가 없으므로 과거분사 driven이 바르게 쓰였다.
① to부정사가 형용사적 용법으로 앞의 someone을 수식하고 있다. someone이 depend의 목적어에 해당하는데, depend는 완전자동사이므로 적절한 전치사 on을 depend 뒤에 써야 한다. (to depend → to depend on) Point 29. to부정사의 역할
③ 선행사(mutual respect, trust, and shared values)가 있고, what 이하의 절에 주어가 없으므로 주격 관계대명사 which 또는 that으로 고쳐야 한다. (what → which/that) Point 43. 관계대명사의 선택
④ cause는 목적격보어에 to부정사를 써야 한다. 따라서 appreciate를 to appreciate로 고쳐야 한다. (appreciate → to appreciate) Point 10. 불완전타동사와 동작의 목적격보어

**[어휘]** ups and downs 우여곡절  forge 구축하다
through thick and thin 좋을 때나 안 좋을 때나  thrive 잘 자라다
appreciate 감사하다

[정답] ②

**286** 밑줄 친 부분에 들어갈 말로 가장 적절한 것은?

> The company's new smartphone is more advanced than _____ released last year, offering enhanced features and performance.

① it
② that
③ those
④ them

**287** 밑줄 친 부분 중 어법상 옳은 것은?

> It goes without saying ① that the importance of warning signals in disasters cannot be overstated. Just last week, a severe storm struck. Experts believed ② what the timely evacuation warnings enabled residents to leave their buildings early, significantly reducing casualties. The proactive measures ③ taking by emergency responders prevented what could have been a ④ dead outcome. Swift and coordinated efforts are crucial for mitigating the effects of natural disasters and ensuring the safety of affected communities.

**288** 밑줄 친 부분 중 어법상 옳지 않은 것은?

> Family members of a 27-year-old man, who was found ① dead in the Bengaluru Lake, said that they suspected foul play. The man, identified as Micheal Kamp, came from Kannada district and was about ② to work as a driver for a hotel in Bengaluru. His family members said "He had no reason to kill himself. We got his mobile phone from one of his friends ③ only to find that all the data had been erased." Obviously, they didn't believe he was suicidal, ④ wasn't he?

**289** 밑줄 친 부분 중 어법상 옳지 않은 것은?

> He ① was offered a perfect opportunity to reverse his career trajectory and silence the negative narrative ② surrounded his former team. He entered the league with high expectations ③ only to cap out his potential as a rookie. It ④ cannot be said too often how enervated he was throughout most of his time on the floor.

## 286 문법포인트 | Point 38. 비교대상의 일치

The company's new smartphone is more advanced than that released last year, offering enhanced features and performance.

[해설] 비교 구문에서 앞에서 언급된 비교대상을 뒤에서 다시 지칭할 때 비교대상이 단수이면 that, 복수이면 those를 사용한다. 비교대상 The company's new smartphone은 단수이므로 정답은 ② that이다.

[어휘] advanced 고급의   release 출시하다   offer 제공하다
feature 기능   performance 성능

정답 ②

## 287 문법포인트 | Point 31. 준동사 주요 표현

It goes without saying ① [that the importance of warning signals in disasters cannot be overstated]. Just last week, a severe storm struck. Experts believed ② [what the timely evacuation warnings enabled residents to leave their buildings early, significantly reducing casualties]. The proactive measures ③ (taking by emergency responders) prevented what could have been a ④ dead outcome. Swift and coordinated efforts are crucial for mitigating the effects of natural disasters and ensuring the safety of affected communities.

[해설]
① '~은 말할 필요도 없다'는 「It goes without saying that S + V」로 표현하며 뒤에 완전한 절이 온다. It은 가주어이고 that절은 진주어이다. 따라서 명사절 접속사 that이 바르게 쓰였다.
② believed의 목적절을 이끄는 접속사가 필요한데, 선행사가 없고 뒤의 절이 완전하므로 명사절 접속사 that으로 고쳐야 한다. (what → that) Point 40. 명사절 접속사의 선택
③ The proactive measures와 분사의 관계가 수동이고, 분사 뒤에 목적어가 없으므로 과거분사로 써야 한다. 따라서 taking을 taken으로 고쳐야 바르다. (taking → taken) Point 32. 현재분사 vs. 과거분사
④ 뒤의 명사 outcome을 수식하는 형용사 자리이다. dead는 '죽은, 침체된'이라는 뜻이므로 의미상 어색하다. 따라서 dead를 deadly(치명적인)로 고쳐 '치명적인 결과'라는 자연스러운 의미가 될 수 있도록 해야 한다. (dead → deadly) Point 35. 주의할 형용사와 부사

[어휘] overstate 과장하다   strike (재난·질병 등이) 발생하다
timely 시기적절한   evacuation 대피   casualty 사상자
responder 구조대원   coordinated 조직적인   mitigate 완화하다

정답 ①

## 288 문법포인트 | Point 02. 의문문의 어순

Family members of a 27-year-old man, who was found ① dead in the Bengaluru Lake, said that they suspected foul play. The man, identified as Micheal Kamp, came from Kannada district and was about ② to work as a driver for a hotel in Bengaluru. His family members said "He had no reason to kill himself. We got his mobile phone from one of his friends ③ only to find that all the data had been erased." Obviously, they didn't believe he was suicidal, ④ wasn't he?
→ did they

[해설]
④ 부가의문문은 주절의 주어와 동사를 기준으로 만든다. 또한 앞 절이 부정이면 긍정을 써야 하고, 앞 절에서 사용된 동사와 같은 종류의 동사, 같은 시제를 사용해야 한다. 앞 절의 형태가 'they didn't believe ~'이므로 wasn't he를 did they로 고쳐야 한다. (wasn't he → did they)
① 불완전타동사 find의 목적격보어로 형용사 dead가 바르게 사용되었다. dead는 형용사로 '죽은'을 뜻하여 '치명적인'을 뜻하는 deadly와는 혼동하지 않아야 한다. Point 35. 주의할 형용사와 부사 / Point 09. 불완전타동사의 목적격보어
② '막~하려던 참이다'라는 의미는 「be about to부정사」로 나타내므로 to부정사가 바르게 쓰였다. Point 31. 준동사 주요 표현
③ 'only to ~'는 '하지만 (결국) ~하게 되다'라는 의미이다. 의미상 휴대폰을 받아서 (결국) 모든 데이터가 삭제된 것을 확인했다는 내용이 자연스러우므로 only to find가 바르게 쓰였다. Point 29. to부정사의 역할

정답 ④

## 289 문법포인트 | Point 32. 현재분사 vs. 과거분사

He ① was offered a perfect opportunity to reverse his career trajectory and silence the negative narrative (② surrounded his former team). He entered the league
→ surrounding
with high expectations ③ only to cap out his potential as a rookie. It ④ cannot be said too often how enervated he was throughout most of his time on the floor.

[해설]
② narrative를 수식하는 분사 surrounded 뒤에 목적어가 있고, 문맥상 능동의 의미이므로 surrounding으로 고쳐야 한다. (surrounded → surrounding)
① 수여동사인 offer는 수동태일 때도 목적어를 가질 수 있고 수동의 의미이므로 was offered가 바르게 쓰였다. Point 17. 동사의 유형별 수동태
③ 「only + to부정사」는 to부정사의 부사적 용법으로 '하지만 결국 ~하다'라는 뜻으로 바르게 쓰였다. Point 29. to부정사의 역할
④ 「cannot ~ too 형/부」는 '아무리 ~해도 지나치지 않다'라는 뜻으로 cannot과 too often이 바르게 쓰였다. Point 18. 조동사의 선택

정답 ②

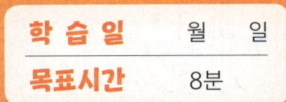

**290** 밑줄 친 부분에 들어갈 말로 가장 적절한 것은?

> The movie was _____ a spectacle that we lost track of time completely.

① such captivating  ② so captivated
③ such captivated   ④ so captivating

**291** 밑줄 친 부분 중 어법상 옳은 것은?

> All the sudden, millions of people just ① disappear the world. Planes ② fall from the sky, cars, trains and machinery with no operators become deadly missiles. At the minute, one man arises with all the answers. The whole world expect he'll restore a peace to them, but he, in fact, is not ③ that he claims he is. But by the time people ④ realize the truth, it will be too late to undo the damage.

**292** 밑줄 친 부분 중 어법상 옳지 않은 것은?

> The so-called Tempietto is a tiny, round tomb ① situated inside the courtyard of the church of San Pietro in Rome, exactly ② where St. Peter was crucified. This small commemorative tomb is considered ③ a masterpiece of Renaissance Italian architecture. This temple was said to have been designed and ④ found by Donato Bramante possibly as early as 1502.

**293** 밑줄 친 부분 중 어법상 옳은 것은?

> The exhibition features different world views from the antiquity and up to the 1600s, and lets you know the meaning of ① that people believed in the old, old days, when the Earth was believed ② to be flat. During the ages, it was accepted that the Earth ③ was round and the Geocentric theory was ④ such firm a belief that many scientists were tried or oppressed for anything related to the heliocentric theory.

## 문장 분석 및 해설

**290** 문법포인트 | Point 23. 관사의 위치 / Point 32. 현재분사 vs. 과거분사

The movie was so captivating a spectacle that we lost track of time completely.

**해설** 「so + 형 + a + 명 + that절」 또는 「such + a + 형 + 명 + that절」은 '매우 ~해서 …하다'라는 뜻이다. 이 어순에 맞는 것은 ②와 ④이다. 또한 사물인 spectacle(구경거리)이 매혹적인 감정을 불러일으키는 것이므로 현재분사인 captivating이 바르다. captivated는 사람 등이 매혹적인 감정을 느낄 때 사용한다. 따라서 정답은 ④ so captivating이다.

**어휘** spectacle 구경거리  lose track of time 시간 가는 줄 모르다  completely 완전히

정답 ④

**291** 문법포인트 | Point 14. 시제일치와 예외

All the sudden, millions of people just ① disappear the world. Planes ② fall from the sky, cars, trains and machinery with no operators become deadly missiles. At the minute, one man arises with all the answers. The whole world expect he'll restore a peace to them, but he, in fact, is not ③ that he claims he is. But by the time people ④ realize the truth, it will be too late to undo the damage.

**해설**
④ 시간, 조건의 부사절에서 미래 시제를 현재 시제로 표현한다. by the time이 시간의 부사절을 이끌고 있으므로 현재 시제인 realize가 바르게 쓰였다.
① disappear는 완전자동사라서 목적어를 취할 수 없다. 의미상 '~에서 사라지다'이므로 전치사 from을 추가해야 한다. (disappear the world → disappear from the world) Point 03. 완전자동사
② 하나의 문장에 두 개의 동사가 있다. become이 동사이므로 fall은 앞선 명사 Planes를 수식하는 분사가 되어야 한다. 문맥상 능동의 관계이므로 falling으로 고쳐야 한다. (fall → falling) Point 01. 문장의 구성
③ 동사 is not의 보어를 구성하는 명사절 안에서 he claims는 삽입절이고 절 안에서 is의 보어가 없으므로 that은 who로 고쳐야 한다. who he is는 '현재의 그'라는 의미이다. (that → who) Point 40. 명사절 접속사의 선택

**어휘** all (of) the sudden 갑자기  machinery 기계류  operator 운전자  deadly 치명적인  minute 순간  arise 나타나다  restore 되찾다  claim 주장하다  realize 깨닫다

정답 ④

**292** 문법포인트 | Point 11. 혼동하기 쉬운 동사의 불규칙 변화

The so-called Tempietto is a tiny, round tomb ① situated inside the courtyard of the church of San Pietro in Rome, exactly ② where St. Peter was crucified. This small commemorative tomb is considered ③ a masterpiece of Renaissance Italian architecture. This temple was said to have been designed and ④ found by Donato Bramante possibly as early as 1502.

**해설**
④ 문맥상 '건설되다'라는 의미이므로 find(찾다)의 과거분사 found가 아닌, found(건설하다)의 과거분사 founded가 와야 한다. (found → founded)
① 수식받는 명사 tomb과 situate는 수동의 관계이므로 과거분사인 situated가 바르게 쓰였다. Point 32. 현재분사 vs. 과거분사
② where 이후의 절이 완전하고, 앞에 the church of San Pietro라는 장소 명사구가 있으므로 관계부사 where의 쓰임이 바르다. Point 44. 관계부사
③ consider는 명사를 목적격보어로 취할 수 있고, 수동태가 될 경우 이 명사 목적격보어는 동사 뒤에 바로 오므로 쓰임이 바르다. Point 09. 불완전 타동사의 목적격보어

**어휘** tomb 무덤  courtyard (보통 성·저택 등에서 건물에 둘러싸인) 뜰  crucify 십자가에 못 박다

정답 ④

**293** 문법포인트 | Point 17. 동사의 유형별 수동태

The exhibition features different world views from the antiquity and up to the 1600s, and lets you know the meaning of ① that people believed in the old, old days, when the Earth was believed ② to be flat. During the ages, it was accepted that the Earth ③ was round and the Geocentric theory was ④ such firm a belief that many scientists were tried or oppressed for anything related to the heliocentric theory.

**해설**
② say나 believe 등의 목적어가 that절인 경우 수동태 전환 시 that절의 주어를 수동태의 주어로 쓰고 that절의 동사는 to부정사로 바꿀 수 있다. they believed that the Earth is flat이 수동태로 바르게 전환되었다.
① that절은 전치사의 목적어가 될 수 없고, believed의 목적어가 없는 불완전한 절이므로 what으로 고쳐야 한다. (that → what) Point 40. 명사절 접속사의 선택
③ 과학적 진리는 시제일치의 적용을 받지 않으므로 현재 시제인 is로 고쳐야 한다. (was → is) Point 14. 시제일치와 예외
④ such ~ that의 부사절 접속사에서 such 뒤에 명사가 부정관사, 형용사와 함께 올 경우에는 반드시 「such + a(n) + 형 +명」의 어순을 취한다. (such firm a belief → such a firm belief) Point 22. 관사의 이해

**어휘** antiquity 고대  Geocentric 지구 중심의  try 재판하다  oppress 억압하다  heliocentric 태양 중심의

정답 ②

**294** 밑줄 친 부분에 들어갈 말로 가장 적절한 것은?

> She promised that she _____ to visit us the following weekend.

① comes     ② came
③ will come     ④ would come

**295** 밑줄 친 부분 중 어법상 옳은 것은?

> The atmospheres were added to the planets after they were formed. This could occur either by material ① bring in by the intense Solar Wind from the young Sun, ② and by comets and by large impacting objects. However, asteroids ③ cannot be the sole source for the water on Earth. If that were the case, we would have ④ 10 more times Xenon in our atmosphere than we do.

**296** 밑줄 친 부분 중 어법상 옳은 것은?

> The two members of the Church said that after finding their priest ① previously convicting, the more they dug, ② the bad the case seemed. Within two weeks, the members ③ were made to resign because they unfairly maligned the priest. The officials of the church said they ④ had informed of the priest's background before he came to this church.

**297** 밑줄 친 부분 중 어법상 옳은 것은?

> We've seen a lot of panic buying ① to occur, with canned goods, water bottles and pasta shelves ② emptying out. But there will be no shortage of food, provided that people ③ behave appropriately. The thing is that it is difficult ④ that higher sales lead to higher profits – the rapid shift can cause high costs in logistics, in extra safety measures, and in hiring new temporary staff to deal with the overload of work.

## 문장 분석 및 해설

**294** 문법포인트 | Point 14. 시제일치와 예외

She promised that she would come to visit us the following weekend.

해설 미래의 의미를 나타내는 부사구 the following weekend가 있으므로 동사 역시 미래의 의미를 가져야 한다. 주절의 시제가 과거이므로 will은 쓸 수 없고 과거에서 본 미래를 나타내는 ④ would come이 들어가야 한다.

어휘 promise 약속하다   visit 찾아가다

정답 ④

**295** 문법포인트 | Point 18. 조동사의 선택

The atmospheres were added to the planets after they were formed. This could occur either by material ① bring in by the intense Solar Wind from the young Sun), ② and by comets and by large impacting objects. However, asteroids ③ cannot be the sole source for the water on Earth. If that were the case, we would have ④ 10 more times Xenon in our atmosphere than we do.

해설
③ cannot은 강한 부정의 추측을 나타내어 '~일 리가 없다'를 뜻한다. 현재 상태에 대한 부정의 추측이 바르게 사용되었다.
① 명사를 수식하는 분사가 와야 할 자리이다. material과 bring의 관계가 수동이므로 과거분사 brought로 고쳐야 한다. (bring in → brought in) Point 32. 현재분사 vs. 과거분사
② 등위상관접속사 either A or B의 구조가 되어야 하므로 and를 or로 고쳐야 한다. (and → or) Point 39. 등위접속사의 병렬 구조
④ 배수사는 비교급 앞에 와야 하므로 배수사 10 times를 more 앞에 오게 해야 한다. (10 more times → 10 times more) Point 37. 비교 사용 표현

어휘 intense 강렬한   comet 혜성   asteroid 소행성
Xenon 크세논: 비활성 기체 원소

정답 ③

**296** 문법포인트 | Point 17. 동사의 유형별 수동태

The two members of the Church said that after finding their priest ① previously convicting, the more they dug, ② the bad the case seemed. Within two weeks, the members ③ were made to resign because they unfairly maligned the priest. The officials of the church said they ④ had informed of the priest's background before he came to this church.

해설
③ 능동태에서 사역동사의 목적격보어는 동사원형이지만, 수동태에서는 to부정사가 되므로 were made to resign이 바르게 쓰였다.
① find의 목적격보어는 목적어와의 관계가 수동일 때 과거분사가 된다. (previously convicting → previously convicted) Point 10. 불완전타동사와 동작의 목적격보어
② '~하면 할수록 더 …하다'라는 말은 「the 비교급 + 주어 + 동사, the 비교급 + 주어 + 동사」로 표현한다. 따라서 the bad를 the worse로 고쳐야 한다. (the bad → the worse) Point 37. 비교 사용 표현
④ 전달하는 시점보다 먼저 일어난 일이므로 과거완료 시제가 바르다. 또한 문맥상 수동의 의미이므로 수동태로 고쳐야 한다. (had informed → had been informed) Point 12. 완료 시제 / Point 16. 능동태 vs. 수동태 구분

어휘 priest 사제   previously 이전에   convict 유죄 판결하다
resign 사직하다   unfairly 부당하게   malign 비방하다

정답 ③

**297** 문법포인트 | Point 14. 시제일치와 예외

We've seen a lot of panic buying ① to occur, with canned goods, water bottles and pasta shelves ② emptying out. But there will be no shortage of food, provided that people ③ behave appropriately. The thing is that it is difficult ④ that higher sales lead to higher profits – the rapid shift can cause high costs in logistics, in extra safety measures, and in hiring new temporary staff to deal with the overload of work.

해설
③ 시간, 조건의 부사절에서 미래 시제 대신 현재 시제를 사용한다. provided (that)이 '~한다면'이라는 조건의 부사절 접속사이므로 미래 시제 대신 현재 시제인 behave가 바르게 쓰였다.
① 지각동사 see는 목적격보어로 동사원형 또는 현재분사를 취한다. 따라서 to부정사를 occur나 occurring으로 고쳐야 한다. (to occur → occur/occurring) Point 10. 불완전타동사와 동작의 목적격보어
② with 분사구문은 「with + 목적어 + 목적격보어」의 형태이다. 이때 목적격보어는 목적어와의 관계가 의미상 수동이면 과거분사를, 능동이면 현재분사를 쓴다. 따라서 진열대가 비어지는 수동의 의미이므로 과거분사인 emptied out으로 고쳐야 한다. (emptying out → emptied out) Point 33. 분사구문
④ 난이형용사가 사용되는 가주어·진주어 구문에서는 that절을 진주어로 사용하지 않고, to부정사를 진주어로 사용해야 한다. 따라서 that higher sales lead는 for higher sales to lead로 고쳐야 한다. (that higher sales lead → for higher sales to lead) Point 35. 주의할 형용사와 부사

어휘 panic buying 사재기   shelf 진열대   empty out ~을 텅텅 비우다
shortage 부족   provided that ~한다면
appropriately 적절하게   The thing is that 중요한 것은 ~이다
shift 변화   logistics 물류   measure 조치   temporary 임시의
overload 과부하

정답 ③

### 298 밑줄 친 부분에 들어갈 말로 가장 적절한 것은?

The old bookstore, _____ shelves were filled with dusty volumes of forgotten tales and timeless classics, was a haven for book lovers.

① which    ② whose
③ whom    ④ what

### 299 밑줄 친 부분 중 어법상 옳지 않은 것은?

Fear of immigrant communities gaining in increasing importance ① has led to the English Only Movement, a campaign by people ② who see other cultures and languages as a threat to the US. They want to make English the only official language of the US and ③ are opposed to allowing students to be taught in other languages or ④ lets people vote using forms printed in another language.

### 300 밑줄 친 부분 중 어법상 옳지 않은 것은?

① Surrounded as it is by technological advancements, the field of biotechnology continues to push the boundaries of healthcare and agriculture. Scientists dare ② to unravel the mysteries of genetic engineering. Never in the history of biology ③ had researchers such powerful tools at their disposal to manipulate and understand genetic information. In this age ④ when personalized therapies are becoming a reality, biotechnology leads reform in healthcare and agriculture.

## 298 〔문법포인트 | Point 43. 관계대명사의 선택〕

The old bookstore, (whose shelves were filled with dusty volumes of forgotten tales and timeless classics), was a haven for book lovers.

**해설** The old bookstore가 주어이고, was가 동사이며, 그 사이에 주어에 대한 부연 설명을 하는 계속적 용법의 관계대명사절이 삽입되었다. 빈칸 이후에 완전한 절이 왔고, 명사 shelves를 수식하면서 주어에 관해 설명해야 하므로 소유격 관계대명사가 필요하다.

**어휘** shelf 진열대   be filled with ~로 가득하다   dusty 먼지투성이의
volume 전집   timeless 세월을 초월한   haven 안식처

**정답** ②

## 299 〔문법포인트 | Point 39. 등위접속사의 병렬 구조〕

Fear of immigrant communities gaining in increasing importance ① has led to the English Only Movement, a campaign by people ② (who see other cultures and languages as a threat to the US). They want to make English the only official language of the US and ③ are opposed to allowing students to be taught in other languages or ④ lets people vote using forms printed in another language.
→ letting

**해설**
④ 등위접속사 or 앞의 구조가 are opposed to allowing으로 전치사 to의 목적어인 동명사가 병렬 구조를 이루어야 하므로 or 뒤의 lets도 동명사인 letting으로 고쳐야 한다. (lets → letting)
① 두려움의 결과로 현재 운동이 벌어지고 있는 상태이므로 현재완료의 결과 용법이 바르게 사용되었다. 또한 주어 Fear가 단수이므로 동사 역시 단수인 has로 바르게 쓰였다. Point 12. 완료 시제 / Point 27. 주어-동사 수 일치
② 앞에 선행사 people이 있고, who 이하에 주어가 없는 불완전한 절이 왔다. 따라서 주격 관계대명사 who가 바르게 쓰였다. 또한 선행사가 복수이므로 복수 동사 see가 바르게 쓰였다. Point 43. 관계대명사의 선택 / Point 27. 주어-동사 수 일치
③ be opposed to에서 to는 전치사이므로 뒤에 동명사인 allowing이 바르게 왔다. 또한 주어가 They이므로 are가 바르게 쓰였다. Point 48. 전치사의 목적어 / Point 27. 주어-동사 수 일치

**어휘** immigrant 이민자   threat 위협   official 공식의
be opposed to ~에 반대하다   form 용지

**정답** ④

## 300 〔문법포인트 | Point 50. 도치〕

① Surrounded as it is by technological advancements, the field of biotechnology continues to push the boundaries of healthcare and agricultural. Scientists dare ② to unravel the mysteries of genetic engineering. (Never in the history of biology) ③ had researchers such powerful tools at their disposal to manipulate and understand genetic information.
→ did researchers have
In this age ④ (when personalized therapies are becoming a reality), biotechnology leads reform in healthcare and agriculture.

**해설**
③ 부정부사구가 문두에 나왔으므로 주어와 동사가 도치되어야 한다. have가 일반동사이므로 do/does/did를 활용해서 도치한다. (had researchers → did researchers have)
① 「형용사/부사/분사/무관사 명사 + as/though 주어 + 동사」의 주요 양보구문이다. 분사인 Surrounded가 문두에 바르게 쓰였다. Point 42. 주요 양보구문
② dare는 '감히 ~하다'의 의미이다. dare가 일반동사인 경우 to부정사를 목적어로 취하므로 to unravel이 바르게 쓰였다. Point 06. 완전타동사와 동작의 목적어
④ 시간을 나타내는 선행사 this age가 있고, when 뒤의 절이 완전하므로 관계부사 when이 바르게 쓰였다. Point 44. 관계부사

**어휘** surround 둘러싸다   technological 기술의   advancement 발전
field 분야   biotechnology 생명공학
push the boundary 경계를 허물다   healthcare 의료
agriculture 농업   unravel 풀다   genetic engineering 유전공학
at one's disposal ~의 마음대로 사용할 수 있는
manipulate 조작하다   personalized 개인 맞춤형   therapy 치료

**정답** ③

# 실전문법 300제 빠른 정답

### DAY 01

| 01 | 02 | 03 | 04 | 05 | 06 | 07 | 08 |
|----|----|----|----|----|----|----|----|
| ④ | ② | ④ | ② | ③ | ④ | ④ | ④ |
| 09 | 10 | 11 | 12 | 13 | 14 | 15 |    |
| ③ | ③ | ② | ② | ① | ① | ③ |    |

### DAY 02

| 16 | 17 | 18 | 19 | 20 | 21 | 22 | 23 |
|----|----|----|----|----|----|----|----|
| ④ | ② | ② | ② | ① | ① | ③ | ② |
| 24 | 25 | 26 | 27 | 28 | 29 | 30 |    |
| ② | ① | ③ | ① | ④ | ② | ① |    |

### DAY 03

| 31 | 32 | 33 | 34 | 35 | 36 | 37 | 38 |
|----|----|----|----|----|----|----|----|
| ② | ② | ③ | ④ | ③ | ④ | ② | ④ |
| 39 | 40 | 41 | 42 | 43 | 44 | 45 |    |
| ② | ① | ③ | ① | ④ | ① | ④ |    |

### DAY 04

| 46 | 47 | 48 | 49 | 50 | 51 | 52 | 53 |
|----|----|----|----|----|----|----|----|
| ① | ④ | ③ | ③ | ④ | ② | ② | ① |
| 54 | 55 | 56 | 57 | 58 | 59 | 60 |    |
| ④ | ③ | ④ | ② | ④ | ② | ④ |    |

### DAY 05

| 61 | 62 | 63 | 64 | 65 | 66 | 67 | 68 |
|----|----|----|----|----|----|----|----|
| ② | ① | ② | ① | ② | ③ | ③ | ① |
| 69 | 70 | 71 | 72 | 73 | 74 | 75 |    |
| ③ | ① | ④ | ④ | ② | ① | ② |    |

### DAY 06

| 76 | 77 | 78 | 79 | 80 | 81 | 82 | 83 |
|----|----|----|----|----|----|----|----|
| ① | ② | ② | ③ | ② | ① | ③ | ② |
| 84 | 85 | 86 | 87 | 88 | 89 | 90 |    |
| ① | ② | ④ | ④ | ① | ② | ④ |    |

### DAY 07

| 91 | 92 | 93 | 94 | 95 | 96 | 97 | 98 |
|----|----|----|----|----|----|----|----|
| ③ | ③ | ① | ④ | ④ | ① | ② | ① |
| 99 | 100 | 101 | 102 | 103 | 104 | 105 |    |
| ① | ① | ② | ④ | ② | ④ | ④ |    |

### DAY 08

| 106 | 107 | 108 | 109 | 110 | 111 | 112 | 113 |
|----|----|----|----|----|----|----|----|
| ③ | ② | ③ | ③ | ① | ④ | ③ | ③ |
| 114 | 115 | 116 | 117 | 118 | 119 | 120 |    |
| ④ | ③ | ② | ③ | ③ | ④ | ② |    |

### DAY 09

| 121 | 122 | 123 | 124 | 125 | 126 | 127 | 128 |
|----|----|----|----|----|----|----|----|
| ③ | ① | ② | ① | ③ | ① | ② | ④ |
| 129 | 130 | 131 | 132 | 133 | 134 | 135 |    |
| ④ | ① | ③ | ② | ④ | ④ | ① |    |

### DAY 10

| 136 | 137 | 138 | 139 | 140 | 141 | 142 | 143 |
|----|----|----|----|----|----|----|----|
| ① | ④ | ④ | ④ | ③ | ① | ④ | ② |
| 144 | 145 | 146 | 147 | 148 | 149 | 150 |    |
| ④ | ④ | ③ | ② | ③ | ① | ③ |    |

### DAY 11

| 151 | 152 | 153 | 154 | 155 | 156 | 157 | 158 |
|----|----|----|----|----|----|----|----|
| ③ | ④ | ④ | ② | ③ | ② | ① | ② |
| 159 | 160 | 161 | 162 | 163 | 164 | 165 |    |
| ② | ① | ② | ③ | ① | ③ | ② |    |

### DAY 12

| 166 | 167 | 168 | 169 | 170 | 171 | 172 | 173 |
|----|----|----|----|----|----|----|----|
| ④ | ③ | ① | ③ | ④ | ① | ② | ① |
| 174 | 175 | 176 | 177 | 178 | 179 | 180 |    |
| ① | ④ | ④ | ③ | ② | ③ | ② |    |

### DAY 13

| 181 | 182 | 183 | 184 | 185 | 186 | 187 | 188 |
|----|----|----|----|----|----|----|----|
| ③ | ③ | ④ | ② | ④ | ② | ① | ③ |
| 189 | 190 | 191 | 192 | 193 | 194 | 195 |    |
| ③ | ② | ① | ③ | ① | ④ | ④ |    |

### DAY 14

| 196 | 197 | 198 | 199 | 200 | 201 | 202 | 203 |
|----|----|----|----|----|----|----|----|
| ② | ① | ② | ③ | ① | ① | ① | ③ |
| 204 | 205 | 206 | 207 | 208 | 209 | 210 |    |
| ④ | ③ | ② | ③ | ④ | ③ | ③ |    |

### DAY 15

| 211 | 212 | 213 | 214 | 215 | 216 | 217 | 218 |
|----|----|----|----|----|----|----|----|
| ③ | ② | ③ | ① | ④ | ③ | ③ | ① |
| 219 | 220 | 221 | 222 | 223 | 224 | 225 |    |
| ④ | ① | ③ | ④ | ④ | ④ | ④ |    |

### DAY 16

| 226 | 227 | 228 | 229 | 230 | 231 | 232 | 233 |
|----|----|----|----|----|----|----|----|
| ③ | ② | ③ | ② | ② | ① | ③ | ② |
| 234 | 235 | 236 | 237 | 238 | 239 | 240 |    |
| ② | ④ | ④ | ④ | ③ | ④ | ④ |    |

### DAY 17

| 241 | 242 | 243 | 244 | 245 | 246 | 247 | 248 |
|----|----|----|----|----|----|----|----|
| ③ | ③ | ② | ④ | ② | ③ | ③ | ④ |
| 249 | 250 | 251 | 252 | 253 | 254 | 255 |    |
| ② | ③ | ③ | ② | ④ | ② | ② |    |

### DAY 18

| 256 | 257 | 258 | 259 | 260 | 261 | 262 | 263 |
|----|----|----|----|----|----|----|----|
| ① | ④ | ④ | ④ | ④ | ③ | ③ | ③ |
| 264 | 265 | 266 | 267 | 268 | 269 | 270 |    |
| ④ | ② | ② | ① | ④ | ④ | ④ |    |

### DAY 19

| 271 | 272 | 273 | 274 | 275 | 276 | 277 | 278 |
|----|----|----|----|----|----|----|----|
| ④ | ① | ① | ② | ③ | ① | ① | ① |
| 279 | 280 | 281 | 282 | 283 | 284 | 285 |    |
| ③ | ② | ② | ① | ④ | ④ | ② |    |

### DAY 20

| 286 | 287 | 288 | 289 | 290 | 291 | 292 | 293 |
|----|----|----|----|----|----|----|----|
| ② | ① | ④ | ③ | ④ | ④ | ④ | ② |
| 294 | 295 | 296 | 297 | 298 | 299 | 300 |    |
| ④ | ③ | ③ | ③ | ② | ④ | ③ |    |

# MEMO

# MEMO

# MEMO

# MEMO

# MEMO